PROMISES OF CITIZENSHIP

RACE, RHETORIC, AND MEDIA SERIES
Davis W. Houck, General Editor

PROMISES OF CITIZENSHIP

Film Recruitment of
African Americans
in World War II

KATHLEEN M. GERMAN

University Press of Mississippi • Jackson

www.upress.state.ms.us

Designed by Peter D. Halverson

The University Press of Mississippi is a member of the Association of American University Presses.

Copyright © 2017 by University Press of Mississippi
All rights reserved

First printing 2017
∞

Library of Congress Cataloging-in-Publication Data

Names: German, Kathleen M. author.
Title: Promises of citizenship : film recruitment of African Americans in World War II / Kathleen M. German.
Description: Jackson : University Press of Mississippi, 2017. | Series: Race, rhetoric, and media series | Includes bibliographical references and index. |
Identifiers: LCCN 2016056635 (print) | LCCN 2017021060 (ebook) | ISBN 9781496812360 (epub single) | ISBN 9781496812377 (epub institutional) | ISBN 9781496812384 (pdf single) | ISBN 9781496812391 (pdf institutional) | ISBN 9781496812353 (cloth : alk. paper)
Subjects: LCSH: African American soldiers in motion pictures. | Race relations in motion pictures. | World War, 1939–1945—Motion pictures and the war. | United States—Armed Forces—African Americans. | United States—Armed Forces—Recruiting, enlistment, etc.—World War, 1939–1945.
Classification: LCC PN1995.9.N4 (ebook) | LCC PN1995.9.N4 G47 2017 (print) | DDC 791.43/652996073—dc23
LC record available at https://lccn.loc.gov/2016056635

British Library Cataloging-in-Publication Data available

Dedication

To the doctors, nurses, and staff at the Barrett Cancer Center, University of Cincinnati, and Ralph—for second chances.

Contents

INTRODUCTION 3

CHAPTER ONE The Dilemma of Racial Identity 11

CHAPTER TWO Military Service and Citizenship 21

CHAPTER THREE Mass Media in the Twentieth Century 41

CHAPTER FOUR *The Negro Soldier* as Conversion Narrative 65

CHAPTER FIVE Conflicting Narratives and Images 90

CHAPTER SIX Military Conditions during World War II 106

CHAPTER SEVEN Attitudinal Barriers to Change 126

CHAPTER EIGHT Social Conditions for Change 150

CHAPTER NINE The Influence of the Black Press 170

CHAPTER TEN The Negotiation of Racial Identity 190

CHAPTER ELEVEN The Challenge of Change in the Aftermath of World War II 201

NOTES 208

BIBLIOGRAPHY 233

INDEX 255

PROMISES OF CITIZENSHIP

Introduction

Once let the black man get upon his person the brass letters, U.S., let him get an eagle on his button, and a musket on his shoulder and bullets in his pockets, and there is no power on earth which can deny that he has earned the right to citizenship in the United States.
—FREDERICK DOUGLASS[1]

Throughout American history, African Americans have lived largely at the margins of society, undereducated, poorly skilled, and underemployed in a nation that separated people by race and limited full citizenship rights to the white majority.[2] While African Americans fought and died in all American wars to guarantee liberty, their own freedom was denied or restricted. Black men and women have participated in military conflicts since the earliest days of the nation, fighting in local skirmishes and in the War of Independence; in every colony, they served in militia units and the Continental army.[3] However, black participation in American military history has been treated ambiguously at best.

Although little research has been done on the colonial conflicts, New England records reveal that blacks joined in militia units in inter-colonial wars and clashes with Native Americans. Some of these men were freedmen and others were probably slaves, but it is not entirely clear if enslaved black men were utilized in similar capacities in the Southern colonies. Southern fear of revolts probably limited arming African Americans in slaveholding regions. Slaves and freedmen were employed as laborers and soldiers in both the Union and the Confederacy during the Civil War. They fought in the Spanish-American War and in every conflict of the twentieth century.

At the end of World War I, black veterans returning from European trenches expected fuller citizenship rights as a reward for their sacrifice. Instead, racial discrimination and segregation continued, especially in the Southern regions of the country. These men's contributions to American freedom—or at least to the freedom of white Americans—are largely absent from the historical record and similarly ignored in popular culture. In addition, African American citizen soldiers who participated in World War II did so despite decades of broken promises of full citizenship. Ronald Krebs summarizes the black experience in American history, explaining that African Americans have "perceived a tight bond between military service and civil rights," volunteering to serve even when it was apparent that the United States would break this basic social contract.[4]

Despite their willingness to fight for freedom, African Americans have been excluded from the national symbolism that valorizes wartime sacrifice.[5] On one occasion—noteworthy because of its rarity—Admiral Chester W. Nimitz, awarding Doris "Dorie" Miller the Navy Cross for bravery during the attack on Pearl Harbor, stated, "This marks the first time in this conflict that such high tribute has been made in the Pacific Fleet to a member of his race and I'm sure that the future will see others similarly honored for brave acts." However, such recognition was slow to arrive. It took executive action and another war before the military became completely integrated.

Only recently has the courage of African Americans been popularly recognized. Films such as *Glory* (1989), Ken Burns's documentary *The Civil War* (1990), and *The Tuskegee Airmen* (1995; 2002) are just beginning to fill historical gaps. We sometimes catch glimpses of African American heroism, as in the character based on navy steward Dorie Miller in the popular film *Pearl Harbor* (2001). Such instances are cameos by prominent actors like Cuba Gooding Jr., and the extent of wartime participation by African Americans remains obscured, the inequities imposed by segregation ignored. Although popular culture resists acknowledging African American contributions to history, there may now be an increasing awareness of the many faces of freedom, especially in recent conflicts in Vietnam, Iraq, and Afghanistan.

The full promise of the American dream still eludes many Americans, among them large numbers of African Americans. Life expectancy, job opportunities, income levels, educational achievement, general health—measured against all of these yardsticks, African Americans often fall short. Their struggle to participate equally in American society continues into the twentieth century. Despite the shortfall, there has been progress toward equality. The points of transition can often be marked on the calendar of history: the Emancipation Proclamation, President Truman's executive order integrating the armed forces, the Civil Rights Bill of 1964, *Brown v. the Board of Education*, and other landmarks. Among these events, perhaps the most far-reaching was World War II.

World War II forced Americans to reckon with the inequities of racial segregation. It was a war fought for liberty by many Americans from whom liberty was withheld. World War II was the stage for massive social, political, and military disruptions that challenged the wisdom of Jim Crow segregation and offered opportunity for change in the decades that followed. John W. Dower claims that World War II was not just about the rise and fall of empires, the shifting fortunes of international powers, but also a race war "fueled by racial pride, arrogance, and rage on many sides. Ultimately, it brought about a revolution in racial consciousness throughout the world that continues to the present day . . . it is a critical aspect which has rarely been examined systematically."[6] World War II revealed core patterns of prejudice that had distorted American society since its inception.

During periods of domestic and international conflict, deeply rooted prejudices are exposed, often fracturing them. Traumatic historical events such as military conflicts often reveal social weaknesses; when societies are disrupted, they must adapt to survive. During these periods of crisis we can discern racial attitudes and behaviors that mark the beginning of change. Among the most potent struggles for the benefits of citizenship are those of minorities and newcomers. As they seize a foothold in their communities, outsiders challenge the assumptions upon which society rests, redefining themselves within the national identity and subsequently recreating the nation. Issues of inclusion and access to political privilege are at the heart of this process.

World War II created an enormous rupture in American society, disrupting entrenched social practices. Achieving the common national goal of victory required cooperation between the races and brought into sharp relief attitudes and behaviors that had previously kept blacks and whites separated by the artificial boundaries of Jim Crow segregation. The war prepared Americans for the challenges of creating a more just society. For all Americans, traditional attitudes and behaviors had to be adjusted in order to accomplish the larger, more encompassing goal of victory. While neither blacks nor whites emerged cured of racial prejudice, American institutions were forced by the crisis of war to confront the inequities of racial separation.

The clashes over civil rights that characterized the 1960s were an outcome of the massive disruptions of the World War II era. The broader convulsions of war converged around primary issues, such as restrictions on military service and discrimination in war industries. These issues, when disclosed and debated, contributed to the reconfiguration of social and political communities—perhaps not immediately, but ultimately inescapably.[7]

We can see the dilemma of race writ large at multiple points in American history: in the *Amistad* case, in newspaper announcements of slave auctions, in popular literature such as Harriet Beecher Stowe's *Uncle Tom's Cabin*, in the *Dred Scott* decision. In each instance, questions of race have percolated to the surface and demanded public attention. Broad understandings of race were codified in federal and state constitutions and subsequent legal decisions. They were further re-enforced by military service and other basic American institutions. As Ronald Krebs argues, "The military's participation (or manpower) policies may constitute a strong signal of how the state would respond to minority citizenship claims, and they may thus shape the process of political contestation."[8] In this way, military institutions function as a microcosm of the larger society and a gateway to its riches. During World War II, the pressures of a two-front war forced Americans to juggle the unrelenting need for manpower with the tradition of social segregation. For African Americans, the political contest to wrest expanded citizenship rights from the nation was exacerbated by the pressures of war. Owing to severe manpower shortages in every sector of the economy and on the European and Pacific battlefronts, they gained a stronger bargaining position. While the national crisis offered a unique opportunity to leverage their demands, it also constrained the violence with which blacks could press them. This dilemma defined the political hazards faced during the "Double V" campaign, referring to the fight for military victory abroad and freedom from segregation for African Americans. It also placed the American majority in a precarious position regarding expansion of citizenship rights and maintenance of segregation. Historian Michael Geyer frames the dilemma eloquently when he writes, "State and society were yoked together by a mutual bond of violence, expressed through conscription and redeemed in the rights of citizenship."[9] This yoke constrained blacks and whites alike, forcing both sides to relinquish some of their prejudices for the common goal of victory.

Today, some scholars argue that there is integration in contemporary public spheres such as military institutions, government organizations, and workplaces, while in the private lives of Americans social barriers persist.[10] Overcoming the history of slavery and blending separate races in the United States has clearly been complicated, with uneven results across various sectors of society. Still, a better understanding of the role of race in American society may contribute to future improvements in human relations.

The difficulties faced by African Americans within the social, political, and economic institutions of American society have stubborn historic roots. It is important to understand the source of fundamental issues framing the African American experience. One vital record of the American experience can be found in the thousands of celluloid images produced during the war. Scholars estimate that between twelve hundred and fifteen hundred nonfiction films were screened in the United States and Britain during World War II.[11] The primary purpose of most of these films was to provide information for civilian and military audiences on topics that ranged from recognizing the enemy to preventing venereal diseases. In addition to their content, these films serve as records of the attitudes and perspectives of a nation at war, waiting to be appraised from a perspective that is distanced by time and culture. In studying the role of films sponsored by the federal government to boost the morale of African Americans and recruit their support for the war, we can investigate the black experience within the dominant culture.

Films produced during World War II have remained largely uninvestigated by scholars. As a result of traditional disciplinary boundaries and limited cross-disciplinary interaction, there are gaps in our understanding of the role of media in military history. Historian R. C. Raack points to the dearth of scholarship about film and its historical consequences.[12] The rationale for examining film in order to understand culture is articulated by Robert M. Entman and Andrew Rojecki in their study of media and race in America: "The media operate both as a barometer of cultural integration and as potential accelerator either to cohesion or to further cultural separation and political conflict–or perhaps to both."[13] For almost fifty years, African American film images have preserved social attitudes. These images are now ripe for examination—from their roots in the eighteenth-century minstrel tradition, to patriotic appeals made by the Office of War Information during World War II. Together, these images reveal the entrenched cultural separation and racial hierarchies of American society. One of the principal films of the war era, *The Negro Soldier*, articulates the complexities of race intensified by the crisis of war. It also fractures the long tradition of degrading minstrel images by presenting a more dignified public image of African Americans. The narrative within *The Negro Soldier* transforms the once "inferior" African American into a competent soldier. This conversion narrative forms the foundation for the evolution of racial attitudes and behavior that eventually followed.

This study lies at the intersection of three disciplines: the history of the African American experience in World War II; the theory of documentary film; and finally, the study of rhetoric, the art of persuasion, as Aristotle defined it, through all available means.[14] These disciplines have not come together before at exactly this point. John E. O'Connor provides the reason:

> Traditional historians tend to neglect the close analysis of the visual image. Cinema scholars may too often rest on their theoretical base, doing injustice to the broader historical context of their discussion; those in communications studies may be too limited in their concern with what can be quantified. We must find ways to integrate the research in the collateral fields of communications and cinema studies into a comprehensive approach to the history of mass media art and industries.[15]

This interdisciplinary vantage point may overcome the limitations of conventional scholarship, although undoubtedly it will introduce other unintended shortfalls. Even so, interdisciplinary approaches offer advantages. Ronald R. Krebs, who departs from more traditional political science studies of conflict, argues, "Political analysis would be richer and more realistic if rhetoric were central to the study of politics."[16] Developing a rhetorical turn in the study of politics as well as military history may allow for a deeper understanding of the complexities of wartime media. By examining *The Negro Soldier*, we can locate the strategies of institutional voices as they maneuvered to secure the allegiance of disgruntled Americans who threatened to derail military victory in their demands for equal rights.

The historical record, preserved in the films of World War II, provides a trail that marks the quest for racial equality in the United States. The symbols and narratives that accompany the forging of national identity are preserved in public discourse offering a rich source of evidence for investigation. The historical backdrop within which critical social issues are encountered framed the debate for the generations that inherited its outcomes. It is culture that makes such public sparring possible, and it is culture that is ultimately transfigured by the arguments. *The Negro Soldier* cannot be excised from its milieu. It is important to understand the social and attitudinal conditions that informed the experience of race in the first half of the twentieth century.

One wonders why African Americans bothered to fight in any American conflict, given their historically marginalized place in American democracy. This conundrum is especially perplexing in the context of World War II, a war to free millions from tyranny. Scholars have neglected to ask the fundamental question: Why did the African American community send thousands of men to fight for a democratic way of life in which they could not fully participate? The answers to this question—and there are undoubtedly many—may shed light on contemporary quandaries, situations that involve military mobilization for the good, not of the whole society, but of narrow constituencies. This is the central question of this book. The following chapters explore the cultural context wherein citizenship for African Americans was negotiated through military service.

Chapter one, "The Dilemma of Racial Identity," explores the historical tension dividing society along racial lines. Chapter two, "Military Service and Citizenship," investigates the links between military service and assumptions about responsibilities and rewards of citizenship in the Western tradition. Chapter three, "Mass Media in the Twentieth Century," explores the long history of African American visual stereotypes from the print era through the celluloid images rooted in the minstrel tradition. Chapter four, "*The Negro Soldier* as Conversion Narrative," focuses on the first film that successfully unified black and white Americans in the common cause of victory and the central narrative strategy it invoked. Chapter five, "Conflicting Narratives and Images," reveals the successful adaptation of the conversion narrative in other Office of War Information films intended to solidify African American support for the war at, even as other military training films employed contradictory messages. Chapter six, "Military Conditions during World War II," considers the paradox of African Americans called upon to serve their nation, often as a last resort and always under the disadvantages of segregation and discrimination. Chapter seven, "Attitudinal Barriers to Change," traces the evolution of American racial attitudes and the violence it engendered among civilians and soldiers during the war. Chapter eight, "Social Conditions for Change," considers the impact of dramatic geographic and social trends that matured during World War II. Chapter nine, "The Influence of the Black Press," identifies the impact of black journalists who shaped minority public opinion and increased racial tensions nationally during World Wars I and II. Chapter ten, "The Negotiation of Racial Identity," analyzes the enduring impact of images from World War II, which reordered social values developed in the cultivation of public patriotism during the war and permanently affected national identity. And the final discussion in Chapter 11, "The Challenge of Change in the Aftermath of World War II," looks at the effects of military desegregation in the wake of World War II, as well as contemporary issues concerning inclusion of women, gays, and other minority populations in American military services.

Among Americans of all racial backgrounds, there are thousands of different experiences of wartime America. One book cannot capture the diversity of those encounters with war. It can, however, explore important themes that circulated in wartime America, helping those of us who did not live through the Second World War to understand the complex historical, social, political, and military influences that shaped lives and communities. In the end, their courage and sacrifice increase our gratitude to those who volunteered and fought on front lines and in factories to support our nation during the greatest conflict of the twentieth century.

CHAPTER ONE

The Dilemma of Racial Identity

We have a wolf by the ears, and we can neither hold him, nor safely let him go. Justice is in one scale, and self-preservation in the other.
—ANDREW JACKSON REFERRING TO THE INSTITUTION OF SLAVERY[1]

Emergence of the idea of a social structure based on race paralleled European colonial expansion, although it had probably been present in other, earlier cultures. In European eyes, the image of nonwhites was profoundly shaped by Christianity, as Europeans encountered and subdued the darker peoples of Africa. Fascination with apes and baboons coincided with the thought that Africans, perceived to be physically similar to African wildlife, were also bestial.[2] European religion provided the framework whereby all things, living and inanimate, were ranked from closest to furthest from God in the great chain of being, a construct that influenced human power relationships for generations.[3] To European colonists, both Africans and Native Americans were originally seen as servants of Satan, as savages without souls. Eventually, Native Americans were acknowledged as fit subjects for conversion—unless they resisted. In that case, they were massacred, their deaths justified because their resistance to Christianity proved they were human manifestations of the devil. Not until the eighteenth century were blacks considered fit subjects for Christian proselytizing.

In North America, the system of rigid racial categories that emerged from colonial conquest produced a social order based on the belief that inferior races required patriarchal protection. This paternalistic hierarchy mirrored the cycle of human development from childhood through adulthood. Nineteenth-century scholars used the concept of human growth to describe the varied development of the races. Blacks were considered fetal, Asians infantile, and whites adult. Lack of beards among the inferior races, as well as their uncomplicated natures, supported this purportedly scientific view.[4] The peculiar institution of slavery and policies of immigration were shaped according to this template.

The hierarchy of privilege that accompanied this racial orientation permeated most aspects of American life and was reinforced by a complex social, economic, political, and legal infrastructure. In one sense, the American institutions that grew from slavery reflected these roots, if not in name, then in the practice of segregation. Among the cultural institutions that preserved racism, by the twentieth century media had become ubiquitous with the advent of film and radio. Ironically, media simultaneously reinforced racial hierarchies and revealed the fissures of an unraveling system of segregation, as Sambo-like caricatures challenged and were rebuffed by white characters. In the land of the free, freedom did not extend to many inhabitants, including African Americans. That apparent contradiction did not seem inconsistent, largely because those disenfranchised were considered incapable of participation as full-fledged citizens; owing to their inferior nature, they lacked the necessary qualities of citizenship.

Federal definitions of race in the United States have relied on the idea of "blood quantum," a measure of how one's heredity can be traced through blood to particular ancestors such as African Americans, Native Americans, Hispanics, and so on. Unlike racial categories that resulted from geographic circumstances, where groups like Asians and Hispanics were protected by strong sovereign territories and governments, Native and African American classifications were "the direct result of conquest and enslavement."[5]

The concept of blood quantum was widely applied in order to prevent the dilution of white blood. The original use of blood quantum can be traced to 1705 and Virginia laws that limited the civil rights of Native Americans and persons who were of half or more Native American ancestry. In practice, many people of mixed ancestry, especially those who "looked white," were blended into the white majority and enjoyed the same privileges as whites—in some places. However, these individuals were restricted by laws like the 1822 Virginia law designating anyone with one African American grandparent as legally "mulatto," and therefore subject to the same restrictions applied to African Americans.

Following the Nat Turner Rebellion of 1831, many state legislatures increased controls over African Americans, and their rights eroded further in the post-Civil War South. For instance, marriage to whites was prohibited to anyone considered black or racially mixed. In the twentieth century, still more restrictive legal definitions of race were enacted. From 1910 to 1930 racial discrimination reached its zenith with implementation of the rigid Jim Crow system in the South and more lax, but still discriminatory racial segregation, in the North and West. Virginia, for example, adopted the "one-drop rule" in its 1924 Racial Integrity Act, making any African ancestry grounds for exclusion as "colored." And the Indian Reorganization Act of 1934 condemned the pollution of white blood by mixing with other races, especially African Americans. Such legal definitions often did not differentiate between African Americans, Native Americans, and others, labeled them all "colored."

The effect of African American blood was so potent that one drop defined a person as black. In application, divisions by race had serious consequences. In 1854, for example, the California Supreme Court in *People v. Hall* held that blacks, mulattoes, Native Americans, and Chinese were not white and therefore could not testify in court against whites. The result was to sanction violence by whites against nonwhites, because eyewitness evidence of nonwhite victims could not be introduced in court. These laws arbitrarily designated Mexican residents as white, while some European immigrants, notably Irish and Italian, were designated as black unless they could demonstrate they were white persons.[6]

The one-drop rule coincided with Jim Crow racial segregation laws, the adoption of eugenics theories by some scientists, and ideas of racial purity that disenfranchised most African Americans by restricting their voting rights, controlling their access to public facilities, and limiting their recourse to education. White-dominated institutions such as state and national legislative bodies, as well as the Supreme Court, reinforced racial restrictions through a network of laws and decisions. *Plessy v. Ferguson* (1896), the most notorious of these decisions, upheld the constitutionality of state laws requiring racial segregation in public facilities under the doctrine of "separate but equal." This standard preserved Jim Crow segregation until its repudiation in *Brown v. Board of Education* (1954), which began the slow legal process of dismantling Jim Crow.

Plessy informed the prevailing social practices and legal standards of World War II. While the Court stipulated that there was no implication of the racial inferiority of African Americans because such would violate the Fourteenth Amendment, it did affirm existing public policies separating people by race. Justice Henry B. Brown summarized the majority opinion that racial separation did not stamp African Americans with "a badge of inferiority," but if inferiority is found, it exists "solely because the colored race chooses to put that construction upon it."[7] Since the court did not find differences in quality between white and black railroad cars in *Plessy*, it assumed that other public facilities were similarly equal. Justice John Marshall Harlan's caustic dissent predicted that the decision would become infamous, but Harlan did not foresee the contradictions that World War II would produce when Asians, who in 1896 were allowed to board the same railroad cars as whites, became the focus of discrimination and relocation to internment camps. *Plessy v. Ferguson* anchored the legal foundation for the separation of races in military institutions; the idea that segregation based on racial classifications remained legal as long as facilities were of equal quality. Ultimately, restrictions based on racial categories informed US military policy during World War II.

The process of racial identification has often been one of reduction, forging a single identity for groups that may be culturally diverse, historically constituted, and ethnically fragmented. Such categorization also dichotomizes societies along a binary scale that classifies as "nonwhite" anyone outside a narrow range, and renders a racial hierarchy of preference for whites at the expense of other racial groups. In practice, the question of race is often complicated by economic and political factors, social interaction, and legal stipulations. And race continues to be debated today, as evident in the 1986 Supreme Court case *Doe v. Louisiana* and publications such as *A Troublesome Inheritance: Genes, Race, and Human History* (2014), by Nicholas Wage.

In effect, racial division in the United States has separated any group deemed nonwhite as racially "other." For much of American history, this practice has protected a narrow group of original settlers, mainly from northern European countries like England, Russia, and Germany, from successive waves of immigration, as well as from the original native inhabitants of the continent. Race, according to Ronald Takaki, "has been a social construction that has historically set apart racial minorities from European immigrant groups."[8] It is not, Takaki argues, equivalent to ethnicity, which derives from the customs and practices of social groups. By contrast, race is the inheritance of immutable physical and psychological characteristics. While the distinction can occasionally be fuzzy, to link race with permanent characteristics justifies racial discrimination because the immutable characteristics that accompany racial groups predetermine their treatment. Hence, the strong prohibition against racial mixing is intended to preserve the innate characteristics of race from dilution. This assumption prompted Mississippi congressman John Rankin to denounce in 1943 the transfusion of black or Japanese blood into white Americans as a communist plot, an attempt to mongrelize America, "to pump Negro or Japanese blood into the veins of our wounded white boys regardless of the dire effect it might have on their children."[9] In essence, racial category dictates social position. For example, this understanding of race explains how Irish immigrants were first classified as nonwhite because they were considered to be pagan and savage, closer to African American slaves than to civilized white men. As a result, the Irish were prohibited from purchasing land, marrying white Europeans, holding office, serving on juries, or testifying in court.[10] In contrast to the straight-laced, hard-working puritan ideal of the European colonists, Irish immigrants were stereotyped as wicked, lazy, morally loose, without manners, inept as farmers and orchard keepers, and thieves who had to be watched carefully.

One ramification of establishing binary racial divisions that preclude change is centralization of power. The immutable characteristics of race establish a permanent border between the powerful and outsiders. Racial definitions preserve the site of decision-making and establish yardsticks for inclusion. The earliest colonial stereotypes of Native Americans, Irish immigrants, and African Americans categorize each group as savage and shiftless, as opposed to white colonists, who exhibited the spirituality and industry of civilized people. The first laws restricting citizenship to land ownership reflected this division between white power elites and disadvantaged others.[11] Throughout the colonies, suffrage was also originally based on property ownership, which assumed that owners of material goods and land had acquired them through dedicated labor and divine providence favoring the godly. Limited access to land and power resulted in tensions that erupted in 1676 in Bacon's Rebellion. In ensuing years, the power base moved from land ownership toward class status, which included property owners as well as indentured and slave classes. Laws once hostile to white servants became more liberal, while those laws restricting the rights of African Americans, who were often enslaved, remained intact, creating a political division based more squarely on skin color.[12] As the criterion for citizenship shifted to encompass social rank rather than land ownership, racial definitions were reinforced—with curious results. Irish and other immigrants, such as Italians, were considered closer to whites, while "blacks were forced to occupy a racially subordinate and stigmatized status, one below all whites regardless of their class."[13] Such racial discrimination protected whites by restricting access to power and defining other groups as nonwhite. This system provided the justification for segregation and, for Native Americans, for forcible removal to reservations. These collective constraints forged a common denominator of powerlessness for those who were excluded by racial restrictions.

During wartime, although legally ambiguous, the social practices of a segregated society were replicated in military institutions. Dichotomization based on race promotes the construction of "the other," those who are located outside the structures of power. Such dichotomization often results in the stigmatization of whole categories of people who, as a consequence, become objects of contempt. Stereotypes about those segregated accompany the stigma of segregation, for those who are "other" are presumed to lack the characteristics valued by the dominant culture. They were seen as inherently unsalvageable, stereotyped as lacking self-control and intelligence, and as carriers of disease. Finally, they were depicted as simultaneously childlike and brutishly savage. The physically distinctive attributes ascribed to African Americans confirmed their innate lack of culturally desirable attributes. And these characteristics, such as a simple nature, were not limited to African Americans, but were also ascribed to other outsiders, such as Native Americans. Vestiges of these stereotypes have persisted unabated into the twenty-first century.

During World War II, both the Allies and the Axis powers expressed racial hatred and practiced systems of racial hierarchy. Intolerance of Jews, homosexuals, gypsies, Poles, and Russians in Axis nations is well documented. The Japanese expressed their racial superiority in atrocities committed against the people of China, Manchuria, and Australia. Americans were not exempt from racial hatred, and sometimes violence, usually targeting African Americans, Japanese, and Hispanics. For some white Americans, hatred of nonwhite races did not distinguish Japanese living in imperial Japan from those living as American citizens. Some conflated all racial groups, lumping Asians together with African Americans.[14] The Japanese, perceived by white Americans as an inferior race, lacking human feelings although possessing manic determination, were more hated than the Germans or the Italians.[15] Racist images were exceedingly graphic and contemptuous, portraying the Japanese as apes, buck-toothed and nearsighted rats, and vermin. Few Americans objected to these depictions.

Such feelings were so commonplace that in 1945 a popular American scientific magazine published an article, "Why Americans Hate Japs more than Nazis" without public protest.[16] Two weeks after the attack on Pearl Harbor, *Life* magazine included diagrams illustrating "How to tell Japs from the Chinese" to help readers distinguish between enemies and allies.[17] American soldiers were issued copies of the *Pocket Guide to China*, a pamphlet illustrated with graphics depicting supposed differences between Asian friends and foes, including skin coloration, eye configuration, and "the wide space between the first and second toes" caused by wooden Japanese sandals.[18] Collectively, the Japanese were understood to be primitive, emotionally deficient, and capable of horrifying atrocities, yet superhuman and fanatically devoted to their emperor. In a 1943 *Atlantic Monthly* article, Virginius Dabney explained the race riots in the United States by blaming African Americans, associating them with the degeneracy of Asians: "Like the natives of Malaysia and Burma the American Negroes are sometimes imbued with the notion that a victory for the yellow race over the white race might also be a victory for them."[19] The link between the Japanese and the African Americans signaled fear that the demands of African Americans for civil rights were somehow associated with the enemy.

Adherence of the Nazis to the doctrine of Aryan superiority provoked a critique of master race arguments, particularly among Western scientists and intellectuals. This examination of theories concerning inherent superior or inferior capabilities of different races began to expose the hypocrisy of racial prejudice in the United States. Anti-Semitism, internment of Japanese American citizens, and demeaning Jim Crow laws were manifestations of American bigotry exposed in the debate over Nazi racism. In the midst of the war, Congress considered revising Oriental exclusion laws, notoriously rooted in attitudes of white racial superiority. As John W. Dower concludes, "In such ways, World War II contributed immeasurably not only to a sharpened awareness of racism within the United States, but also to more radical demands and militant tactics on the part of the victims of discrimination."[20]

Intellectual uneasiness regarding racism was more broadly introduced into the public discussion by other challengers. The popular works of Ruth Benedict, *Patterns of Culture* (1934) and *The Races of Mankind* (1943), became epicenters of controversy. They were banned by the army and civilian United service organizations, as well as denounced by the Military Affairs Committee of the House of Representatives as communist propaganda because they critiqued racism— in particular, American racial injustice.[21] These actions reflected the racial views of many Americans, who were not receptive to reconsidering racial issues or inclusive viewpoints. Their racial attitudes derived from historical precedent and were embedded in public institutions. But the social tensions and severe disruptions introduced by global war necessitated closer inspection of unjust attitudes and practices.

At a time when white Americans overwhelmingly supported segregation, the federal government was obliged to acknowledge positive African American capabilities in order to generate support for African American enlistments, while simultaneously avoiding black demands for expanded civil rights. The most successful federal effort was *The Negro Soldier*, a film praised by white and black viewers alike. Focusing on the common goal of victory, filmmakers plundered the past, retelling America's story while highlighting African American contributions. This revised history generated an unmistakably integrationist message for black viewers but reassured whites that victory was the ultimate goal of temporary cooperation.

Previously African American stereotypes helped to justify rigid social structures found in segregation and Jim Crow policies. But in order to utilize African Americans as military personnel, the federal government needed to revise stereotyped constructions, updating them in ways that would serve military goals without alienating either black or white Americans. Thus, African Americans formerly designated as "other" were now included, at least superficially, in the pursuit of military victory.

The challenge was complicated by the patchwork application of segregation laws and practices. Northern and Western regions often differed significantly from their Southern neighbors, and practices were not consistent even within regions. Both black and white Americans stationed in Hawaii, for example, were subject to racial understandings that drew distinctions between native Hawaiians and others. In Hawaii, people of African descent were considered Puerto Ricans, and thus fell into the Caucasian category, along with whites of European extraction.[22] Conventions of racial segregation that worked locally in peacetime began to unravel during World War II, as thousands of displaced Americans confronted inconsistent regional racial practices.

In addition, the myth of white omnipotence was shattered for Americans in the wake of the initial Japanese victories in the Pacific theater of war. Contrary to the tenets of the white superiority dogma, nonwhite Japanese developed sophisticated battle strategies, mastered advanced technologies, performed fearlessly in battle, and executed skillful, although brutal, management of conquered territories. Unlike Americans who often were oblivious of racial discrimination, the Japanese were well informed on various aspects of American racism: the policies of segregation, the lynching of blacks, and the published racist statements of American leaders.[23] Such examples of American racial intolerance appeared frequently in Japanese propaganda pointing out the white supremacist attitudes of many Americans. For example, a 1944 Japanese magazine article, "Naming the Western Barbarians," caricatures Americans as demons recognizable by their gross physical features and treatment of all nonwhites as domestic animals.[24]

The cracks that appeared in the racist superstructure, combined with the need for all Americans to unite for victory, help to explain the enthusiastic reception of films that celebrated African American contributions to the war effort. Release of such films would have been unimaginable even a few years before the war. Films like the signal corps's *The Negro Soldier* bear witness to the struggle between the dominant ideologies of racism and patriotism, which came to a head in World War II. These films articulate ideologies that support government and military institutions. In doing so, they negotiated a compromise between black and white Americans, subordinating the individual interests of each group to the collective national goal of military victory. The central theme of the films' texts is American patriotism. The growing influence of mass media, particularly film, aided broad circulation of images of patriotic Africans Americans and paved the way for dramatic social changes in the second half of the twentieth century.

Film penetrates the private spaces of our lives, an effect that usually goes unnoticed because it masquerades as entertainment. Inevitably, because film is "experienced" it becomes part of the fabric of our reality, perceived as personal rather than ideological in its impact and rarely raising critical questions about how its subject matter is presented. Because military service and the conduct of war are grounded in historical traditions of patriotism and citizenship, we forget that films depicting these subjects are imbued with ideologies rooted in culture. The way societies represent war becomes a repository of their social ideologies. When films are screened and accepted without critical examination, their ideologies compound the problems of unexamined nationalism.

The Negro Soldier has been dismissed by some historians. John Modell, Marc Goulden, and Sigurdur Magnusson characterize the film as a "saccharine confection . . . bathed in almost hysterical acclaim" that "would leave more recent viewers squirming in embarrassment."[25] From a contemporary perspective, perhaps their point is well taken. However, when viewed from the vantage point of mid-World War II, in the context of segregation and violent racial intolerance, another conclusion is warranted. At any rate, the film invites further examination, this time as a response, however incomplete, to a complex web of issues, attitudes, and audiences. It provides the first positive projection of African Americans, creating a startling contrast to the uniformly negative media images of earlier years.

Since the advent of mass media, the range of images for African Americans has been narrow. From the minstrel era that spanned early to mid-nineteenth century, popular culture portrayed African Americans as shiftless, infantile, and ignorant, with exaggerated physical features that mirrored a propensity for bestiality. Cultural roles accessible to African Americans were limited as well, with most of them relegated to service functions. Encoded in these images and roles is the message of African American inferiority. In the bulk of Hollywood entertainment films, even those depicting African themes, black actors rarely appeared as more than narrative props. In films like *Tarzan of the Apes* (1918), for example, Africans are marginalized, serving as a backdrop for European American actors.[26]

It was likely that both races carried prejudices into the ranks of the military, attitudes that were largely suppressed for the duration of the war by various institutional and organizational forces that enforced segregation. But racial prejudice reemerged with the declaration of peace.[27] It would be simplistic to claim that a few positive film images created a new place in society for African Americans, but these images did plant seeds that would later mature into demands for a more inclusive society. It remained for activists in the 1960s to tackle institutionalized racism, and through the civil rights movement capitalize on the promises made to African Americans who defended democracy during the war years.

As events following the Allied victory attest, it would take decades to redress injustices perpetrated for generations. As in the war years, "emerging demographic diversity" continues to raise "fundamental questions about America's identity and culture."[28] Even after Hollywood studio heads recognized the restrictive nature of stereotypical screen images of whites and blacks, Patricia Turner recollected, these images were translated to television: "Our images were few and far between, and we hungered for more of them. . . . In subtle ways they did communicate a sense of fractured possibility and a near resignation to second-class citizenship."[29] One could argue that contemporary media continue to represent society in ways that are skewed toward heterosexual, white, young, wealthy males, while avoiding a more realistic depiction of the true diversity of American society.

CHAPTER TWO

Military Service and Citizenship

In our culture there has always been a direct connection between military service and citizenship.
—MARY CHEH[1]

In the Western tradition, military service has been linked directly to citizenship both as a responsibility and as a right ever since the first wars fought by the soldiers of ancient Greece and Rome. As Antonio Santosuosso concluded in his study of classical societies, "The identity of citizens was inextricably linked to the identity of the soldier . . . and the person who had the privilege of being a citizen of the polis also had the duty to defend or to advance the power of his city."[2] The defense of their city-state was a fundamental responsibility of citizens of Athens, Sparta, Crete, and later Rome. Ironically, the defenders of Gaul, Germania, and other territories invaded by Roman legions were also exercising their obligation to defend themselves as members of their respective tribes. In Western societies, military service has been a function of citizenship since the era of ancient city-states, perhaps fluctuating in its objectives, but always tied to the rights of citizens.

Among the social institutions that describe nations, military organizations reveal both the internal character of the nation and its external intentions toward others. Consider, for instance, the demanding bushido code of the Japanese, the Ayran superiority of the German soldier, or the citizen soldier of the United States. Each unique military philosophy accompanied an orientation toward others that rested on fundamental principles. The Japanese valued loyalty and self-sacrifice; the Nazis elevated the superiority of purity; and the Americans championed the common citizen. As in the military forces of the Japanese and Germans, an important influence shaping the armed forces of the United States has been the extent to which the military reflects national purpose and identity. As the United States changed from a colony fashioned from British traditions into a modern international force, its military institutions were shaped by the changing national vision, evolving from their initial function as domestic protection to international police force. What once was a volunteer organization of local inhabitants protecting their homes became a conscripted force, as citizens taking up arms transformed into trained professionals. Yet throughout these historical changes, citizenship has remained the underlying presumption of military service.

It is important to understand that citizenship is generally a central component of individual well-being and success, that citizenship brings economic, community, and political advantages not available to outsiders.[3] Individuals and groups advance in social hierarchies to the extent that they assume the rights and benefits, along with the responsibilities of their nation.[4] Nations protect the lives and property of individuals and groups, but they can also limit privileges and, by extension, political power, by denying citizenship to individuals or groups. As Christopher Parker elaborates, citizenship is dependent on social conventions "determined by membership in this or that ascriptive category. Put differently, citizenship is inherently political, the result of a process by which individuals are ultimately proclaimed fit or unfit for membership in the political community, often on the basis of one's race or sex."[5] And historically, outsiders could often advance their social standing through military service. For generations, military service has been a direct means of earning American citizenship. But slavery, segregation, and racism limited such possibilities for African Americans, a direct result of the reluctance of the larger society to grant them the opportunities and privileges of full citizenship.[6]

For African Americans the primary obstacle to full citizenship was the persistent belief that the black race was fundamentally inferior to the white race. This belief in black inferiority underlay most arguments prohibiting equal opportunities for African Americans to secure the benefits of education, voting, and civil rights exercised by other citizens.[7] The key to challenging social segregation, according to Mary Cheh, lies in military service: "The story of African-Americans claiming their rightful places as full citizens is mirrored in their ability to shatter policies of exclusion and segregation in the Armed Forces."[8] It follows that those who could not come to the defense of their country could not lay claim to the rights of full-fledged citizenship. A review of Supreme Court rulings on the Fourteenth Amendment reveals the extent of the interconnectedness of citizenship and military service in American history and practice.[9]

Although African Americans have been present since the first colonial militias took up arms against Native Americans, the British, and the French, blacks' service and sacrifice did not yield equality or citizenship. Even while shouldering the obligation to defend their communities, they were excluded from the benefits of living there. This chapter will examine the origins of the citizen soldier concept in the colonial militia, the tension between the citizen soldier and the professional standing army, and the role of the military in instilling American values as well as in excluding American citizens, especially during World War II. Finally, this chapter will consider how various disenfranchised groups continue to establish their case for full participation through military service.

Origins of the Citizen Soldier

As previously noted, the Western tradition of military service as an obligation of citizenship has roots in the city-states of ancient Greece and Rome.[10] While it has waxed and waned, this connection of citizenship to military service persisted through the Middle Ages and on into modern Western civilization and is evident in the philosophies of Machiavelli, Hegel, and others, as well as in practices of various nation states.[11] Participation in the armed forces stood as a test of commitment to the nation, an essential ingredient of citizenship. Historian Otto Hintze summarizes the claim: "Whoever puts himself in the service of the state must logically and fairly be granted the regular rights of citizenship."[12]

Citizenship is grounded in the twin values of military service and civic participation. In this tradition, if a resident desires to reap the benefits of a society, he must share in the responsibility to defend it against external enemies. In practice, military service requirements vary among nations, but they always carry an implicit responsibility to take up arms in defense of the nation.[13] In this respect, nations are more than geographical locations, people, and buildings. They exist as symbolic formations, systems of representation that produce identification within communities. Citizenship is a symbolic representation that binds an individual to the fundamental symbols of group identity. These symbols gain potency in times of crisis as the heightened identification of nationalism when they can override basic human needs in their call for ultimate sacrifices.[14]

Rather than concentrating power in the hands of a powerful few as in European monarchies, universal service distributed responsibility among citizens, who were most invested in the nation and most likely to benefit from the bonds of the state. R. Claire Snyder identifies the roots of the tension between these political models: "In the American case, the republican founders, coming from England, were well-versed in the problems inherent in a standing army; they believed that only a military consisting of temporary citizen soldiers would be willing and able to maintain peace, preserve liberty, and minimize the omnipresent possibility of tyranny."[15] As a result, founders of the New World colonies invested heavily in guaranteeing to every able-bodied man the right to bear arms as an expression of commitment to their communities and nation. This citizen soldier would answer only to his community, because that is where his home, family, and livelihood were invested. By contrast, the standing armies of European monarchies (replicated in many South American nations), exhibited broad political power and, on various occasions, deposed established governments, replacing them with military dictatorships. The citizen soldier prevented the development of a powerful autonomous military establishment outside the checks and balances of the democratic process—at least, some would argue, until the emergence of the "military industrial complex" foreseen by Dwight D. Eisenhower.[16]

In European history, because it challenged the relationship of the citizen to civic duty, the French Revolution was a crucial point in the evolution of modern military establishments. These daring challenges sent shock waves throughout Europe that reverberated across the ocean in the newly developing Americas. At the end of the eighteenth century, the French people broke decisively with the assumptions of the monarchy, reverting to the ideal of the Greco-Roman citizen soldier. They determined that common citizens could be fully armed, share military power, and influence political decisions that directly impacted their lives. In the years following this reassertion of the citizen as soldier, they introduced the idea that common men could advance to become military leaders based on merit rather than birth, a revolutionary concept. Prior to the French Revolution, under feudal and aristocratic governments, militaries were officered by men chosen from the nobility. Armed forces were manned by the poor, who were pressed into service, and supplemented with adventurers and mercenaries. The French Revolution marked a return to the fundamental idea of the citizen soldier, a figure that had originated in Greek city-states and the early Roman republic. The result was the emergence of an ideal of citizenship expressed in citizen armies that in time operationalized American democracy.[17]

The idea of the citizen soldier was transported to the Americas by the first European settlers, who were often obliged to fight native inhabitants and each other for a foothold in the New World. Thousands of miles of ocean prohibited more traditional reliance on national armies for defense. As R. Claire Snyder summarizes, "The United States has historically seen a conceptual linkage between military service and first-class citizenship, a connection embodied in the 'citizen-soldier' ideal of civic republicanism."[18] Owing to its Greco-Roman heritage, this civic republican tradition locates military service and citizenship in the citizen soldier ideal.[19] The isolation of the early colonists engendered a fierce independence that included self-defense.

In the early colonies the fortunes of African Americans as citizens rose and fell from generation to generation. Before the mid- 1790s, black slaves and freedmen enjoyed many legal rights and relatively unrestricted lives. After 1800, most Southern states codified their restrictions on slaves, possibly as a response to anti-slavery agitation, the threat of slave revolts, and the increased presence of freedmen.[20] From 1790 to 1810 the portion of freedmen rose from 8 percent to over 13 percent of the total black population in Southern regions, and attempts to deal with the presence of freedmen contributed to shifting attitudes as well as more restrictive legal boundaries, especially regarding the bearing of arms.

African American slaves were usually prevented from bearing arms or discharging militia service when the security of the colonies was threatened by enemies, although slaves who fought were occasionally granted their freedom in return.[21] Their emancipation depended on the willingness or ability of the colonial governments to compensate masters for the loss of their property.[22] It was usually practical necessity that lead to the arming of slaves. However, there was no consistent policy regarding slave enlistments. For example, lacking alternative sources of manpower in 1703, South Carolina promised freedom to any slave who killed or captured an enemy soldier, provided that the slave "could produce a white person who witnessed the deed."[23] On the other hand, precautions were taken in neighboring Virginia to prevent the arming of slaves, because of the lingering fear of rebellion. The number of slaves in the New England states was too small to make an impact.

Despite its inconsistent implementation, the link between military service and freedom for African Americans was firmly established in colonial practices. African American military service was recorded as early as 1708, when armed slaves served as mounted soldiers protecting Charleston, South Carolina, from Indian raids. Their exemplary service was recognized by the colonial legislature in a 1747 resolution. During the same period, armed slaves served in the state militia, although by law they were required to be accompanied by two armed white men at all times, presumably to ensure faithfulness.²⁴ Before 1776, the British colonies formed part-time militias to counter the dangers posed by Indians and by rival French and Spanish colonial powers. All of the colonies, except Quaker-dominated Pennsylvania, compelled enlistment of citizens under universal military service laws that applied to all males of appropriate age. Eventually, even Pennsylvania, which had created a voluntary militia in 1755, made military service compulsory in 1775. Beginning early in the French and Indian Wars, in 1755, these colonial militias operated as supplementary units with the British regular army.

From its colonial British roots, the United States inherited a military tradition that included both citizen soldiers and regulars, together with inevitable friction between them. The first standing army established by the Second Continental Congress in June 14, 1775, was modeled on the British regular army. An army was raised by offering volunteers cash bonuses and tracts of free land in the West at the conclusion of the Revolutionary War. These incentives did not attract enough men, and those who enlisted often fulfilled the terms of their enlistment before the end of the war, leaving the militia without sufficient manpower. Thus, General Washington was forced to rely on state militias for soldiers. This relationship was a rocky one. State militias were made up of citizens, were often poorly trained, inadequately lead, and prone to desert to tend their farms. Crops needed planting and harvesting during the spring and fall; those seasons were also best suited for military combat, further complicating citizen soldiers' devotion to duty. To supplement troop strength, some state governments offered African Americans their freedom for volunteering and completing military service, thus formalizing the direct connection between citizenship and service.²⁵

Citizenship was indirectly, and sometimes directly, related to race. In 1790 a law provided that only white persons could become United States citizens. This legal restriction was reasserted in 1922, when the United States Supreme Court concluded that Takao Ozawa, an immigrant from Japan, was not entitled to naturalized citizenship because he was not Caucasian. Two years later, Congress enacted immigration legislation that included a provision prohibiting the entry of any person ineligible for citizenship, reinforcing the Supreme Court restriction on citizenship for Japanese immigrants. While this stance on Japanese citizenship was a response to immigration pressures of the period, it also indirectly reinforced the limitation of full citizenship rights for African Americans who, like the Japanese, were clearly not Caucasian. This limitation was not reversed until the 1952 McCarran-Walter Act.

Evolution of the Citizen Soldier Concept

Development of the ideal of the citizen soldier can be seen in the reaction of the fledgling American democracy to the excesses of its European masters, with the colonists designating terms of citizenship in the essential documents of the new democracy.[26] The founding fathers rejected the British model of the professional soldier, and instead reverted to the concept of citizenship that arose during the French Revolution. The Second Amendment to the Constitution illustrates the central importance of citizens as soldiers. Under the Second Amendment, all citizens have the right to organize militias for the "defense of a free state." The Militia Act of 1792 also articulated the responsibility of military service by establishing the principle of universal military obligation. It required every white, able-bodied male citizen between eighteen and forty-five to serve in the militia of his state.[27] Restrictions on full citizenship, based on gender and race as well as age and physical condition, were inscribed into law, codifying informal practices. This codification allowed for a small standing army, staffed by volunteers and subject to public control, to safeguard the new nation. American self-defense rested on its commitment to the citizen soldier and rejection of European-inspired professional armies.

The first test of the American military model came with the break from Britain. Both the colonial governments and the British relied on slaves to provide labor and bear arms. British commanders promised freedom to any slave who fought for the king and remained loyal to the throne. Colonial governments also promised rewards to the masters of slaves who served government interests. As many as five thousand African Americans, both slave and freemen, constituting almost 3 percent of all military personnel, fought in the Colonial Army against the British. Several thousand slaves acquired freedom based on this military service.[28] As Bernard C. Nalty concludes, "The Revolutionary War lent credence to the belief, which later would become almost an article of faith among blacks, that military service in wartime represented a path toward freedom and greater postwar opportunity."[29]

Following the Revolutionary War the terms of citizenship were again revised, and the previous requirement of property ownership for suffrage gave way to demands for enfranchisement by veterans regardless of their financial status. Recognition of military service as a condition for suffrage effectively excluded women, who sometimes could meet the property requirement, but rarely found the opportunity for military service.[30] African

American slaves were also disenfranchised, because while many were freed, they were prevented from voting.

The ragtag Continental Army was replaced by a smaller force that became the nucleus of the regular army recognized by the Constitution in 1789. The Second Amendment to the Constitution, enacted in 1791, reflected the compulsory service militia mandate that had existed since the earliest colonial wars. In spite of the support of presidents Washington, Adams, Jefferson, and Madison for a military system that would register men for service and assign them to regular units for training, the army remained small and decentralized. Both the standing army and militias were opposed by advocates who feared that a military coup d'état like those witnessed in Europe would threaten liberty. Those voices might have prevailed except for the continuing friction with Native Americans and the ominous presence of Great Britain and France in North America. Still, the standing army and militia numbered fewer than twenty-five thousand as late as 1898, the eve of the Spanish-American War.

Whether the United States adopted a militia system or a standing army, neither structure affected the status of African Americans, who were completely excluded except in periods of extreme need. In spite of their service in the War of 1812, African Americans were legally barred from joining the regular army or state militias. The New York legislature, for example, claimed that blacks were unfit for the duties of citizenship regardless of the military service they had provided. Similar illogical claims were made in other states. The 1857 Supreme Court decision in the *Dred Scott* case also denied citizenship to enslaved African Americans. The decision did little more than reflect the status of African Americans that existed in most parts of the nation. In the eyes of the law, slaves were articles of property. In the period following the Civil War, many free African Americans were not much better off than slaves, subject to segregation, denied equal legal rights, brutalized with mob violence and lynchings, and prevented from voting to change their conditions.

Debates over employment of slaves and freedmen in North and South during the Civil War renewed the association of military service and citizenship. In 1863 the Emancipation Proclamation allowed African Americans to join Union military forces and provided the opportunity for them to demonstrate their responsibility as citizens. It challenged the Southern presumption of sovereignty by nullifying slave legislation. As former slave turned abolitionist leader Frederick Douglass concluded, "The black man deserves the right to vote for what he has done, to aid in suppressing the rebellion both by fighting and by assisting the Federal soldier wherever he was found.... If he knows enough to shoulder a musket and to fight for the flag, fight for the government, he knows enough to vote."[31] His point is reinforced by the recognition that immigrants who volunteered to serve during the war were granted citizenship in both the North and the South. After the Northern victory, black men served in state militias, but the Southern white backlash that followed Reconstruction created a segregated military force at state and federal levels.

For black Americans, the relationship between bearing arms and full citizenship was summed up after the Civil War by Douglass: "The Negro had been a citizen three times in the history of the government, in 1776, 1812, and 1865, and in the time of trouble the Negro was a citizen and in time of peace he was an alien."[32] In the chaos of the reconstruction period following the Civil War, through spokesmen like Douglass, African Americans pressed their demand for citizenship, recalling their sacrifices for the Union. By invoking their collective military record, they hoped to seize citizenship opportunities, to force the nation to reward the loyalties of black troops, but one of the failures of Reconstruction was its inability to permanently upgrade the political circumstances of newly freed black men and women.[33]

While roots of the segregated military system were buried deep in the antebellum period, the system itself received its justification from the persistent and relatively unchallenged assumption of the innate inferiority of the darker races. In 1863 William Wells Brown, a self-taught escaped slave, wrote in his book *The Black Man: His Antecedents, His Genius, and His Achievements*, "Two and a half centuries of the negro's enslavement have created, in many minds, the opinion that he is intellectually inferior to the rest of mankind ... it has been asserted, and from high authority in the government, that the natural inferiority of the negro makes it impossible for him to live on this continent with the white man, unless in the state of bondage."[34] The wild success of Brown's book—ten printings in three years—suggests the controversial nature of his argument. Even though Brown questioned the premise of African American inferiority, the stubborn persistence of early attitudes of racial differences continued into the twentieth century, serving as a justification for racial segregation and discrimination. In some ways, African Americans traded one form of slavery for another. As Judith Shklar concludes, "To be less than a full citizen is at the very least to approach the dreaded condition of a slave. To be a second-class citizen is to suffer derogation and the loss of respectable standing. It has also meant being ruled by others, if not wholly as the slave was, at least more so than free male citizens were."³⁵ The system of Jim Crow that replaced slavery specifically targeted African Americans, just as other manifestations of racism arose in the restrictive immigration laws that excluded Asians and the reservation system that confined those Native Americans not decimated by conflict and disease.³⁶

As evidenced by conflicts beginning with the Civil War and extending into the twentieth century's world wars, several objections persisted to the enlistment of Negro troops and, by extension, to granting them full citizenship. Deep-seated racial prejudice, the belief that European Americans were racially superior to African Americans, was primary. In addition, most European Americans believed that African Americans were too cowardly or stupid to make good soldiers. These beliefs buttressed each other and, as a result, African Americans were generally not given opportunities for military service. Hampered by substandard conditions and inadequate training, their subsequent poor performance reinforced the view that they were unable to perform in combat. Even when African American soldiers proved themselves in combat, their abilities were ignored, and they were assigned in disproportionate numbers to heavy labor and menial tasks in order to release white troops for combat.³⁷

Citizen Soldier Versus Professional Army

Another source of controversy with regard to universal citizenship was the tension between the citizen soldier, a legacy of the colonial roots of the nation, and the professional soldier, a common source of military strength for European nations. During periods of relative peace militias were disbanded, and citizen soldiers returned to their civilian lives, leaving little opportunity for African Americans to acquire citizenship through military service. To the extent that the United States used professional soldiers, their ranks were closed to African Americans.

As the frontier receded westward, the need for military defense was centered on the Indian threat in the plains territories. Atlantic coast and mid-American towns and cities retained volunteer militia companies, although their function shifted during peacetime. In the last half of the nineteenth century, most military units did not fight, but they remained a vital part of community life. According to Russell F. Weigley, "These companies achieved a remarkable vitality, and their drill competitions became a vehicle for expressing rivalries between towns and cities before the heyday of organized athletics."[38] Perhaps more than an outlet for town spirit, local militias encouraged a continued identification of military values with local citizenship, retaining the direct connection between national identity and military responsibility. Given the historical connections between local communities and their militias, African Americans hoped for full citizenship through military service. Stanley Sandler concludes, "Traditionally, black Americans have looked upon entry into the armed forces of their nation as one of the most effective ways to open doors to their fuller participation in American life."[39] Rhetorically, the significance of the citizen soldier held sway even when the United States was not engaged in war, an ideal that persists in contemporary works on American military.[40]

Even though the fight for independence rested upon the rejection of a patriarchal system, represented by the British monarchy and the assertion of the colonists' right to make their own political decisions, the privileges of citizenship were not inclusive. Enslaved persons, Native Americans, and women were mostly excluded as unsuitable for citizenship because they were considered morally and genetically weak. They were, according to popular belief, unable to fulfill the duties of citizenship. Among those duties were the obligations to pay taxes, to avoid vagrancy, to serve on juries, to refrain from treason, and to risk one's life in military service.[41] These obligations imposed particular hardships on African Americans who, especially in the years immediately following the Civil War, found it difficult to demonstrate that engagement in productive labor. They often had little money, few material possessions, limited skills, no residence or land, and no observable means of employment. Thus, citizenship was constructed in ways that prevented African Americans from attaining it during peacetime. The obligation of military service remained an insurmountable barrier, even though African Americans gradually gained employment and acquired property.

The primary obstacle to full citizenship for African Americans was the persistent belief that the black race was inferior to the white race. This tenacious belief in black deficiency underlay the patriarchal system of segregation, which, at its best, was intended to provide patriarchal protection for a people incapable of governing itself. The same belief supported the argument against granting African Americans equal opportunities in education, voting privileges, and civil rights–they simply could not benefit from such opportunities.[42]

Well before the advent of hostilities in the first worldwide conflict, W. E. B. Du Bois warned that opportunities in both civilian and military roles were being closed to African Americans. At the annual Niagara Movement meeting in Oberlin, Ohio, in August 1908, Du Bois addressed the issue of opportunity in the armed services. His words held an uncanny prediction of both world wars: "Once we were told: Be worthy and fit and the ways are open . . . . Today the avenues of advancement in the army, navy and civil service, and even in business and professional life, are continually closed to black applicants of proven fitness, simply on the bald excuse of race and color."[43] Similarly, pervasive restrictions on citizenship were grounded in the unquestioned belief in innate African American inferiority. For example, in a debate in the Mississippi State Senate over a bill to provide special civics textbooks for Negro pupils—books that did not contain information on voting or government—senator H. L. Davis stated, "Under the Constitution the Negro is a citizen . . . . But he can never expect to be given the same educational and social privileges with the white man and he doesn't expect them. The best education we can give him is to use his hands because that's how he must earn his living. It always has and always will be."[44] The Mississippi bill passed by a vote of thirty-seven to nine.

Instilling American Values

African Americans were not the only people to seek citizenship by volunteering to fight America's wars. As history records, successive waves of immigrants claimed their rights as citizens by virtue of their military service—from Irish participation in the Civil War, through the Hispanic presence in twenty-first-century conflicts in Iraq and Afghanistan.[45] This route to citizenship was encouraged because military service was an effective means to integrate newcomers into America and a quick way for recent arrivals to demonstrate their loyalty. In spite of this logic, resistance to inclusion of African Americans remained stubbornly intact. Only when they were presented with a choice between sustaining complete exclusion of African Americans from vital military functions or ensuring military victory did white Americans choose the latter. After all, a democracy's espoused ideal of equality would be meaningless if the nation was destroyed by fascist aggressors.

Each successive wave of immigration reinforced the notion that the military must not just protect the nation from its enemies, but also must foster and sustain democratic values between soldiers and hopeful newcomers alike.[46] The citizen soldier concept increased in importance with the tremendous waves of immigration that began early in the twentieth century, and reached its apogee during World War II. The qualities of citizenship—patriotism, sacrifice, discipline—were articulated through military service. Antonio Santosuosso claims, "It was inevitable that war should reflect all the main values of the warring societies in its symbolism and propaganda. What is remarkable at least to modern eyes, which look at armed conflicts as a deviant behavior, is that war was not just a normal feature of ancient life but also the element that best defined society."[47] Greeks spoke of freedom as they fought the Persians, and Romans who went into battle were convinced that they fought in the name of honesty.[48] Similarly, American military institutions elicit pride in their demonstration of American democratic virtues.[49]

Colonial communities celebrated the citizen soldier in various rituals of civic life. For example, artillery day celebrations, commemorations of battles such as the Battle of Bunker Hill, public executions, and national memorials like the Fourth of July provided opportunities for military displays like parades and canon fire, as well as sermons and lectures that illustrated civic values.[50] Prominent members of the community extolled the virtues of the heroic citizen soldier with florid oratory. Perhaps one of the most famous of such addresses, delivered by Edward Everett, was a two-hour speech dedicating the Soldier's National Cemetery in Gettysburg, Pennsylvania, on November 19, 1863. Everett's description of General George Pickett's charge raised the common soldier's sacrifice to new heights.[51] President Abraham Lincoln's five-minute speech is now cherished, while Everett has been forgotten, but at the time, the words of Edward Everett were celebrated throughout the North.[52] These speeches and rituals venerated the virtues of civic life, essential for sustaining a democratic republic. They provided models for citizens to emulate in fulfilling the military and civic duties of their communities. And most importantly, they reunited the nation after the horrors of each conflict.

The complex connection between citizenship, masculinity, and military service was also well entrenched, and the definitions of masculinity were rooted in stereotypical characteristics of whites: fearlessness, godliness, intelligence.[53] The process of military socialization that produced troops for the defense of the nation was undertaken by the entire population. The uniformed marching company was a well-known sight in the local festivals "that animate[d] American politics during the nineteenth century"; these spectacles channeled political participation into martial rituals.⁵⁴ Even though later legislation such as the Dick Act of 1903 and the National Defense Act of 1916 would concentrate military service under the auspices of the federal government, and increase the gravitation of power away from states and localities to Washington, DC, military service would continue to be an important responsibility for the community and an occasion for local celebration of masculine virtues.

National identity took on an aspect of anti-immigrant sentiment at the beginning of the twentieth century. This is not a surprising reaction considering the waves of immigrants who were landing on American shores. Thousands of new arrivals added a new dimension to the concept of citizenship. The pressure of their presence probably hardened attitudes of dominant groups intent on excluding outsiders. There was considerable debate about the role of immigrants in American society, accompanied by opposition to their military service in World War I.⁵⁵ Scott Malcomson makes a critical distinction between loyalty and citizenship. He labels the difference "Americanization" during World War I: "Loyalty was not too difficult to prove in wartime. You proved it by risking your life, or at least not saying or doing anything against the national cause. One faced a greater challenge in proving one's Americaness. Americanization programs provided some help, showing newcomers how to dress, speaking English, cook properly, ventilate their tiny apartments, bake bread rather than buy it from the store."⁵⁶ Differences in dress, language, and customs set immigrants apart from those who had settled in the New World in earlier decades. Most immigrants found themselves competing with African Americans for housing and jobs on the bottom rung of the social ladder. According to one pamphlet titled *Americanization*, "Folks who used to be just human beings are being classified into American and un-American, according to their willingness to agree or disagree with the Americanizers as to what their social, economic and political ideals should be."⁵⁷ Because they did not conform to accepted social standards, African Americans often found themselves ostracized with new immigrants.

Many leaders have turned to the armed forces to create a cohesive national identity, to divert attention from domestic issues, and to mold political communities. In the United States, it is clear from historical evidence that requirements for citizenship tightened at the turn of the nineteenth century at the same time that immigration threatened to swamp Americans with alien peoples perceived as a threat to the national interest. President Theodore Roosevelt, for example, took aggressive action in foreign matters and simultaneously extolled the virtues of military service.[58] Together with other civic leaders, Roosevelt was convinced that military service would ignite patriotic allegiance in hordes of newcomers and ingrain the virtues of American life in them at the same time. Military service became the means of transforming a rabble of immigrants into members of a cohesive society.[59] Across time and geography, military institutions have been viewed as the key to transmission of social values and national cohesion.[60]

Immediately after the United States entered World War I, in response to concern about potential disloyalty among African Americans, President Woodrow Wilson sent William G. Willcox, president of the New York City board of education and chairman of the board of trustees of Tuskegee Institute, as an emissary to boost African American morale in the Southern states.[61] According to Willcox, African Americans would "prove their right to stand shoulder to shoulder with their white brothers in answer to their country's call, and, if the supreme test must come, prove that their blood is as red, their hearts as true, their courage as steadfast to do and die in service."[62] Dr. Hollis B. Frissell, principal of Hampton Institute in Virginia, was alarmed at charges of African American disloyalty, but he assured the nation's leaders that "the colored man is going to secure recognition, not by demanding his rights, but by deserving them."[63]

The question of African American citizenship remained unresolved well into the twentieth century. Three generations after the Emancipation Proclamation legally provided African Americans with the opportunity to participate in the responsibilities of citizenship, full realization of citizenship's corresponding rights was not forthcoming. At the conclusion of World War II, James Burk explains, "The United States found itself locked in a struggle to define and defend what democratic society stood for in contrast with the claims of totalitarian societies on the right and left."[64] The performance of African American servicemen and the nation's need for their willingness to fight in defense of democracy, brought the contradictions of segregation and racism within military ranks to the forefront. James Burk identifies the expectations that followed African Americans' contributions to World War II: "African Americans supposed their efforts would be rewarded by a reduction in the intensity of racism and an increase in recognition of their worth and status as citizens. And again they were disappointed. Black veterans were not welcomed home after the war to participate as equals in American society."[65]

In 1948, President Harry S. Truman ordered the desegregation of the armed forces in Executive Order 9981, but racial integration was not implemented in the military until the end of the Korean War. By the onset of the Vietnam War, all vestiges of military segregation for men had disappeared. Since then, steady progress has been made toward ending the stigma of race in the military, which often provides a model for other American institutions. And, not surprisingly, current efforts to obtain equal rights for women and gays are being made within the ranks of the military.[66] James Burk sums up the importance of the struggle for recognition of the role of African Americans in World War II: "What is important for the persistence of democracy is that minority groups, whose interests are neglected, are able to mobilize and compete for support for their point of view. If democracy rested on anything, it was on a set of formal procedures that allowed virtually all people, views, and positions to be heard and respected."[67] The inclusion of African Americans in World War II ultimately revised the definition of citizenship so that the practice of responsibilities of military service became a reality in democratic participation.

Contemporary debates have been waged over the inclusion of women and openly gay individuals in the military. The link between citizenship and military service assumes that American values—at least those of the nation's dominant white culture—will be demonstrated by its citizens in uniform. This assumption partially explains why individuals considered deviant, such as homosexuals and conscientious objectors, were rejected for military service. Sexual orientation and gender continue to be problematic issues for military institutions and divisive topics for public debate. The admission of women to the Virginia Military Institute, for example, was met with extreme resistance by those who claimed women would require segregated facilities, would change the bonding experience of men, and would not be able to meet expectations of physical rigor, mental stress and desirable values required by the military.[68] Similar arguments have been made regarding the inclusion of openly gay individuals in the military. Both women and gays have been shunned because they ostensibly have the potential to distract and disrupt men, considered to be more serious soldiers. While these issues are beyond the scope of this study, it is interesting to note that the same arguments were used to prevent the integration of African American men into branches of the military during World War II.

Military Service as a Condition of Citizenship during World War II

Frederick Douglass's explanation of the relationship between military service and citizenship, although made in the nineteenth century, applied equally well almost a century later at the start of World War II. According to Mary Patrick Motley, "The black community knew very well that the refusal of the service branches to accept black recruits was part of a deliberate effort to prevent the exercise of rights of citizenship. If they were ever to be full-fledged citizens, black Americans had constantly to demand full participation in the war effort."[69] However, most branches of the armed services were resistant to those demands for equal participation. The marines refused to enlist anyone of color. Other services allowed some African Americans to serve, but only in menial jobs, mostly as laborers. Only the coast guard was integrated, although African Americans were clustered in the bottom ranks. For the most part, military institutions were unwilling to include anyone considered inferior by nature, and historical evidence suggests that such attitudes were entrenched.

In the midst of the vast migration of African Americans from the rural South to the urban North, W. E. B. Du Bois was poised to understand the dynamic of race relations at the turn of the century. Du Bois framed his idea of what it meant to be a minority within a majority culture, and drawing from this understanding, posited the concept of "double consciousness" to capture the unique consequences of this experience. Concerning double consciousness, Du Bois writes, "The history of the American Negro is the history of this strife—this longing to attain self-conscious manhood, to merge his double self into a better and truer self. . . . He simply wishes to make it possible for a man to be both a Negro and an American, without having the doors of opportunity closed roughly in his face."[70] These words capture the essence of African American citizenship. Throughout the course of American history, blacks' status, particularly in times of military conflict, has been paradoxical. Society asks for their sacrifice, while simultaneously subjecting African Americans to the frustrations and humiliations of secondary citizenship. The discrimination was part of the legal code, as evidenced by Jim Crow laws. And it was ingrained in practices of the military services.

In many minds the appeal of communism for African Americans was based in the philosophy's recognition of the class struggle—a fundamental tenet of Marxism experienced in every aspect of African American life. A supplementary resolution, printed in the *Socialist Appeal* on November 9, 1940, contains a statement that perceptively summarizes this relationship:

> The system of Jim Crowism in the armed forces demonstrates very clearly to the Negro the hypocrisy of slogans about "war for democracy." But the ruling class maintains Jim Crowism in the armed forces. For it cannot wipe out the system in the armed forces without endangering the whole system of Jim Crowism practiced in "civilian life": in industry, and civil service, on relief, at the ballot booth, in housing, theaters, restaurants—economically, politically, socially. The capitalists fear that *no Negro trained to handle a gun would peacefully go back to the old life of discrimination, segregation, disfranchisement, an insult, after training in an army where he was treated as an equal with white soldiers* (italics in the original).[71]

This socialist resolution clearly comprehends that the segregation of African Americans rests uneasily on keeping African Americans from seizing equality. Both blacks and whites recognized that arming African Americans was the most likely route to changing the status quo, either peacefully through citizenship or through violence. Military policies and practices themselves were an acute sign of the problems of racism, and they were rooted solidly in the injustices that stemmed from segregation.

Fully a year before the United States entered World War II, President Franklin D. Roosevelt addressed the nation on the need for a selective service. While it was clear to many political leaders that war was inevitable, popular opinion strongly favored isolation. Roosevelt began his address by linking military obligations to citizenship: "America has adopted selective service in time of peace, and, in doing so, has broadened and enriched our basic concept of citizenship. Beside the clear democratic ideals of equal rights, equal privileges and equal opportunities, we have set forth the underlying other duties, obligations and responsibilities of equal service." Roosevelt drew a quick historical sketch of national defense, referring to the militia system that imposed the obligation of military service upon every American. Its roots in common law "brought to this continent by our forefathers" were understood to include citizens who reported for military duty, armed with their own weapons and their training in frontier hardships.

While conditions had changed, the underlying responsibility for military service had not. Roosevelt outlined the selective service system as organized and controlled by communities of "patriotic citizens," who would select and provide individuals for military service, for "Americans from all walks of life, rich and poor, country-bred and city raised, farmer, student, manual laborer and white collar worker, will learn to live side by side, to depend upon each other in military drills and maneuvers, and to appreciate each other's dignity as American citizens." Finally, recognizing the inevitable spread of the European conflict, he asserted, "Universal service will bring not only greater preparedness to meet the threat of war, but a wider distribution of tolerance and understanding to enjoy the blessings of peace."[72] This promise was problematic but necessary to ensure the cooperation and loyalty of every American in the upcoming crisis. The cooperation of all Americans, including African Americans, was a critical part of military preparedness, requiring the support of civilians as laborers in military industries and agriculture. The promise of future rewards acknowledged, as never before, the link of military sacrifice to citizenship. The hopes of generations of African Americans appeared closer to being fulfilled than they had been in previous wars.

Establishing the Case for Citizenship

For whites, citizenship and military service continued to be closely related concepts well into the twentieth century. First slavery and then second-class citizenship were considered naturally ordained for African Americans; the laws of God and nature relegated them to servitude. Any efforts to elevate their status would fly in the face of nature. This assumption was reflected in an entire social infrastructure, from religion to government to community practice, that functioned to keep African Americans in a subservient position. Barriers to citizenship are sustained by the inferiority argument, the same argument that underlay the treatment of Native Americans, Asians, and others.[73]

This legacy of decades of racism did not easily yield to change. Change first required that the assumption of racial inferiority be broached. One arena where this could occur was on the battlefield, because courage under extreme conditions was a direct demonstration of loyalty. The central question of racial equality revolves around military equality, as Stanley Sandler suggests in his study of army air force segregation during World War II: "How could whites be accepted or drafted into the military and face death or mutilation while blacks escaped? Here, indeed, was the rationale for black participation in each of America's conflicts since at least the time of the Civil War."[74] In addition, military service demonstrated willingness to sacrifice everything for one's country.

Contemporary restrictions on military service continue to reflect the inherent link between citizenship and military service. For example, the federal government awarded United States citizenship posthumously to soldiers killed in Iraq and Afghanistan during military service. And lawmakers agreed to decrease the waiting period—from five to three years—for those immigrants who fought in Operation Iraqi Freedom to obtain citizenship. In July 2002, citing the war on terrorism, President George W. Bush signed an executive order eliminating the waiting period, making service personnel immediately eligible for US citizenship. Although the Pentagon does not track foreign nationals serving in the military, it is estimated that thirty-seven thousand active-duty service personnel serving during the Iraq War were not American citizens. Nearly 20 percent took advantage of President Bush's July 2002 order. The Pentagon confirmed that as of June 5, 2003, twelve noncitizens in US military uniform had died in the Iraq war.[75]

CHAPTER THREE

Mass Media in the Twentieth Century

Movies were a tool, free of language barriers, transferring the social mores and popular culture of the day at the expense of the cultural realities and social existence of Black Americans.
—PEARL BOWSER[1]

In the spring of 1942, as the United States was entering the first months of World War II, delegates from the National Association for the Advancement of Colored People met with several Hollywood studio heads to codify changes in film portrayals of African Americans.[2] Studios agreed to forego placing African Americans in roles that emphasized stereotypes, to cast black characters as extras in credible parts, and to integrate production crews. In return, the NAACP would suspend their boycotts and public protests of popular films.[3] For years, protests had accompanied releases that pictured African Americans in demeaning roles. Films like *The Birth of a Nation* (1915) and *Gone with the Wind* (1939) drew public condemnation, protests, and boycotts from African Americans and others. While the agreement between the NAACP and the Hollywood studios only affected the employment of a few hundred African Americans, it did signal awareness that film was a powerful force in the perpetuation of stereotypes. It would take decades for film, and later television, to redress the inequities of negative portrayals of African Americans, but World War II initiated the process of changing media stereotypes.

Films such as *The Negro Soldier* were produced by the signal corps in 1944 to ease racial hostility and promote harmony in order to achieve military victory. These films negotiate a compromise between racial factions, subsuming the individual interests of each group to the collective national goal of military victory. A central vehicle of the negotiated text is the patriotism of black Americans, demonstrated in their contributions to military history. The growing influence of mass media, particularly film, allowed for broad circulation of these positive images of Africans Americans. For the first time in American history, African Americans were presented with dignity, converting decades of demeaning images. This chapter begins with a look at the rising popularity of mass media with roots in earlier modes, the popular appeal of director Frank Capra, and government use of film in both world wars.

The Rising Power of Mass Media

The concept of the movie theater as a potential forum for democracy became apparent even before World War I, when hundreds of Americans flocked to see films and newsreels in the first decade of the century. The promise of film as a propaganda tool immediately became apparent, and film eventually served the national goals of each major combatant in World War I. Studies of the impact of propaganda conducted by the Committee on Public Information during World War I concluded that film had powerful effects on viewers, and although by current social sciences standards the studies are considered flawed because they failed to control for outside variables, at the time the research persuaded government officials that media produced broad and powerful effects on people's behaviors.[4] War Department experts on race relations were convinced that film could be used to instill patriotic fervor in apathetic viewers and to steer that enthusiasm toward military victory. Documentary films, at least those produced by most American filmmakers associated with the war effort, were considered to be factual, relying on truth telling to achieve their persuasive effects. As a result, there were few ethical qualms about using film to influence public opinion. While the films of other combatants were considered propaganda, officials were convinced that American films merely provided information.

The potential audience for propaganda films was vast. By the time hostilities broke out in Europe preceding the American entry into World War II, most Americans saw a film every week. By 1946 a weekly average of ninety million Americans—roughly 75 percent of the country's total population—attended the movies.[6] Although radio was a more pervasive presence in American life, film attracted audiences because it coupled images with sound in a way few could resist. During the war years, average profits of theaters rose 200 percent.[7] In addition, films were increasingly used as a means to train and indoctrinate military recruits. Along with the production of government films for military use came acute interest in the potential of film to influence civilian audiences. On the eve of Pearl Harbor, cinema going was a deeply rooted social habit throughout the United States. It was inevitable that motion pictures, newsreels, and documentary shorts would become powerful weapons of war; along with news and entertainment, films disseminated democratic ideology.[8]

The centrality and power of motion pictures in World War II were confirmed by *Variety* columnist John C. Flynn several days after the outbreak of war in Europe. Flynn proposed that, in times of crisis, film theaters should be thought of as "places of public assembly, meeting halls of democracy ... where the 'trend of national thought' was discernible, and that emphasis on this political function of the theater in the social life of the community could bring new prestige to the industry," becoming a new civic space, an American "town hall."[9] The designation of commercial theaters, formerly places of entertainment and commerce, as sites of political engagement is curious unless one considers that these are the very places fundamental American values such as individualism, self-reliance, and family.

On the eve of World War II, it was clear that government-sponsored films would serve as the most effective means of advocating national causes in wartime. Lectures, pamphlets, comic books, and other media had been employed to educate civilians and soldiers, but most Americans preferred films. The establishment of the signal corps and recruitment of Hollywood directors, actors, and technicians provided the federal government with a steady supply of top quality films for the duration of the war. And it is not surprising that the signal corps would turn to popular filmmakers like Frank Capra to articulate the American dream for fighting men and women. As Robert Sklar and Vito Zagarrio conclude, "As far as the army and Roosevelt were concerned, during the war Hollywood was the ideal instrument for American propaganda, at home as well as abroad, and Capra its prophet."[10]

During World War II, in the United States alone, the budget for nonfiction film production and distribution exceeded $50 million a year for each year of the war.[11] Similar amounts were spent by the British and other allies, even as Axis nations contended with acute shortages of film stock and other materials critical for movie production.[12] Scholars estimate that between twelve hundred and fifteen hundred nonfiction films were produced in the United States and Britain during World War II. The primary purpose of most of these films was to provide information for civilian and military audiences. But despite of the tremendous resources devoted to film, the scope and practices of film production during World War II have remained largely unexplored by scholars.[13]

Throughout the war, Hollywood cooperated closely with the federal government, especially branches of the military. Because it provided morale-boosting films, Hollywood was declared an essential war industry. The federal government considered men like Ronald Reagan, Jimmie Stewart, Gary Cooper, and Frank Capra more effective in their roles as actors and producers than as soldiers serving in regular army units. Hollywood personnel were reassigned from regular military duties, and studios were guaranteed necessary quantities of film stock.[14] The industry's special status enabled Hollywood filmmakers to continue producing approximately 440 feature movies per year, down only slightly from the five hundred annual features produced during the 1930s.

While both Hollywood and the federal government benefitted from this wartime arrangement, tensions developed. Filmmakers bristled at intervention by the Office of War Information, while government agencies resented Hollywood's resistance. Overall, filmmakers were more interested in selling tickets than in pushing overt propaganda, but government agents insisted that allies be shown positively in order to dramatize the differences between them and the enemy. Patriotism won out. As Susan L. Carruthers notes, "Wartime cinemas generally sharpened the contours of national identity by projecting it in opposition to enemy 'Others.'"[15] The Office of War Information was particularly sensitive to the racist policies of Nazi Germany and anxious to minimize the difficulties of race relations within the United States.

During the twentieth century, mass media became a primary source of information and entertainment for most of American society. During World War II, the federal government was quick to realize and utilize mass media to shape public opinion, just as it had attempted to do during the First World War. These mediated messages are important sites for excavating the construction of race, because the federal government had a critical stake in promoting particular clarifications or representations of race, unlike the commercial film industry, whose primary goal was making money. In spite of pervasive government use of media for military purposes, there was little government publicity about the success of the African Americans in uniform—owing to racism, not military secrecy. News and photos of African Americans in uniform were systematically deleted, never appearing in mainstream media.[16] War correspondents from the black press had to rely on government provided sources such as handouts or approved interviews. Images of African Americans in uniform were entirely absent in mainstream media. African Americans appear in only one photo in *Life's*

Picture History of World War II, a popular reminiscence about the good war. Even today, popular commemorations of the war rarely document African American participation.[17]

The signal corps films, produced for the federal government by teams of Hollywood directors, scriptwriters, animators, and others, including Frank Capra, are classics of wartime cinematic propaganda. Considering that more than fifty military and civilian agencies in Washington were involved in most aspects of development, from script approval to final screening and aspects of distribution, each film is a remarkable feat.[18] But Hollywood, whose directors, writers, and crew had been drafted and assigned to the signal corps, was essential to translating the American dream into military victory. Frank Capra was a pivotal figure in many of these productions.

The Popular Appeal of Frank Capra

The populist ideals underlying Hollywood entertainment films produced during the years between the world wars pitted the individual against the organization, the powerless against the powerful. Among Hollywood directors, Frank Capra was among the most successful in capturing these prevailing sentiments of Americans in film. He contributed to the national myths of individual heroism and grassroots populism in films like *Mr. Deeds Goes to Town* (1936), *Mr. Smith Goes to Washington* (1939), and *Meet John Doe* (1941).[19] Capra had an unerring sense of American popular sentiment, which earned him a number of Academy Awards. More than personal style or individual authorship, Capra succeeded because he retold American myths on the screen.

Capra enlisted heroic characters in fundamental American myths for propaganda purposes as he developed films like the *Why We Fight* series and *The Negro Soldier* for the signal corps. As if following one of his own Hollywood scripts, Capra celebrated the common man in these pro-war documentary style films. He shared a heroic vision of the world, one featuring uniformed Americans in central roles. The individual became the everyman American hero, a figure made flesh by prewar characters like Mr. Deeds, Mr. Smith, and John Doe. The value of the individual was a premise Americans believed in, forming "the logical point of view that the cinema of the 1930s offered itself to *all*, in a universality of social classes and ... values."[20]

Among the Capraesque themes that resonated with American viewers is the construction of small town America, the site of the American dream, standing defiantly against the enemy of freedom, usually corrupt, ruthless figures who are the antithesis of the small-town hero. This populist appeal was based on nostalgia, "the dream of an impossible return to a mythologically idyllic past."[21] For Capra, the importance of situating the hero in tradition was critical because the past was not just "an inventory of intact traditions and ongoing myths. It was a social force that he was able to salvage."[22] The past is refracted in the present, not static but alive in the actions of the hero, whose sacrifice proves to be the salvation of the future. It is no surprise then that Capra's government films are heavily weighted with historical explanations, as they celebrate an idealized vision of the common American.

Capra's wartime propaganda films were characterized by a simple working idea: If Americans could see the Axis glorification of a master race, they would understand the threat to democracy.[23] Typically, Capra would edit millions of feet of captured Axis film until stark images of menacing enemies emerged. His films are laced with contrast and counterpoint, in which he juxtaposed images of the enemy against those of the Allies. The promise of a better postwar world in which peace and democracy would prevail leads to the idealistic conclusions of his wartime films, which reprised the happy endings of his prewar Hollywood releases.[24]

By contrast, Japanese and German propaganda critiqued domestic American racism by asking questions about the treatment of Native Americans and African Americans. For example, *The Way of the Subject*, issued by the Japanese Ministry of Education in 1941, presented Western history "as a chronicle of destructive values, exploitative practices, and brutal wars."[25] The arrogance of white Americans who looked down on all other races and cultures was highlighted in the pamphlet. Axis propaganda exploited the inherent contradiction of American democracy, which professed freedom as an ideal but in practice denied it to millions of Americans. In his depictions of Germany and Japan, Capra's strategy was to let the enemy damn itself, showcasing the startling vision of cherished national images crushed by enemy actions. This exploitation of fundamental features of a people and culture is evident in all of Capra's films, including *The Negro Soldier* and *The Navy Steward*, which feature stories set in a church and in a newspaper office, locations essential to African American communities. Capra provided a snapshot of African American lives never represented in other mainstream media.[26]

The close cooperation between Hollywood and the United States military has a long. It is estimated that the War Department provided approximately $15 million of personnel and services for the production of *Wings*

(1927) and millions more for films promoting patriotic themes in World War II. According to Katharine Q. Seelye, "The military establishment has been cooperating with Hollywood for nearly a century, with a noticeable break in the Vietnam years."[27] During World War II the War Department not only supplied expertise and occasionally military backdrops, members of the Office of War Information and other government agencies were assigned to review proposed Hollywood scripts and preview films with an eye to recommending changes. Hollywood directors, actors, and technicians were drafted and assigned to the signal corps for production of government films. Much of the cartooning and graphics work in films like Frank Capra's *Why We Fight* series was produced in cooperative arrangement with the Disney studios.

As domestic racial tensions escalated, the Office of War Information made efforts to encourage the use of positive images of African Americans in popular films. Hollywood generally ignored these requests. A 1945 study of one hundred African American roles in wartime films conducted by researchers at Columbia University discovered that seventy-five film roles perpetuated stereotypes, thirteen were neutral, and only twelve were positive.[28] Even with the primary goal of winning the war, the Office of War Information was relatively ineffective in its attempts to encourage positive images of African Americans in a commercial film content. As a result, the Office of War Information turned to its own internal signal corps to address racial issues in military ranks. And it is not surprising that the signal corps would turn to Frank Capra to articulate the American dream for fighting men and women. Film was the ideal vehicle for displaying democratic ideals "and Capra its prophet."[29]

The first signal corps production, *The Negro Soldier*, resulted from the government conviction that film would be the most effective means to recruit African Americans to replenish military ranks, to overcome racial tensions by creating a more positive view of African American contributions, and to stir patriotism among apathetic African American communities. The goal was to unite African Americans behind the war effort while postponing African American demands for an immediate end to discrimination. *The Negro Soldier* also reassured white viewers that African Americans were capable of military service. This film is especially important because it signaled a dramatic shift in government policy regarding the abilities of African Americans. By admitting their suitability for service as well as their contributions in past wars, the government implicitly sanctioned African American claims to full citizenship.[30]

Evolution of African American Images

A review of the evolution of African American screen images from their roots in the eighteenth century minstrel tradition to the eve of World War II reveals a long-standing cultural separation of blacks and whites. Black characters in the earliest American films shuffled, sang, and danced, presenting little threat to dominate white society. Images of blacks were suspended in a white world that ignored the supporting network of black institutions like families and churches. The racial schism was rooted in the popular culture of the antebellum period, which created a hierarchy of slaves and masters. In the early American theater and literature, the rationale for slavery was articulated in popular entertainment.[31]

The myth of the happy Southern plantation was everywhere in American cinema. Jim Pines argues, "It embodies the essential ingredients of American racial-cultural ideology, it is the cradle of race methodology, and it determined the form and content of all plasticized black images. During the initial years of film this process was largely inspired by a white, paternalistic conception of plantation vernacular . . . from the early 1900s on words racism embedded in the black movie image became more pronounced."[32] Several classical racial motifs dominated the early period of American film: the faithful servant, the buffoon, the savage. These images glorified the institution of slavery and Southern chivalry, with its attendant myth of white racial purity. Romanticized images of the Old South are replete with compliant blacks, while mulatto characters who inevitably reached a bad end dealt with issues of miscegenation, interracial mixing, and uppity blacks who did not know their places. Films like *The Debt* (1912) and *In Slavery Days* (1913) depict African Americans as objectified problems.

The first appearances of African American characters on the cinema screen were stagy and overblown, tied to vaudeville and minstrel show antecedents with distorted broad smiles, double takes, illiterate dialects, outlandish gestures, swaggering movements, and exaggerated levels of energy. Such images appeared normal, and their unconscious acceptance in the dominant culture perpetuated broadly disseminated messages of racism. Even a cursory glance at popular film titles reveals the extent of the problem. These include: *Pickanniny Dance* (1892), *Pickaninnies* (1894), *Negro Dancers* (1895), *A Watermelon Feast* (1896), *Dancing Darkies* (1897), *Chicken Thieves* (1897), *Dancing Darkey Boy* (1897), *Sambo and Aunt Jemima* (1900), *A Night in Blackville* (1903), *Prizefight in Coon Town* (1904), *The Wooing and Wedding of a Coon* (1905), *Coon Song* (1908), *How Rastus Got His Chicken*

(1911), *How Rastus Got His Turkey* (1914), *Rastus in Zululand* (1914), and many others. The plot of *An Interrupted Crap Game* (1903) follows black gamblers who are distracted from their game trying to capture a chicken to eat. Slapstick antics and dancing were prominent in such films. One of the last silent films, a Warner Bros. production, was *Ham and Eggs at the Front* (1927) advertised as "Two darkies' hair raising adventures with girls, ghosts, and guns in No-Man's Land."[33] The dire consequences of mixing the races form the themes of many other films, including *The Nigger* (1916) and *The Bride of Hate* (1917).

The stereotypes of the plantation tradition that flourished into the twentieth century can be seen in the paternalistic treatment of African American characters when they appear in white films. Folk dialect and ethnic naturalism, professedly liberal treatments of African Americans, depicted black characters as objectified others, inferior to the white viewer. Films like *Nigger* (1915) are typical of this pattern of representation. In this respect there was little fundamental difference between white liberal and conservative viewpoints in the conception of black life. Both were superficial, rooted in traditional depictions of the black slave. Such images were intensely popular in American cinema. They were especially nonthreatening when black stereotypes were coupled with idealized white images like American sweetheart Shirley Temple in *The Little Colonel* (1935), *The Littlest Rebel* (1935), and *In Old Kentucky* (1936). Other films, such as *Prestige* (1932), *So Red the Rose* (1936), and *The Prisoner of Shark Island* (1936), exploited racial characters and situations overtly.

Such representations reinforced the ideology of racism for audiences who absorbed the caricatures along with the entertainment. Historian Robert Toll captures the underlying process: "Blackface performers were like puppets operated by a white puppet master. Their physical appearance proclaimed their non-humanity; yet they could be manipulated not only to mock themselves but also to act like human beings.... Blackface minstrelsy's dominance of popular entertainment amounted to a half a century of inurement to the uses of white supremacy."[34] These stereotypes migrated virtually unchanged to film.

Part of this phenomenon was the acceptance of white actors in blackface. This version of racial posturing reportedly began during a New York City minstrel show in 1843, in which white men smeared their faces with burnt cork and pretended to be African Americans. The blackface caricature was a wild success. Soon after, "Jim Crow," allegedly derived from Thomas Dartmouth Rice, an early minstrel performer whose song about

Jim Crow yielded the phrase, became synonymous with institutionalized racism.[35] Blackface performances by white actors depended on the belief that African Americans could not effectively portray members of their own race because they could not act. In conjunction with this belief, the economic stranglehold of white financiers on film production relegated black performers to demeaning roles and further humiliations, even as white actors in blackface performed in key roles. African American actors and actresses who challenged stereotypes and insisted on better treatment did not get work.

Al Jolson exemplifies the peak of the minstrel-inspired caricature in one of the first sound films, *The Jazz Singer* (1927), followed by the less known *The Singing Fool* (1928). Within two years, the Warner production *Big Boy* (1930) featured Al Jolson in blackface playing a faithful Negro jockey. By this point, the use of blackface, except in comedy routines, had largely disappeared. Even so, casting calls for African Americans were limited to Negro character roles. Only the genre of prison films, popular throughout the 1930s, offered African Americans more than a few background parts. With few exceptions, African Americans characters were not written into radio or film productions. One noteworthy exception was the part of Rochester, Jack Benny's valet. This radio character proved controversial because even though Rochester appeared in an otherwise white medium, the pairing of Benny and Anderson was based on comedy routines of the white master and his Uncle Tom slave, a legacy of the minstrel era.

In addition to the widely accepted belief that blacks could not act, a number of other stereotypes were conveyed in film. For example, films often emphasized superstitious aspects of black religion in patronizing ways. Fear of the devil, inaccurate but humorous biblical citations, and zealous religiosity became elements in the religious stereotyping of African Americans.[36] Even all-black movies such as *Green Pastures* (1936) and *Cabin in the Sky* (1943) dramatized religious practices in this way. But the most popular show, *Amos 'n' Andy* (1928–55), appealed to Americans because, as Cookie Lommel explains, the two black Southern characters "represented comforting familiarity as well as perpetuating stereotypes drawn from the minstrel era."[37]

A survey of films released between 1915 and 1920 revealed that during this five-year period, more than 50 percent of black actors played maids, stable boys, or other servile roles. During the next decade, the number rose to more than 80 percent. Most films set in the South had a mammy or "faithful colored servitor," continuing the Civil War tradition by recreating slavery.³⁸ Hollywood stereotyping of African Americans was so potent that it influenced European filmmaking, which faithfully reproduced American stereotypes.

Film presentations of African American physical attributes were often grotesque. Expressions were exaggerated, eyeballs bulged out, feet shuffled due to inherent laziness, and these characters spoke in ungrammatical local dialect. Rooted in assumptions about blacks' inferiority, these depictions of African Americans showed them as childlike, easily fooled, and satisfied by simple, almost bestial pleasures. African American men were simultaneously feminized and hyper-sexualized, with an irresistible attraction to white women. They were afraid of the dark, intolerant of cold weather, and unable to learn higher-level skills such as operating machinery. No matter how ridiculous the characters and the plot, white audiences overlooked the exaggerations, entertained by actors who rolled their eyes, staged pratfalls, and imitated stupidity.³⁹ The popular Rastus film series and the Sambo comedies all depicted African Americans as fools or clowns with minimal intelligence.⁴⁰

Portrayal of African Americans as heroes did not emerge smoothly. It was a long process of self-discovery, as black awareness emerged with the new century. The Pan African Congress of 1900, held in London, elevated awareness of African identity among blacks, and seminal leaders like Booker T. Washington and W. E. B. Du Bois contributed to African American consciousness. Organizations such as the NAACP urged collective action for political and economic justice, and Marcus Garvey's Universal Negro Improvement Association promoted racial pride among thousands of followers. The period prior to World War II was marked by growing recognition of African American culture. The great migration that brought thousands of African Americans into the urban centers of the North and West contributed to the momentum of black consciousness. The artists and visionaries of the Harlem Renaissance encouraged the African American cultural tradition. Arising from many different sources, these voices helped to redefine African Americans and their place in the American community. African Americans rallied with increased racial pride that found itself expressed politically with a movement away from accommodation to more radical demands for equality.

For many years, since the advent of mass media as popular entertainment, African Americans had protested their portrayal in popular entertainment. The National Urban League, the NAACP, and other organizations often spearheaded the protests and interviewed with business interests and media groups on behalf of African Americans. In a 1943 speech, Walter White, spokesman for the NAACP, pointed to the power of film, arguing, "The matter of treatment of the Negro in the motion pictures is of such importance that it takes rank over some other phases of our work." He concluded, "The importance of these media by which ideas are formed and propagated is more critical than the making of guns and planes."[41] Under pressure from church groups and community organizations, the film industry did censor itself during the 1920s, but the resulting codes and formulas were concerned with African American images only in instances of miscegenation that would offend white viewers.

Films depicting African Americans in uniform offer a unique departure from otherwise negative treatments. Several of these films were produced between 1916 and 1918, including *The Heroic Black Soldiers of the War*, *The Battle of Mt. Ariat*, *Colored Invincibles*, *Jim Bludso*, *Trooper of Company K*, *The Greatest Thing in Life*, and *Our Hell Fighters*. Although such depictions are rare, they offered a vision of African Americans that was neither exaggerated nor inadequate. Even though these films showed African Americans in unfamiliar, dignified images, they simultaneously relied on entrenched stereotypes of both black and white social roles. For example, Shiftless Joe, the main character in *Trooper of Company K*, was transformed into a good soldier—but only through the efforts of white officers. This narrative offers hope for African Americans, but reassures white viewers of their unaltered racial superiority.

Other African American images in military films were either ambiguous or unrealistic. For example, *How Uncle Sam Prepares* (1917) and *The Lost Battalion* (1919) depicted integrated armed forces, defying the reality of military life. In another production, *The Slacker* (1917), a composite of racially diverse faces magically merged into an American flag, provided a compelling but highly improbable visual metaphor. More typical is *Pershing's Crusaders* (1918), which included black units playing a background role. Not surprisingly, the film was poorly received in the South. More typical were films like *America's Answer* (1918), which included dancing black troops for comic effect.

By the mid 1920s, film had supplanted popular literature and the minstrel stage as the primary conduit for cultural images of African Americans.[42] With the exception of radio, film reached more people than any other medium. But the representation of minority characters was consistent across media. Silent films and early talkies both preserved and exaggerated stereotypes perpetuated by earlier media. Film, with its visual dimension, presented a perfect opportunity to exploit stereotyped images of African Americans. At first, nuances of individual character were difficult to express, given primitive technology, so many films featured black characters who sang and danced, reinforcing the common belief that African Americans are naturally rhythmic.[43]

Before Edwin S. Porter's innovations in film editing allowed crosscutting and the development of secondary story lines, films were shot entirely as one entity. In 1898, Thomas Edison produced *The Colored Troops Disembarking* and *The Ninth Negro Cavalry Watering Horses*. Both films showed uniformed African American soldiers as central subjects of interest. Less than six years later, when the process of editing film allowed, Thomas Edison began to use African Americans in cutaway sequences for entertainment purposes. In *A Watermelon Contest* (1896) and *Ten Pickaninnies* (1908), groups of African Americans became objects of entertainment.[44] This treatment was repeated in other films that copied Edison's success. In spite of NAACP protests, the first decades of film production saw hundreds of degrading images in films like *The Nigger* (1914) and *The Birth of a Nation* (1915).

Even though new editing techniques allowed for greater range in character and plot development, the roles of African Americans began to shrink further, more closely resembling constricted social roles than Southern literary forms.[45] After 1908, the range of racial experience depicted on the screen had narrowed, perhaps as a collective response to audience resistance to controversial topics, reluctance of film financiers to such topics, and conservative social attitudes among the majority audience. In this context, it would have been difficult for filmmakers, even if they had wished to do so, to break away from fixed racial stereotypes and narratives.

While African American viewers did have the option of seeing black productions, this was a limited answer to the problematic films of Hollywood. African Americans faired little better in all-black films shown in segregated theaters. By the late 1920s, there were more than seven hundred movie houses in the black communities of America. At least thirty black film production companies were operating, among them Ebony Films in Chicago, Gate City Film Corp. in Kansas City, Temple Studios in Philadelphia, and of course, Oscar Micheaux's productions.[46] Black productions were often technically poor, made quickly and cheaply with limited access to studio facilities that, even at their best, did not rival those of the white production studios in Hollywood. Just as the production infrastructure was controlled by whites, most cinemas were owned by whites who believed black viewers enjoyed burlesque depictions of their own race.[47] Even cinemas catering to black audiences routinely showed demeaning caricatures and stereotypical depictions of African Americans. The belief that blacks not only conformed to accepted stereotypes, but endorsed them wholeheartedly affirmed white belief in the innate inferiority of blacks.[48]

The advent of sound technology augmented images in a way that allowed greater cinematic realism, giving greater credibility to film images. The racial caricatures previously demonstrated through movement and facial expression alone could now exploit the vernacular expressions of African Americans. Racial images did not change in their orientation, they were simply refined by the addition of black talk. The immediate impact was profound. The addition of sound effects projected a sense of realism that added new credibility to racist images. While other technological advances in film stock and color sharpened the picture itself, sound added an entirely new dimension to the cinema experience, compounding the impact of the images by reaching new heights of realism. Stereotyped images of African American films were amplified.

The transition from radio to film spelled doom for some white actors who were cast as black characters in radio, but clearly could not play them in film. But this cutback did not provide opportunities for diversifying African American characters. Black performers were usually required to master thick dialects fixed in racial stereotyping. Female actresses like Louise Beavers were stuck in mammy and servants roles that required them to gain weight. Others, like Stephen Fetchit, Hattie McDaniel, and Butterfly McQueen, found it almost impossible to break free of menial roles.

The rationale for maintaining traditional images of African Americans, and often, separating all-black sequences from their film context was purely economic. Studios could cut costs by employing an African American cast and crew on a much lower wage scale, and could also ensure acceptance from Southern censors because Jim Crow laws would not be challenged. Big budget Hollywood films often included musical numbers inserted into films in segments that could easily be edited out if the musicians were African Americans unacceptable in the South.[49] While Southern audiences constituted only a segment of moviegoers, their economic impact on Hollywood films was apparent. Rather than risking boycotts over black characters or racial themes that might be censored in the South, the film industry found it financially profitable to stick with traditional depictions of African Americans. The film *Hallelujah* (1929), for example, was banned by the Southern Theater Federation because its lead character was African

American. Ultimately, it was more convenient for the studios to maintain the status quo rather than disrupt the romanticized memory of the Old South, regardless of where the films were screened. Thus, the Southern market became the touchstone for the development of African American images. Often, two versions of a film would be released, one shown in the North and the other shown below the Mason-Dixon line.

Preservation of old stereotypes did not go unchallenged. The NAACP protested, claiming that millions of white Americans had limited interaction with blacks, except for mostly negative film images. The organization denounced the limited casting of African Americans as clowns, crooks, and thieves, characters pictured as ignorant, unethical, vulgar, and cowardly. Years later the NAACP observed the same problem with the *Amos 'n' Andy* television show: "An entire race of 15,000,000 Americans is being slandered each week by this one-sided caricature on television, over the Columbia Broadcasting System, sponsored by the Blatz Brewing Company, to advertise and sell Blatz beer."[50] Demeaning stereotypes survived unaltered as this popular entertainment passed through depression and war, transitioning from stage minstrel shows to radio, film, then television broadcast entertainment. Some of the resistance to change was undoubtedly fear of offending financial backers.

Even though protesters targeted individual films, and sometimes even filmmakers, they did not attack the underlying cultural assumptions that sustained racial imagery. And usually their efforts, even when small-scale, were unsuccessful. Probably the most controversial film, D. W. Griffith's epic drama of the Civil War, *The Birth of the Nation* (1915), provoked indignation from many quarters of the nation. It was banned in New York for a period of time, as well as in Connecticut, Illinois, Kansas, Massachusetts, Minnesota, New Jersey, Ohio, Wisconsin, and other states. The unabashedly white supremacist portrayal of white domination was offensive to many. As James Murray concludes, "The film was a passionate and persuasive avowal of the inferiority of the Negro."[51] Still, thousands of Americans bought tickets, and protests ultimately did little to affect social consciousness, particularly in former strongholds of the Confederacy.

Despite protests over the stereotypes projected through its characters, the *Amos 'n' Andy* radio show was wildly popular with white and African American audiences alike. Along with *Amos 'n' Andy*, other radio shows like *Beulah*, *The Goldbergs*, *The New Adventures of Charlie Chan*, and *The Lone Ranger* projected stereotypes that dominated radio and film and eventually won favor with television audiences. According to Donald Bogle, "Any cultural experiences or attitudes—except those of the generic white American—remained a source of derision for years. Everything that seemed 'foreign' or 'alien' was fodder for laughs or condescension: from the way the characters spoke to the way they dressed to the ideas they espoused."[52] First radio and film, then television were overwhelmingly populated by racist ideologies. And, except for largely ignored pockets of protestors, these images reproduced a widely embraced, racially divided society.

But black and white audiences read film performances in entirely different ways. Black viewers understood the stereotypes as barriers because of their own experiences, so from that vantage point, even demeaned black characters could be considered heroic. And black characters appeared so rarely in mass media that black viewers could be excited by the mere presence of an actor who looked like them.[53]

True to their capitalistic underpinnings, Hollywood feature films remained largely conservative in their depiction of racial themes and images. That is to say, most films reinforced traditional stereotypes and rarely broached sensitive topics, including racial discrimination. While individual directors occasionally tested the boundaries by engaging racial themes and images that reflected a more liberal attitude, as in *The Petrified Forest* (1936) and *They Won't Forget* (1937), not until the late 1940s did a transition in black images begin on a broader scale, becoming a more Americanized image.[54] Even then, forceful black characters were often negative figures, eventually falling victim to their own arrogance and thereby preserving traditional racial constructs.

World War I

Several pioneering one-reel films chronicled daily life for black troops in short, unedited records of everyday life. As early as 1898, the Ninth Negro Cavalry was documented watering horses, and African American infantry troops were filmed disembarking from a troop transport.[55] Among later narrative films, *The Realization of a Negro's Ambition* (1917) told the success story of a Tuskegee graduate, and *The Trooper of Troop K* (1917) recorded African American contributions to General Pershing's actions against Mexican revolutionary Pancho Villa. While popular with African American audiences, neither film was a profitable venture in mainstream white theaters, which may explain the absence of subsequent films with similar themes.[56]

By the time the United States entered World War I, the credibility of motion pictures as propaganda was well established. Major European combatants, already at war for several years, used films to manipulate soldiers and civilians alike by the. For this reason, the US War Department had provided financial assistance to the producers of two general preparedness films, *The Eagle's Wings* (1916) and *Uncle Sam Awake* (1916), with the expectation that Americans might be drawn into the European conflict.

With Executive Order 2594, President Woodrow Wilson created the Committee on Public Information (CPI) in April 1917. The committee's role was to promote participation in the war to defend American democratic ideals. Film quickly became a primary means of galvanizing public opinion. At first, the CPI had to rely on the army signal corps for its film stock, but the corps was an unreliable source of footage. By September, steps were taken to better coordinate the CPI and the signal corps by creating a division of films. By the end of the war, the Division of Films was producing its own feature-length films and documentaries. Among them, *The Training of Colored Troops* (1918) serves as a forerunner of World War II era appeals for African American support. *The Training of Colored Troops* eased white anxieties about arming blacks by relying upon a dignified presentation of African Americans within the parameters of subservient stereotypes. *The Training of Colored Troops* and another similar film, *Our Colored Fighters* (1918), were probably distributed erratically and, as a consequence, not widely viewed, although viewership is not well documented. *Our Colored Fighters*, featuring black soldiers as laborers, appears to have been in heavy demand in African American churches and social organizations.[57] One explanation for this lopsided distribution may be that the film was officially available only to black audiences.[58]

The similarities between *The Training of Colored Troops* and films produced twenty-six years later during World War II are striking. *The Training of Colored Troops* follows Edward Johnson, a recruit from Louisville, Kentucky, as he goes through boot camp and then is shipped with the Engineering Corps to France. Johnson communicates with the folks back home through personal letters. In the final scene, Edward Johnson's latest letter is read aloud to the enthusiastic and excited family, grouped nearby. The story of Edward Johnson's military career is told against a backdrop of actual footage of black recruits in barracks, in military drill exercises, and at boot camp.[59] *The Training of Colored Troops*'s basic narrative structure and visual design are repeated in *The Negro Soldier*.

The primary message of World War I government documentaries was promotion of unity across racial boundaries while simultaneously preserving the inequities inherent in a segregated society.[60] Cued by movie stereotypes and generations of negative representations, however, disparaging images of African Americans dominated newsreels and other documentary films during the war. African Americans were shown in comic sequences for entertainment effect in newsreels, such as when several African Americans are arrested after a midnight chicken coop raid. Even in more serious treatments, African Americans stereotypes persisted. For example, one newsreel contrasted battle-ready white Americans with "a black soldier with a French lesson book in hand, scratching his head and gazing at the book in bewilderment."[61] Ironically, the French lesson book may refer to African Americans serving primarily in French military units. In reality, most African American recruits were placed in segregated non-combat units with little prospect of seeing the enemy. The contributions of the few black troops fighting in the French front lines were ignored. Throughout the war, positive images of African Americans were scarce, and images of African Americans in uniform were equally rare.

To deflect anxieties about African Americans being trained to use arms, government films usually rendered black soldiers harmless by showing them through the lens of racial stereotypes—eating watermelons, loafing, singing, and dancing. Such familiar depictions would be less likely to upset the social hierarchy. Films also focused on activities in training camps and avoided images of African Americans engaged in battle. As Thomas Winter concludes in his study of World War I films, the overall message is clear: "African Americans, even if trained for soldierly duties, would remain harmless, contented denizens at the lower rungs of America's social ladder."[62] And if they should elude the direct surveillance of their white officers, they would revert to predictable behavior patterns. The comforting message was that while blacks could be disciplined, they were childlike outside the dominant structure of white authority, making the presence of white officers essential.

The strategic absence of African Americans from combat eased any lingering anxieties about arming African Americans. Excluding African American soldiers from the front lines had the added benefit of reassuring blacks whose cowardice, it was felt, might keep them from enlisting. As Thomas Winter concludes, "Seeing a black man ready and eager to engage an enemy, instead of being scared by the mere thought, was a rare sight in films of the time."[63] Focusing on the impressive spectacle of black troops in marching formations had the added advantage of deflecting rumors about the horrendous conditions typical in African American boot camps.

Since records were not kept, the impact of World War I government films on the attitudes of African Americans can only be guessed. On the one hand, the films offered images of African Americans unavailable in other venues. However, the films never questioned Jim Crow practices and ignored the pervasive presence of racism in American society. The legacy of World War I training films can be found in the 1944 World War II productions, *The Negro Soldier* and *The Navy Steward*. In both wars, appeals to racial pride with references to black contributions to earlier American wars formed the persuasive strategy of the films. The films included African American families and communities to remind viewers of what was at stake.

In the period between the wars, most Hollywood releases unabashedly celebrated American imperialism, focusing on white victories and patronizing defeated foes. The virtues of white soldiers justified their victories and, in turn, affirmed the righteousness of the democratic way of life. Black characters reverted to their prewar stereotypes. In addition, they appeared in action films as colonized or enslaved primitives who deserved to be destroyed by superior forces. Prison films were also popular during the interval, and they exhibited a pattern of white dominance over black criminals that was associated with justice.[64]

Despite the presence of diverse racial groups in American society, movies offered a homogeneous vision of white Americans and motifs inspired by their lives. Hollywood producers resisted attempts to portray black urban life and social themes, partially because there was little financial incentive, only huge profit risks. And owing to the financing required to underwrite a film through the sales of tickets in theaters, whites controlled most economic aspects of the film industry. By the end of the decade, however, subtle changes had worked their way into Hollywood productions, and World War II offered glimpses of social changes to come.[65]

World War II

The political and social disruptions of World War II introduced new ideas about race, religion, and daily life that slowly, but inevitably, corroded monolithic white culture. Harold Cruse has described the effects of this transition on African Americans: "America's entry into World War II had marked the beginning of the end of Negro ethnic group insularity; an entirely new phase of American Negro life was under way."[66] Following the war, the emergence of a black middle-class, greater economic advantages for most African Americans, and an increased range of labor skills available to them gave weight to blacks' demands for greater inclusion in American society.

The centrality and power of the Hollywood film industry were recognized within days of the outbreak of war in Europe, as social commentators in newspapers and magazines proposed that films should serve the national interests. John C. Flynn designated film theaters "places of public assembly, meeting halls of democracy," where the social life of citizens could flourish in a new civic space that would intersect with the national purpose.[67] The elevation of commercial theaters, formerly places of escape and commerce, to sites of political engagement seems curious unless one considers that these are the very places fundamental American values had always been articulated, albeit on a movie screen.

In an effort to ease the transition to overseas postings, information about cultural differences was provided for soldiers through films. For example, the movie *A Welcome to Britain* (1943), starring Burgess Meredith, was required viewing for servicemen assigned to British posts. The film addressed different cultural practices and attitudes, warning servicemen that the British—in particular British women—were less conscious of racial barriers than many Americans. This approach to forestalling intercultural conflict was well intentioned, but certainly not foolproof. Determined commanders could circumvent these attempts to ease racial relations. Overall, problems caused by race were not as pervasive in England as in the United States and other overseas postings. British tolerance of racial differences and the attitude of acceptance that prevailed among British commanders probably greatly contributed to the acceptance of African Americans.

The B-movie genre, churned out with production-line efficiency and constituting the majority of Hollywood fare, did not reflect the changes precipitated by war. The new conditions did not significantly alter the films' essential narratives, traditional characterizations, or implicit ideologies. Still used mostly as backdrops or villains, African Americans gradually began to appear in more popular Hollywood pictures like *The Maltese Falcon* (1941), *Tarzan's Desert Mystery* (1941), *Bataan* (1943), *Crash Dive* (1943), *The Ox-Bow Incident* (1943), and *Lifeboat* (1944). Mostly, the wartime need to visualize the locales of foreign theaters of war was met by posing African Americans as exotics. Exceptional characterizations, such as Joe, the black crewman in Alfred Hitchcock's *Lifeboat*, preserved social roles. Joe is never really part of the group, and he is the only survivor to perform janitorial duties aboard the small craft. Joe is a reformed pickpocket, leaving the viewer to wonder if absent the positive influence of his white shipmates he would revert to his former larceny.

Gradually, the images of African Americans presented by Hollywood filmmakers and the signal corps began offering more positive portrayals of African Americans, redefined by wartime needs for a unified nation. Censorship regulations were stringent owing to the War Department's consciousness of the tension between white expectations and black images. The result was so effective British civilians were often surprised that African American soldiers were less homogeneous than their Hollywood cinema images.[68] In order to avoid fallout at home, all photographs—including amateur photographs—sent through the mails were censored, especially if they showed African American soldiers with white women, regardless of the circumstances. In response to the protests of black families, General Eisenhower lifted the ban on personal photographs in March 1945, but the absence of blacks in newsreels, popular magazines, and other public media continued.

The World War I practice of using African Americans for comic relief was repeated in World War II newsreels, such as the 1944 fundraising short film, *At Their Side*, in which African Americans clown for the camera.[69] Lack of satisfactory images on the screen left a vacuum for black viewers as James Murray notes: "For years, black audiences identified with heroes in Hollywood films–heroes who were invariably white. Black children playing cowboy in front of tenement buildings wanted to be Alan Ladd, Gary Cooper, and John Wayne.... Black women envisioned estates with luxurious mansions and scores of servants as the real and finest way to live."[70] In the absence of black celebrities, African Americans processed and bleached their hair and used skin brighteners in an attempt to copy the appearance of white screen actors and actresses, as if copying them would somehow bring dignity and respect. Rare media appearances of African Americans would send waves of excitement through black communities.

The sentiment that Patricia Turner identifies in television probably characterized African Americans watching themselves in movie theaters a decade earlier: "Our images were few and far between, and we hungered for more of them.... In subtle ways they did communicate a sense of fractured possibility and a near resignation to second-class citizenship."[71] The message of inferiority was encoded in these depictions. Since the minstrel era of the early to mid-nineteenth century, popular culture had portrayed African Americans as shiftless, infantile, and ignorant, with exaggerated physical features that mirrored a propensity to bestiality. In most Hollywood entertainment films, like *Tarzan of the Apes* (1918), African peoples were marginalized, serving as a background for white actors.[72] The implicit message to viewers was that African Americans were inferior.

Old signal corps footage was sometimes edited into black films such as Robert Rossen and Jack Goldberg's *The Unknown Soldier Speaks* (1934), a remembrance of the black soldier's contribution to American wars. The poor lighting, jerky quality, and graininess of this footage were probably expected by black audiences, who were accustomed to the poor production quality of black films. Production quality deteriorated as black producers languished in the mid 1930s. Their films failed to draw audiences, financing evaporated, and black talent migrated to mainstream studios. Both black movie houses and black production companies continued their decline in the late 1940s, as Hollywood began to target black audiences, television eroded cinema audiences, and white financial backing evaporated.[73]

Aftermath

In the last months of the war, Lawrence Reddick compiled a list of damaging black stereotypes drawn from the feature films of 1944: the savage African, the contented slave, the devoted servant, the immoral politician, the petty thief, the social delinquent, the knife and gun toting criminal, the sexual superman, the pompous athlete, the born cook, the primitive musician, the superstitious churchgoer, the chicken and watermelon eater, the uninhibited expressionist, and the illiterate minion.[74] Stubborn images of black inferiority such as these had persisted virtually unchanged since the first African Americans appeared on screen. For over thirty years, racial prejudices were perpetuated in the plots and characters of film entertainment. In the postwar period, some films addressed segregation directly, beginning a cycle in which African American racial identity is problematized. Among the more popular "problem pictures" are these 1949 releases: *Pinky, Home of the Brave, Intruder in the Dust,* and *Lost Boundaries.*

Without alternative images, many moviegoers had simply accepted the outrageous portraits of blacks as historically and socially accurate. While it might be expected that stereotypes would dominate films set in the South, even films featuring other locales "were scarcely an improvement. In the main, the black men on screen continued to be presented as emasculated, easily frightened semi-literates while the women were shown as fat, excessively jolly menials. Blacks of both sexes were to be found cleaning, cooking, or carrying suitcases; their place was in the fields, the kitchen, the stable, or the train station."[75] Not until the late 1940s did the film industry begin gradually to depart from the stereotypes entrenched in earlier films, even though many films continued to caricature and denigrate blacks with unflattering images.[76]

Eventual modification of the conventional image of African Americans can be found in films dealing with social issues. In addition, a more liberal group of Hollywood filmmakers, many of them refugees from Europe, influenced movie themes and images in the late 1940s and early 1950s. The exploration of new themes clashed with conservative media images of African Americans. And, overall, departures from tradition were suppressed somewhat by investigations by the House Committee on Un-American Activities, which targeted influential Hollywood liberals.

In the immediate postwar years, a handful of films diverged from the traditional stereotypes in their treatment of African Americans. However, traditional stereotypes continued to dominate the screen well into the 1950s.[77] African Americans were still predominately shown as maids and menial workers. They were servants, ignorant and superstitious savages in the Tarzan series and, of course, slaves in historical films. Sidney Poitier became one of the first black celebrities acceptable to white audiences. However, even he had limits. Between 1958 and 1966, Poitier appeared in thirteen movies, but was only once cast in a romantic role. Bowing to social constraints, his partner in *Paris Blues* was Diahann Caroll.[78]

Eventually, commercial considerations won out, and black moviegoers' desire to see black actors on the screen was exploited during the 1950s and 1960s. However, lighter-skinned blacks were favored in the lead roles, while villains and comic figures were darker-skinned and spoke in dialect. The musical continued to be the most prevalent form of all-black movie. All these films mostly skirted difficult social issues. For example, the film *Lost Boundaries* (1949), based on the true story of Dr. Albert H. Johnston, who passed for white in the Midwest, dealt superficially with racial prejudice, but the film skipped over many of the complex issues raised in the original book written by William H. White.

In retrospective films, the armed forces are often depicted as integrated, clearly not reflecting history accurately. In *Judgment at Nuremberg* (1961), black military policemen work side-by-side with whites at a 1948 war crimes trial, even though President Harry Truman had not yet ordered the desegregation of the armed forces.[79] Recent Hollywood films also portray World War II inaccurately, showing integrated troops more typical of wars that followed the Korean conflict. From its very beginnings, film has operated as a cultural barometer, sharpening racial distinctions and excluding African Americans from the silver screen.[80]

CHAPTER FOUR

The Negro Soldier as Conversion Narrative

Movies were a tool, free of language barriers, transferring the social mores and popular culture of the day at the expense of the cultural realities and social existence of Black Americans.
—PEARL BOWER[1]

The Negro Soldier has been called a "watershed in the use of film to promote racial tolerance."[2] It provided visual evidence of African American capabilities while remaining ambiguous about integration, thus providing hope for thousands of black Americans while reassuring supporters of segregation that the status quo would not be challenged. The film offered a vision of African Americans that went far beyond decades of stereotypical depictions at a time when the institution of military segregation was strained by the crisis of war and massive social disruption. *The Negro Soldier* provided a short-term compromise but foreshadowed the strife that would gather momentum in the ensuing years, coming to a climax in the civil rights movement to end Jim Crow segregation in the 1960s.

The signal corps's production of *The Negro Soldier* resulted from the government's conviction that film would be the most effective means of overcoming racial tensions, uniting African Americans behind the war effort while postponing slowdowns, strikes, and riots protesting discrimination. Following an increase in racial disturbances in 1943, the War Department was eager to stifle public dissent and unify citizens to win the war.[3] It was also pressured by competing demands of African Americans, who sought better treatment in military roles, and by the dire need to reinforce fighting units decimated on the front lines, particularly after the Battle of the Bulge.

This film is especially important because it signaled a dramatic shift in tactics for addressing the military service of African Americans. By admitting blacks' suitability for service as well as their contributions in past wars, the federal government implicitly sanctioned African American claims to full citizenship. In this way, the film serves as a marker for the beginning of the struggle for integration of the military, a change that eventually rippled through society, becoming the foundation of the civil rights movement.[4] *The Negro Soldier* acted as a catalyst for social change because it provided dignified images of African Americans. It is a cultural signpost for the transformation of citizenship. It appeared at the intersection of a complex network of voices, audiences, and purposes during a time when equality was demanded but delayed because of wartime constraints and entrenched attitudes. The film emanated from the context of crisis, responding to the voices of people existing on the margins of society and witnessed by an entrenched majority resistant to change.

The Negro Soldier offers an opportunity to see how powerful entrenched forces function at multiple levels: institutional, social, historical, personal. It presents an inclusive egalitarian vision of military services, yet falls short of promising integration after the war. The rhetoric of the film worked because it was "open," an ambiguous text that could be interpreted differently by diverse audiences. It did not alarm white viewers, yet it offered hope to African Americans. It tempered wartime aspirations of black communities seeking to leverage their critical manpower at a time when unity was essential to victory.

We can only estimate the effect of the film on Americans because few surveys were completed at the time, particularly surveys of civilians. Millions viewed the film in civilian and military theaters. More than likely, it modified perspectives and at the same time quieted demands for equality until military victory could be won. The film is significant because it is a record of government attempts to manage social attitudes to best serve the national interests. The American perception of race in relationship to the war was manipulated through mass exposure to this film.

This chapter examines how *The Negro Soldier* negotiated harmony within a social context of racial tension, soothing those who refused to acknowledge the ability of African Americans to fight on an equal footing with whites. The film rewrote the historical narrative of promises of military service and citizenship, mostly broken during the peace that followed wars, that encouraged African Americans to respond to the national crisis by making common cause.

The Social Context

Formulating an appropriate response to a complex rhetorical situation in 1943 required the reconciliation of coexisting and competing demands.[5] Contradictory interests existed on several planes—between white and black, army and civilian, national and international, domestic and military. Government and military leaders, including President Roosevelt, argued that racial change would threaten victory, while "civil rights leaders countered that the status quo jeopardized it even more by denying the nation the full contribution of blacks to victory, the ideological difference from racist enemies it needed, and the image abroad it wanted to cultivate."[6] *The Negro Soldier* was the official response to this complex rhetorical situation, as the War Department attempted to foster civilian cooperation and to meet its recruitment needs in the midst of racial tensions, all while protecting the policies of exclusion that pervaded all branches of the service except the coast guard.[7] As in past conflicts, America faced the problem of race, a quandary that ebbed and flowed through the history of American wars, recurring when the cooperation of all of citizens was essential to victory.[8]

The Negro Soldier was intended to accomplish several objectives. It was primarily meant to overcome racial tensions by uniting all Americans behind the war effort, while postponing African American demands for immediate equality.[9] Since racial problems were viewed as the result of their demands for change, African Americans were the principal target of the film. There were several secondary goals. The federal government needed to resolve the military manpower shortage following the German counteroffensive in the Ardennes, commonly known as the Battle of the Bulge, to provide a positive propaganda response to international political pressure, to secure African American loyalty in the face of potential fifth column activity, and to suppress the threat of domestic strikes in key war industries. This film addressed these issues while simultaneously signifying a subtle shift in the government's position. It skirted any promises of change, controversial historical claims, and insinuations of civil rights concessions.[10]

Audience

For much of the war, government offices like the Office of War Information (OWI), the Office of Facts and Figures (OFF), and others had carefully reviewed the status of African Americans. They collected and analyzed data about officer promotions, editorials and articles in black newspapers, summaries of racial incidents by category, complaints about military practices, and statistics about the general profile of black soldiers. In 1943 an OWI official report on the status of racial relations concluded that the problems of race could not be solved during wartime. Instead, racial segregation was a long- range problem, and in the short term the "media should be fed all the material we can develop" to convince the black soldier that he had an interest in the "institutions of liberty."[11] This policy echoed the federal commitment to victory without integration, and it endorsed a vigorous media campaign to secure African American compliance. *The Negro Soldier* was the cornerstone of that campaign. Director George Barnes charged that OWI should "use methods that will bring the quickest, most positive results . . . [which means] filling the Negro with information about his stake in the war, in effect, a direct and powerful Negro propaganda effort as distinct from a crusade for Negro rights."[12] The goals and procedures of the OWI paralleled those of the military: to recruit and use black manpower within the current racial policies of segregation, and postpone the problems of integration. Any adjustments regarding racial discrimination in military ranks would not be made during the war.

In the initial stages of pre-production, two primary audiences were identified. *The Negro Soldier* was intended for African American soldiers in uniform, serving as a means of stopping violence on military bases, and it was planned as a classroom film to accompany *Leadership and the Negro Soldier* (1944), a training manual for white officers who dealt with black troops.[13] Before it could be released, the film also had to be screened and approved by white upper echelons of the army, which included skeptics as well as supporters such as General Lyman Munson, who was considered the political power behind the development and eventual distribution of the film. Chief of Staff George C. Marshall also was a strong proponent of the general use of films to motivate both soldiers and civilians. Prior experimentation with comic books, lectures, pamphlets, and other media proved that films had a greater impact on audiences than other media.[14] In particular, Marshall supported the use of documentary film to motivate black troops and quell increasing racial tensions.[15] Like others, Marshall thought that the power of documentary film derived from its factual nature, which contrasted with the lies perpetuated in Axis propaganda films.

Prior to the development of *The Negro Soldier*, the armed forces had investigated comic books as a primary tool for disseminating ideas and information. Psychologists assigned to the Office of War Information had observed that the billion-dollar civilian comic book market offered heroes who overcame insurmountable odds and were invincible in the face of enemy assaults.[16] By contemporary standards, comics were insensitive to race and gender, but at the time comic books were a major source of information for millions of Americans, especially young men of draft age who sometimes read little else. Comic books were so compelling as a propaganda medium that the Office of War Information printed a memorable biography of Franklin Delano Roosevelt in that format. According to one scholar, "Comic books had a direct psychological and political impact on their audience. They reinforced stereotypical individuals, groups, and situations and tapped the basest emotions. Clearly, the comic book provided the reader with the kind of emotional gratification that was unavailable in the daily experience of home front America."[17] The same vicarious participation in heroics was offered up even more intensely on the cinema screen. For that reason, director Frank Capra, who had originally tried comic books as a channel for justifying American participation in the war, turned to the more effective medium of film with his *Why We Fight* series.[18] Because it could engage large groups in an intense visual experience, film seemed to be a more compelling choice for addressing the problem of race.

Groups within the Army Information and Education Division argued that both white and black audiences, military and civilian, would benefit from viewing the film. After considerable debate about who should see the film, it was screened before a "safe" audience of troops at a camp outside San Diego. Their wildly enthusiastic reaction was unanticipated, giving weight to arguments that the film should be shown to a broader audience than originally intended.

Convinced that *The Negro Soldier* would not provoke a racial backlash, army officers made recommendations for several changes before releasing it to civilian audiences. In particular, scenes that included visual references to black officers, an extended combat sequence involving black infantry, and a white nurse tending an injured black soldier were all cut. To avoid completely misleading construction corps about their primary assignment, scenes showing black troops engaged in labor battalions were added. Within weeks, surveys reported that black troops stationed at Camp Pickett, Virginia, previewed the film and overwhelmingly wanted it shown to white troops. Almost 80 percent of both black and white troops (949 responses) thought the film should be shown to civilians. From February 1944 until the end of the war, *The Negro Soldier* was required viewing as part of the standard orientation program for every recruit in the United States Army.

The War Department allowed the film industry to handle civilian distribution of *The Negro Soldier*. Instead of being distributed through a single, major studio as was standard practice, "It was parceled out to a number of distributors in various regions of the country: the film then was made available to those exhibitors who requested it."[19] The film, along with others, such as *Teamwork* (1943) and *Negro Colleges* (1944), were still in use in 1948, when Truman's executive order limited their value.

Elmer Davis, head of the Office of War Information, approved *The Negro Soldier* for release to civilian audiences after a private showing at the Pentagon for two hundred black journalists, who were uniformly delighted with it. Even the omission of slavery and segregation did not dampen the enthusiasm of the reporters, although several noted the "painfully mild" treatment of difficult topics and "questionable" gilding of racial issues.[20] When interviewed by *Time* magazine, Carlton Moss stated that the movie would "mean more to Negroes than most white men could imagine."[21]

The Negro Soldier proved problematic for civilian theater owners in its original forty-three minute format because it was too long to be used as a short film before the main feature and too short for a main feature. Still, 16,203 theaters requested the original uncut film, and records show that approximately 1,819 theaters included it as part of their weekly program. This was remarkable considering the length of the film. *The Negro Soldier* was later re-cut to a twenty-minute length that proved more popular, eventually showing in five thousand theaters. Black newspapers as well as the National Council of Negro Women and the Los Angeles Civic Unity Committee also sponsored *The Negro Soldier* in a variety of noncommercial venues. The Office of War Information produced 150 prints of *The Negro Soldier* in the last six months of 1944. They were released and viewed by approximately 3.1 million Americans.[22] In April 1944 the Office of War Information was granted permission to offer the film for viewing in public libraries, schools, and colleges throughout the nation. Attendance at these events is estimated at approximately 7.5 million yearly.[23] In total, by the end of World War II more than ten million civilians had seen *The Negro Soldier*.

Jack Goldberg, president of The Negro Marches On, Inc., produced an independent film, *We've Come a Long, Long Way* (1944), for his chain of mainly black movie houses. Goldberg's film was based on the Office of War Information pamphlet *Negroes and the War* (1943), and it was intended to compete with *The Negro Soldier*. *We've Come a Long, Long Way* was sponsored by Elder Lightfoot Solomon Michaux, a radio evangelist who was popular in the black community. After some controversy over circulation practices involving the NAACP, Nelson Rockefeller, Cardinal Spellman, and several prominent newspaper editors, the case was decided against Goldberg in court, and subsequently *We've Come a Long, Long Way* was withdrawn from his movie theaters.

As the Goldberg case suggests, American audiences were by no means homogeneous. Various factions formed the viewing audience, some with clear political positions and some nonaligned. However, *The Negro Soldier* was soon shown everywhere, from base camps to civilian theaters across the United States and abroad. Southern as well as Northern audiences responded positively to the film, although opinions varied within the generally enthusiastic reception.[24] The NAACP, black newspapers, African American churches, the socialist party, Negro leaders like A. Philip Randolph–these voices representing the black community applauded the film, although many wanted it to go farther. The NAACP responded by praising the film, concluding that *The Negro Soldier* "has enormous potentialities for good . . . in educating white Americans to the true place of their fellow citizens in our country."[25] The NAACP press release regarding the film suggested that the white viewer would learn about the valuable part that blacks played in the national cause. William White, executive secretary of the NAACP, touted the film in a 1943 speech to the leftist UCLA Writers' Congress as "an outstanding contribution to the morale of Negro troops and civilians."[26] The National Negro Congress, an organization to the left of the NAACP, praised the film as "the best ever done," and the headline "Army Shows Hollywood the Way" topped the story about the film that appeared in the new magazine *Negro*.[27] Other viewers, including white civilians, international allies, and potential white recruits, were reassured about the patriotism of African Americans and felt more confident in blacks' ability to contribute to the war. Although it is impossible to prove so directly, the film probably accomplished many of its objectives by blunting racial violence, suppressing the potential for backlash of white civilians and soldiers, and motivating African Americans to champion the war.

The Army Information and Education Division, a group of leading social scientists overseen by Brigadier General Frederick H. Osborn, used cutting-edge research methods to investigate the impact of films like *The Negro Soldier* on viewers. Samuel Stouffer, a sociologist from the University of Chicago, headed the research branch of the Army Information and Education Division. Stouffer, along with Donald Young, the War Department's official expert on race, was convinced that films could be used to instill democratic values in viewers.[28] They were keenly aware of the value of this sort of informational film. Their confidence in the motivational value of films reinforced the Office of War Information's decision to share *The Negro Soldier* with all American and Allied civilians and soldiers. Although by most definitions films like *The Negro Soldier* are steeped in ideology, their creators considered them documentaries. Documentary films, at least those produced by most American filmmakers associated with the war effort, were considered factual, relying on truth telling to achieve effects. They felt that Axis propaganda, by contrast, was built on lies.

The wartime climate fostered coexisting and competing demands for white and black Americans. It was through military service that African Americans fully realized their place in American society, one that had not been secured in previous wars. The differences between white and black attitudes toward military service are summarized by M. S. Sherry: "Whites volunteered without any social or political thought about the action; for blacks the 'privilege' of serving pointed out the inferior status of blacks—exploitation of their lives without a clear distinction of their equality."[29] These divergent vantage points account for African American protests and the resulting white backlash. *The Negro Soldier*, with dignified but nonthreatening images of African American soldiers, offered a temporary compromise.

For black audiences, *The Negro Soldier* highlights past African American triumphs and glorifies personal sacrifices. By doing so, it extends the invitation to equality. The emphasis on African American contributions to the historical development of the United States implies citizenship, earned through military sacrifice. The shuffling, ignorant black caricature preserved in other media is replaced with a proud, competent soldier who is committed to defending his country. For white audiences, this film asserts that acceptance of African Americans will not upset social norms, but will ensure American victory. Visual images of menial labor like road building and ship loading suggest that military segregation is preserved. Opportunities offered to African Americans appear to be consistent with their subordinate station and limited abilities. In addition, black soldiers are commanded by white officers and restricted to interactions within their race.

All viewers are urged to move from individual ambition to collective patriotism. Because the visual medium invites vicarious participation, "The viewer associates, often subconsciously, his prior experiences and attitudes to arrive at new interpretations and conclusions."[30] As in most films, images in *The Negro Soldier* are open to interpretation, depending on the audience to determine their meaning, although by placing them within the larger struggle against a common foe, the film encourages viewers to think of their patriotic obligations. *The Negro Soldier* offered a more dignified image of the African American soldier, one that clashed with the restrictive practices of Jim Crow segregation.[31] *The Negro Soldier* encouraged adoption of alternatives to enduring stereotypes. The mammy image was avoided, the black soldier could read, and black troops appeared to engage the enemy. The effect was electrifying, as Walter Fisher, a black officer in the Army Instruction and Education Division, attests: It was "one of the finest things that ever happened to America."[32] The film shows African Americans in a revised historical chronology that includes them as important contributors to building the nation. Thomas Cripps and David Culbert posit that by shattering deeply rooted media stereotypes of blacks, War Department films such as *The Negro Soldier* provided a model for postwar Hollywood.[33] It was a watershed moment in the evolution of American civil rights; these films broke through previous demeaning images to allow for a new vision of African Americans.

The Negro Soldier

The original forty-three-minute black-and-white film, *The Negro Soldier*, was a blend of cinematic themes, a hybrid of the theatrical newsreel, a *Life* magazine feature article, and grand Hollywood entertainment.[34] It originated in the War Department but quickly engaged Hollywood talent drafted and assigned to the signal corps to make government films during the war. Frank Capra and various government offices contributed to this production. For example, the Research Branch, headed by sociologist Donald Young, provided Frank Capra with a list of associations to avoid when depicting black characters in government films. Young cautioned against showing an affinity for watermelon and pork, pronounced Negroid features, or friends and leaders of the race such as Abraham Lincoln. These dictates may explain the absence of slavery, emancipation, or political leadership in references to the Civil War. Young also treated the difficult issue of African American officers, who he regarded as upsetting the racial order, by telling Capra to show black officers, while adding, "Don't play them up too much."[35]

Capra appointed Stuart Heisler to direct the film. Several drafts of a script for *The Negro Soldier* were prepared. The first by Marc Connelly (*Green Pastures*, 1930) was rejected as overly dramatic; the second by Ben Hecht and Jo Swerling also failed to fit the requirements of a factual representation. Carlton Moss, who was personally authorized by Heisler, wrote the final script.

The setting for the film is a church service in which the congregation is made up of African American families, a choir and soloist sing patriotic background music, and a minister, played by scriptwriter Carlton Moss, uses his sermon to discuss the war. In the opening sequence, white congregants file into their church, and black worshipers enter a separate building, visually preserving Jim Crow segregation. Using a communal gathering place for African Americans justified grouping them apart from white Americans in a visually segregated setting, in addition exploiting the powerful influence of organized religion in African American lives.

The story then moves inside the black church. Within this fictional framework, the black minister addresses his congregation, saying, "I think I am going to depart from my prepared sermon. While I was listening to the sergeant's solo, I kept looking up at our service flag."[36] This announcement is followed by a comparison of Joe Louis's comeback match against Max Schmeling with the current world war pitting America against Germany. Schmeling, Hitler's favorite, had beaten Louis two years earlier, but in 1938 Louis took revenge in Yankee Stadium by knocking out Schmeling two minutes into the fight. The hypocrisy of a nation cheering Joe Louis, the Brown Bomber, while discriminating against his African American brothers in uniform is probably blunted because the boxing match is presented as an ideological contest between democracy and fascism.

The reference to Joe Louis is followed by a recounting of African American contributions to military history via an individual soldier's experiences in the US military, related a letter read by his mother, a member of the congregation, and an inventory of African American participation in the current war. The film concludes with the minister's allusion to Joe Louis, as he exhorts his congregation to unite in defeating the enemy: "The job isn't finished. This is only the beginning. To win the final victory over Germany and Japan, our blows must be dealt harder and faster and with all our strength. There can be no let up in supplies. More food, equipment, and ammunition must reach our troops in the battle areas. More airports, landingfields, docks, bridges and roads...." The swell of patriotic music, along with images of African American gangs building roads and the sounds of battle in the distance reinforce the minister's call for solidarity. Defeating the Axis requires that racial diversity be shown as a source of strength, not weakness, in direct contrast to Aryan ideology.[37]

The underlying theme of the film emphasizes the need to form a common front against fascism. This message is delivered as the "voice of God" through the minister, whose narration reminds listeners of the African

American role in the European conflict. Writing about Carlton Moss, the de facto director of the film, Clyde Taylor argues, "Moss brought a degree of poetry to his screen image by inventing the device of a Negro preacher as a pulpit narrator. And the sweep of his montage and elevated images approached epic grandeur."[38] The abstract idea of patriotism is situated in an eloquent description of black heroism in America's wars. Given the centrality of the church in the African American community, the minister functions as a credible source for the film's pro-government message.

This grand vision pivots on the retelling of American military history. Fully a quarter of the film chronicles black contributions to past American wars. As the minister recalls the African American role in earlier conflicts, he seeks to remind viewers that these were times of national unity when individuals put aside their differences for the greater good of the nation.[39] Beginning with the phrase "Americans have always guarded liberty," the minister identifies the first casualty for American freedom as Crispus Attucks, an African American who died in the line of fire in 1770 on the Boston square "in freedom's cause." Like Attucks, other brave African Americans died at Concord Bridge, Bunker Hill, Lexington, Valley Forge, and in the War of 1812. The Civil War is acknowledged in only two lines, both quotations from Abraham Lincoln. The problem of slavery is strategically omitted, as is Reconstruction and Jim Crow segregation. Then, identification of African Americans in military service is continued through the character "Jim," who recollects his participation in the Spanish-American War. Later, Jim builds the Panama Canal, and his sons fight in World War I. Their units and battle service are listed. As the historical chronicle unfolds through Jim and his sons, other African Americans are visually commemorated through photographs, tombstones, and battlefield monuments. At one point, a black navy steward takes up a gunner's weapon to join a battle. Clearly this is a reference to Dorie Miller, whose bravery during the attack on Pearl Harbor would undoubtedly resonate with African American viewers. The overall impact of this retelling builds an argument for patriotism through military duty.

The transition to World War II is accompanied by footage of Nazis blowing up the French monument commemorating African American soldiers who served in World War I. The startling image of this destruction serves as a direct assault on African American heroism. At this point, the minister switches to a recitation of the social, cultural, and scientific achievements of black civilians like Booker T. Washington, George Washington Carver, and others, followed by a listing of African American universities and colleges.

African American contributions are rehearsed as a string of individual accomplishments against a collective backdrop of American wars and institutions. This reconstruction of the American story highlighting individual African Americans strengthens the relationship between the civilians seated in the congregation and national symbols that dominate the conclusion of the film. Owing to the African American heritage of sacrifice in American wars, history becomes an argument for individual obligation to military duty.[40]

The film progresses in a linear fashion, and the church with its minister as narrator weaves an invisible framework for the narration. The viewer follows the African American soldier, vicariously experiencing the events that unfold on the screen. Because narrative techniques like flashbacks are unobtrusive, the action proceeds seamlessly for the viewer. The film offers up a slice of real life, with the viewer engaging vicariously participating. Ironically, the film, which functions as a documentary, does not recognize its own cinematic conventions.

Although it may seem inconsequential, government funding of *The Negro Soldier* ensured technical superiority rarely seen in the movies typically screened in African American theaters. Production qualities such as flashback devices, a clean soundtrack, excellent lighting, superb editing, and precise camera work in *The Negro Soldier* outshone those of black productions, adding credibility to the final product. The impact of the technical quality of the film cannot be underestimated; "Never before had a film purporting to document black American achievement been made with such professional competence."[41] The technical quality of the film must have dazzled its viewers. Combined with the film's unique message of dignity, the film showed competent African Americans that markedly depart from generations of shuffling, grinning servant depictions. The effect was nothing less than spectacular. Essentially, *The Negro Soldier* offered a new image that integrated the African American with the national cause and, in doing so, elevated his station.

The Strategy of Conversion

The Negro Soldier addressed both African American and white audiences simultaneously. The text is polysemic, open to interpretation on several levels by multiple audiences. For African Americans, the film increased race consciousness, as it offered images of African Americans as heroes. For white audiences the film displayed black soldiers patriotically serving the national cause, something the nation required to win the war. To accomplish its polysemic message, examples are rendered strategically ambiguous, such as when the chaplain helps the African American soldier with a letter to his folks. Indirectly this scene addresses the issue of illiteracy. It is not clear if the soldier needs help writing the letter because he is illiterate, or if he only needs guidance with the content of the letter. The scene is open to various interpretations, depending on the assumptions of any given viewer.

Within the film, two frames interconnect: first the church, which is intimate, and second, the boot camp, which is public. The second frame is nested within the first, making military duty a personal obligation. Reinforcing this nesting of visual frames, the minister talks about "soldiering," employing what is a friendlier, more colloquial term than "fighting." The decision to "soldier" is made within the context of the familiar, intimate church service, with the credibility of the minister and endorsement of family and friends to sanction it. Within the context of past American wars, soldiering becomes a symbolic invitation to join with family and community in the American cause.

The Negro Soldier emerges as a site of compromise between the dominant chronicle of national patriotism and the opposition of disenfranchised African Americans. The film works for both black and white audiences by negotiating a truce between competing social interests through a sophisticated mix of compelling images, historical reconstruction, American myths, and sophisticated framing. The central vehicle for persuasion is the renegotiated image of dignity for African American soldiers, a conversion from inept minstrel stereotypes rooted in the mythic plantation and into capable patriots.

The Conversion Narrative

Human responsiveness to narrative has been demonstrated in multiple forms, from myths to movies.[42] The potential of narrative to invoke nationalism during wartime is noted by critic Michael Osborn, who argues that such a story "needs to center on the relationships among symbols and social control."[43] During hostilities, need for social control is particularly acute, requiring combatants to harness potent national symbols in order to justify the sacrifice of millions of citizens. In the wartime propaganda film, the relationship between the viewer and symbols of national identity is constructed through a narrative that often includes the viewer as a central heroic figure in the story of the conflict.[44] In this process, the narrative replaces individual sacrifice with national glory. Thus, the relationship between symbols and social control is completed through the narrative of heroism. In World War II, filmmakers employed a conversion narrative in which "men and women saw that authority lay in savior institutions and patriotic goals ... strong ethnic loyalties and criticism of class and gender arrangements were seen as alien to the American way."[45] Thus, individual goals were subsumed in the national cause, and the war hero became the symbol of the national cause.

Derived from popular film, the conversion narrative shows individuals overcoming divisive factions to work together for the common good. In 1930, the conversion narrative was absent from Hollywood films but accounted for 20 percent of the film plots eight years later.[46] Perhaps the collective economic crisis of the Great Depression required a national narrative of unity that found expression in the films of the period. Whatever its source, the conversion narrative tells the story of a hero whose selfish personal concerns are transformed through a series of events so that he reaches out to others, and together they solve common problems. During World War II, films such as *Bataan* (1943), *The Fighting Sullivans* (1944), and *Life Boat* (1945) featured this transformation of rugged individualism into group solidarity for a common cause. The conversion narrative celebrated teamwork and institutional loyalty critical for military victory.

The conversion narrative was adopted as the fundamental perspective in *The Negro Soldier*, inspiring white and black audiences to unite for the national defense. For both whites and blacks, the film redirected attention from divisive racial strife to shared problems, encouraging every viewer to recognize that cooperation was a prerequisite to winning the war. While the immediate goal of the film was to foster support for the war, its long-term impact involved reshaping American culture and political ideology. The positive portrayal of African Americans made it difficult to dismiss them as unable or unwilling to cooperate. Simultaneously, African American viewers were required to relinquish convictions that collided with patriotism as individual demands for equality were converted into collective victory. Thus, the confrontation over equal rights was temporarily postponed, as individuals put aside selfish interests in favor of long-term national success.

From the opening frames of the film, viewers are immersed in the patriotic cause. To this end, national myths and symbols are reworked to include African Americans, a step that indirectly changes the nature of their relationship to the national identity and sets the stage for postwar claims for equality. The film situates African Americans within the military struggle by exploiting socio-religious culture, appropriating black history, and appropriating personal experience.

THE NEGRO SOLDIER EXPLOITS SOCIO-RELIGIOUS CULTURE

The setting for the film is a church service in which the congregation consists of African American families, a choir and soloist sing patriotic background music, and a minister uses his sermon to comment on the war. Since conversion is a fundamental part of the religious experience, this setting is rich in symbolism. In addition, the importance of religion and community for African Americans during the first half of the twentieth century was a key component of black identity.[47] The influence of the unofficial grapevine in the African American community, together with the opinion leadership of ministers, servicemen's letters home, and the church congregation give credibility to the film's message. The power of the religious framework is exploited to advance national interests. As the visual backdrop for the story of the war, the church service contributes "to the reproduction of knowledge, beliefs, attitudes, ideologies, norms, or values" of viewers and functions as a major avenue for the reproduction of cultural identity.[48]

Early in the film, the minister assumes the role of government spokesperson, explaining, "I think I am going to depart from my prepared sermon." He offers a justification in support of the Allies over the Axis, replacing the conventional Bible reading with a passage from *Mein Kampf* that reveals Hitler to be an unmitigated racist. The comparison casts the war as a contest between democracy and fascism, mimicking the spiritual battle between good and evil, God and Satan. This contrast implies American commitment to the inherent equality of all races; the common foe of racism is personified in Hitler. The assaults on Nazi evil require that racial diversity be shown as a source of strength, not weakness, as Hitler asserts, a message to which African Americans responded as positively as whites.[49]

In particular, the black minister functions as a community leader in a historically oral culture.[50] His relationship to his parishioners is reciprocal when he engages them and they respond. This call-response formula sets up testimonials on behalf of the military, as the film's mock church service unfolds and members of the congregation speak. In a key sequence, added specifically to improve the credibility of the film, a soldier's mother reads a letter detailing his experiences as a recent inductee and army officer candidate. During casting, producers were careful to specify that the mother be portrayed as a well-dressed middle-class woman. They instructed, "The woman should not be a 'mammy.' Her race should be determinable only by her color; not by her dress or manner."[51] This direction demonstrates that the producers were conscious of creating positive visual images that broke from traditionally demeaning stereotypes.

The interaction of the minister and his congregation further exploits the formula of the church service. The dynamic call and response protocol of many African American churches, in which speakers and listeners both contribute to the formation of the message, creates a bond between the congregation and the minister, who asks questions, recognizes individuals within the group, and otherwise encourages them to become involved in the worship service. The result is that boundaries between individuals are blurred with personal interaction. As Gladstone L. Yearwood explains, "In black cultural expression, the audience exists in a dialectical relationship, which is more readily observed in those parts that favor interpersonal performances and involve oratory, music and dance."[52] *The Negro Soldier* recreates this performance through the interaction of the minister with his congregants, the soldier's mother, a WAC in her service uniform, and other enlisted men. By extension, a space is preserved for the viewer, who becomes part of the congregation.

THE NEGRO SOLDIER APPROPRIATES BLACK HISTORY

Reminding his congregants that "Americans have always guarded liberty," the minister recalls the long tradition of African American participation in earlier conflicts, when black soldiers and civilians put aside their individual differences for the greater good of the nation.[53] In the quest for victory, national unity demanded personal sacrifice, and the list of martyrs who "have always guarded liberty" begins with Crispus Attucks, who died "in freedom's cause." Key events in American history such as the colonial defense at Lexington and Washington's winter at Valley Forge are woven together with African American contributions, thus implicitly recognizing the latter's value in building the nation. As the historical chronicle unfolds, African Americans become part of the story and part of the national legacy of military responsibility to the nation.

The contributions of African Americans are expanded beyond military service to include social, cultural, and scientific achievements. The individual leadership of men like Booker T. Washington and George Washington

Carver are celebrated as highlights in American history. The recitation of accomplishments creates a bond of pride and obligation. Social control is thus established through narrative symbols that engage listeners in a common legacy.[54] History appropriates black participation with an argument that obligates African Americans to continue to support their nation in spite of personal preferences. Owing to their sacrifices for the common good, individuals like Washington, Carver, and the generic "Jim" who fought in the Spanish-American War provide potent models.

The historical chronology rehearsed within the framework of the church service reveals differences in narrative styles preferred by black and white audiences. White narrative tends to be factual and subject to little embellishment or exaggeration. It adheres to strict chronological time frames. Narratives for African Americans are often less formulaic, acknowledging for individuality of the storyteller, and are often episodic rather than strictly chronological. They provide observations and interject commentary as the narrative progresses, not constrained by preordained conclusions. White narratives, because of their form, reaffirm group membership and behavioral norms. African American narratives, on the other hand, assert individual strengths and powers.[55]

The structural differences between black and white narratives are evident in *The Negro Soldier*. Allowing for typical African American narrative structure, the film is episodic and does not reach a definitive conclusion. It revolves around strong, independent main characters. While using these features of African American narrative, by copying the style of documentary film *The Negro Soldier* also appears factual; it is given to little exaggeration or few embellishments. The film follows a time frame that is roughly chronological. Thus both black and white narrative traditions are incorporated into *The Negro Soldier*.

Many inaccuracies and ambiguities exist in the film's review of history. Precision of historical chronology, however, is incidental to the function of the conversion narrative in the film. As David Thelan suggests in a study of collective memory, "The important question is not how accurately a recollection fitted some piece of a past reality, but why historical actors constructed their memories in a particular way at a particular time."[56] The rationale for government portrayal of African American history is apparent. Reconstruction of the past ignores mistreatment of black soldiers, instead stressing their contributions. Such discourse operates in an ideological context where the reconstruction of history is shaped by values of nationalism framed by circumstances of war. The government position prevails by demonstrating the African American stake in the war by means of patriotic images that capture the dominant ideology in a common history. To that extent, the "mobilization of memory is . . . a vital political resource."[57] The appropriation of African American history, as it is re-envisioned through images, is an essential condition for commitment to the war. The past is selectively resurrected to serve the present without mention of the problems of slavery, the Civil War, Reconstruction, and Jim Crow segregation.

THE NEGRO SOLDIER APPROPRIATES PERSONAL EXPERIENCE

In its attempts to amplify patriotism, *The Negro Soldier* is dominated by images of individuals and their personal relationships to national goals. The reconstruction of history through individual African American servicemen transforms past events into present experience at a personal level. This recounting of African American triumph in past wars is tapped and translated into the personal obligation to fight in the current conflict. As director Frank Capra put it, "Done with taste and repression, this may not only be an information picture, but may also serve as an emotional glorification of the Negro war effort."[58] Once emotions are stimulated by situating the war as a personal obligation, they can be redirected to defuse current hostility. Thus, military history is susceptible to error to the extent that "it seeks not so much to render an accurate account of the past as to reintroduce us to feelings about the past."[59] In one sense, the film reforms the historical past to serve immediate ends.

The soldiers in the film demonstrate personal development that presumably they did not attain as civilians. As they are transformed through uniforms and training into efficient columns of marching soldiers, they become part of an army unit. Uniformed African Americans demonstrate for their civilian viewers correct ways to salute officers, use rifles, and drive jeeps. Viewers are reassured that individual problems are also treated seriously. For example, the narrator explains that the soldier can see his chaplain about financial, romantic, and military problems: "Now, I don't want to give you the impression that it is only for religious services or advice that you can come to the chaplain. You can come to him anytime. For example, if you get into trouble with your girlfriend, she doesn't write to you anymore, you want to know how to propose, why just come to the chaplain and he'll give you some advice." In another scene, a new GI meets a woman he'd be proud to introduce to mom, "a real apple pie girl. Just the right size and everything." She is black, so racial barriers are preserved. Such scenarios present the military establishment as benevolent, reassuring viewers that African Americans will be guided through the complexities of military life.

The suitability of black soldiers for military duty is reinforced in their transformation from civilians to soldiers. Black civilians start out as "all thumbs," but soon drill and march in unison as part of a disciplined column. Meanwhile, white soldiers consistently appear in roles of authority. In the visual text, black soldiers are foregrounded against white soldiers. In battle scenes, black troops appear to attack enemy installations in the foreground against a backdrop of white soldiers. The racial composite, achieved by superimposing film images, serves as a metaphor for harmony and mutual respect. And old stereotypes are replaced by new characterizations of blacks as capable soldiers who work peacefully alongside whites.[60] African American soldiers also assume responsibility making beds, washing clothes, and cleaning floors. Visually, *The Negro Soldier* offers a message of inclusion that emphasizes these men's abilities, while at the same time truthfully showing the menial tasks they will doubtless perform in segregated units.

By the conclusion of the film, the individual is subsumed within the military unit, replacing private ambitions with teamwork. The black recruit has learned how to become a soldier and, in the process, has grown as an individual. Graeme Turner observes, "The etiology of a film does not take the form of direct statements or reflections on the culture. It lies in the narrative structure and in the discourses employed—the images, myths, conventions, and visual styles."[61] Within the story of *The Negro Soldier*, the African American soldier has become part of a larger military institution. His transformation is visually reinforced as the awkward civilian becomes part of an impressive military formation, able to march, execute orders, and function as a unit. In this way, the etiology conveyed through narrative structure, rather than didactic observations, provides the argument for unity in support of the war. This message clearly worked in the cause of the federal government, but it also provided a window on dominant cultural etiology for the critic. It offers an insight into the meaning systems of the culture and into the ways such systems are imbedded in social practice. The film co-opts the viewer with a narrative that supports the segregation of the war.[62]

Repercussions of the Conversion Narration

The power of the conversion construct is evident in reactions to the film. First seen by military personnel, *The Negro Soldier* was widely praised by both black and white soldiers as honest and inspiring. The film received equally laudatory responses when it was released for civilian audiences in June 1944, even in generally hostile Southern cities.[63] Capitalizing on this success, within months the navy released *The Negro Sailor* to bolster its tarnished image. Other films, including *Teamwork* (1943), *Negro Colleges* (1944), and *The House I Live In* (1945) employed similar formats and themes.

The filmmakers provided personal frames of church and community as well as frames of public institutions and shared American history in *The Negro Soldier* in order to manipulate viewers' opinions regarding the war.[64] The nation's interests are promoted through the conversion narrative that re-imagines African Americans in their historical roles and in the contemporary. The reconstruction of African American socio-religious culture, history, and personal experience serves to intensify solidarity for the sake of the war effort while ignoring injustice and discrimination. In general, the conversion narrative serves the national ideology of democracy.

National ideology is embedded in the retelling of history that includes African Americans in American wars, scientific discoveries, and educational achievements. In this reconfigured form, both dominant and minority viewers can participate in the same narrative. The conversion of African Americans makes them acceptable to viewers who had rejected their presence while simultaneously providing the dignified images craved by black audiences.[65] Ambiguity allows viewers to interpret the film in sometimes contradictory ways. Scenes such as those of black soldiers marching with white troops on the same parade ground may imply integration for some and segregation for others. The film simultaneously brings historical events into sharper focus and obscures racial divisions in favor of transcendent national identity. Thus, the ideological dimension of the narrative is achieved through the process of conversion. The basic premise of nationalism is embedded in the film in patriotic actions endorsed by family, church, and community.

A primary goal for the film's producers was to quell African American protests against discrimination, and to boost morale, which, in turn, would encourage cooperation and support for the war effort. In order to achieve these ends, *The Negro Soldier* overlooks tough issues. It avoids the problems of military segregation and the contradictions of the historical chronicle. Most importantly, it ignores the existing practices of exclusion, as blacks are denied opportunities in military, social, and political arenas. In spite of these limitations, the film does declare the first premise of the argument for full citizenship that foreshadows the civil rights movement of a decade later: Soldiering has consistently been an invitation to full citizenship.[66] This premise leads to the conclusion, "If they could fight as equals, then blacks could expect to be rewarded as equals. Military service thus became central to the whole campaign for civil rights," a powerful force for change prompted by the circumstances of the war, which "started the breakup of segregation and led in the immediate postwar period to the beginning of total integration in the American forces."[67]

The identity of African Americans, which had been evolving since the First World War, was newly visualized in *The Negro Soldier*. The tremendous growth of film reached its zenith during World War II, when millions of Americans were repeatedly exposed to the cinematic messages of Hollywood and the federal government. Then, as today, film was a primary conduit for the construction of cultural identities.[68] In the process of forging identity, films and other media texts organize signs and symbols around potent values. They offer discourses that validate identity through constructions of socially valued concepts.[69] In essence, the hero is the idealization of the common man. In *The Negro Soldier*, for example, Joe Louis and Max Schmeling appear, not just as boxers who mimic the struggle between their respective nations, but as icons upholding the values of their respective cultures. Joe Louis represents resolute democracy, while Max Schmeling epitomizes a government that makes men into machines.

In his classic study of the hero, Joseph Campbell identifies the potency of such heroic images whose purpose was "to conduct people across those difficult thresholds of transformation that demand a change in the patterns not only of conscious but also of unconscious life."[70] The hero, standing in for the nation, undergoes a transformation that requires self-sacrifice, setting up a model for others to follow. The physical transformations of the hero's journey represent a moral regeneration. Following the heroic formula, Louis emerged from defeat to triumph over Schmeling. The pattern of heroism is paralleled in *The Negro Soldier* as the African American recruit leaves home to undergo the challenge of military training. The power of the hero myth, echoed in the boxing match and in boot camp, engages the viewer in the transformation that informs the compelling appeal of heroism.

Much like the ambiguous final scenes of films like *Thelma and Louise* (1991), *The 400 Blows* (1959) *Gallipoli* (1981), and *Butch Cassidy and the Sundance Kid* (1969), the conclusion of *The Negro Soldier* is left to the viewer's imagination. In this way, the hero's actions become "the filmic equivalent of commemorative statues of the soldier erected in small towns.... Its ideology is the same."[71] Similarly, the unresolved ending of *The Negro Soldier* places the viewer in the critical position of determining the outcome of the story, thus generating a personal connection to the film. Some viewers were more likely to see the African American soldier as rising beyond his customary incompetence, while others saw new opportunities connected with his transformation. The ending of the film has theological implications that spin out from the narrative and, although individual audience members' reactions undoubtedly varied, it is likely that this orientation affected their interpretations.

In addition, because the film's conclusion is open-ended, allowing the viewer to reach closure that is comfortable, the world of the viewer is sustained in the ambiguous final scenes of *The Negro Soldier*. This personal control over the meaning of the film narrative explains how racial threats were reduced for white viewers. Manthia Diawara argues, "The dominant cinema situates black characters primarily for the pleasure of white spectators (male or female). To illustrate this point, one may know how black male characters in contemporary Hollywood films are made less threatening to whites either by white domestication of black customs and culture— a process of deracination and isolation—or by stories in which blacks are depicted playing by the rules of white society and losing."[72] Even though Diawara is evaluating contemporary films like *Trading Places* (1983), *Forty-Eight Hours* (1982), and *Beverly Hills Cops I* and *II* (1984, 1987), if we alter the conclusion of the stories, allowing for an ambiguous ending, this idea can be adapted to films of the World War II era. In this way, the films place white spectators in their customary privileged positions by depicting African Americans playing by the white military's rules. The threat to the social order is diminished because black soldiers follow rules and fight to protect a segregated society.

In *The Negro Soldier* the diverse backgrounds of soldiers were narrowed to a common image of the new recruit whose experiences condensed military service into events experienced by all recruits, regardless of race. There is an additional common denominator–a: All Americans were civilians in uniform. Stephen Ambrose has popularized the ideal of the citizen soldier, ordinary men molded into genuine heroes.[73] The symbolic citizen soldier promoted what many Americans wanted to believe about their country: that it stood for freedom for all. The title of the film captures its equivocation as a narrative device. The "negro soldier" could refer to the primary character in the film, a single anonymous black soldier, or it could indicate black soldiers as a group. In any case, the solitary soldier represents his race.

The ambiguous identity of the black soldier is also reflected in the visual narrative of the film, as the African American soldier is presented only in relation to a military institution that is overwhelmingly white. Rather than emphasizing justice, integration, and equal opportunities, *The Negro Soldier* shows the African American recruit eager to fight under current conditions. The visual images of the film reflect a segregated army in subtle ways that seem natural. For example, although Carlton Moss provides the on-screen narration, an off-screen voice of white authority introduces the film, provides transitions, and states conclusions. The two congregations, white and black, remain separated during the film, and sequences that show both white and black soldiers foreground one race while backgrounding the other. The races are never mixed, so black identity is defined within dominant white culture in an extension of W. E. B. Du Bois's double consciousness, "a 'twoness' of American racial code."[74] The tension between the ideals of democracy and the reality of segregation was only temporarily eased by the conversion of the African American soldier.

The function of *The Negro Soldier* as a vehicle for the dominant ideology becomes apparent in the structuring absences of the film narrative—that is, the gaps in historical reconstructions. The film overlooks tough issues. It avoids the problems of military segregation and the contradictions within its historical chronicle. Most importantly, it neglects the legacy of excluding blacks from opportunities in military, social, and political fields. It sidesteps then current racial conflict, ignoring riots on military bases and in the surrounding civilian communities. Contentious topics like equal military pay, the potential for promotion in rank, integration of military base facilities, and courts martial for the Port Chicago protestors are also absent. Even the recreated American military history, although inclusive of individual African American heroes, fails to mention the lack of memorials to them or the complete absence of African Americans in general military histories.

On potentially contentious issues, *The Negro Soldier* avoids controversy through visual or verbal omissions. These structuring absences shift the viewer's attention to other subjects. For example, the Civil War is almost entirely ignored, despite its centrality to the question of racial history. In its place, there is increased attention to black contributions in other wars, which surely created pride among viewers. The threat of racial violence is similarly reduced by excluding scenes with armed black soldiers, and by having training sequences eschew direct combat techniques. Visual racial stereotypes are also absent from *The Negro Soldier*. In their place, a more dignified African American soldier encounters the same issues any white soldier might face. On the other hand, he cannot solve his own problems with women or finances, in childlike fashion seeking the advice of white officers and chaplains. It appears that African Americans must be led, bolstering current military practices. The visual image of white officers guiding black soldiers forestalls the controversy of military integration. Demonstrating that African Americans are trainable becomes a central theme of *The Negro Soldier* in a manner that promises opportunities to black viewers, but soothes supporters of segregation with messages of subordination. The faithful, docile black man is equated with the good American, ensuring that social disruptions of the war will be minimized.

The social reality in *The Negro Soldier* is a segregated military fighting abroad in the name of democracy for limited rights for many American citizens. This reality is presented as inevitable and impervious to change. Vincent F. Rocchio offers insight into this situation with his description of the contemporary film *Driving Miss Daisy* (1989), where the "codes of realism and appropriation of history" serve to render segregation "as a natural occurrence—the unintended result of a specific history, rather than a particular and contingent social formation maintained through a variety of social forces and interactions."[75] Although the social reality of the segregated nation is an imposed, inevitable reality that dominates institutions, individuals "cannot change, but can ultimately rise above [segregation] in their own interpersonal relationships."[76] The solution lies, not at the institutional level, but in interpersonal relationships. As *The Negro Soldier* reveals, it is the personal commitment of the individual black soldier, with the support of members of his community, that results in African American pride. The individual achieves his potential within the institutional structure, activating the American myth of individualism and bypassing questions of social justice. The bootstraps philosophy of the American dream is used to naturalize white privilege and black subordination. This appeal invites, as bell hooks would contend, a call for replacing the ethic of individualism with a vision of communalism.[77]

The Aftermath

In 1943, in *The Negro Soldier*, the War Department constructed the public memory of past heroism and recognition of African American competence as soldiers. The result was inclusion of African Americans in a sanctioned national history that quieted immediate wartime racial tensions, but set the stage for future confrontation. As a popular magazine summarized the issue "America, having proved finally that all men are equal in her military graves, is faced with the necessity of matching the generosity of black soldiers by proving that all men are equal on her ambiguous streets."[78] The claim for the rights of equal citizenship had been substantiated in a government film that created a dignified image of African Americans.

In the process of adapting the conversion narrative to achieve its immediate goals, the War Department included African Americans in national symbolism. It also sowed seeds for civil rights activism in the long term by suggesting that equality for African Americans was earned through military sacrifice. The American experience has always been filled with contradictions between ideals of democracy and its practices, which frequently fall short of achieving the dream. As *The Negro Soldier* put in place a new narrative that challenged past stereotypes of incompetence, it began to close the gap between the promise of democracy and its fulfillment. While the evolution of dignified mainstream media images required many more years, this film marks a dramatic departure from prior images of degradation and situates African Americans as worthy citizens in the American story.

CHAPTER FIVE

Conflicting Narratives and Images

Freedom is never given; it is won.
—A. PHILIP RANDOLPH, OCTOBER 15, 1937[1]

The American dilemma, identified by Gunnar Myrdal in 1944, was the fundamental contradiction between professed ideals of equality and the reality of racial discrimination. But a combination of factors, including severe shortages of manpower and mounting racial violence, accompanied by more positive images of African Americans began to change the way Americans conceptualized equality.[2] Eventually, the fabric of segregation unraveled, erupting in the civil rights movement of the 1960s and the final dismantling of segregation. Heralding the looming racial conflict, *The Negro Soldier* disrupted the long-standing tradition of servile media images of African Americans by offering portrayals of competent black men in uniform. This revolutionary way of visualizing race would shape the thinking of future generations.

The Negro Soldier reshaped American discourse about race in popular media, initially to win victory, but eventually to change society. Long-term implications for African Americans drew upon the historical claims to citizenship that had percolated through society since the first colonial militias included black volunteers. The hopes of African Americans were encouraged by promises of citizenship in exchange for African American military service and industrial labor. But these promises were rarely followed by serious action. On August 28, 1963, Martin Luther King Jr. reminded Americans in his famous "I Have a Dream" speech that the check had come due, a call that resonated across decades of broken promises.

The Negro Soldier offered the first glimmer of change in racial relationships because it provided novel images of dignified African Americans in uniform. Several other films produced between 1942 and 1944, such as *The Negro Sailor, Teamwork, Henry Browne, Farmer*, and *Negro Colleges in Wartime*, added other positive images. But their distribution was limited.

Unfortunately, these positive portrayals were far outnumbered by persistent denigrating film stereotypes or the complete absence of African Americans on the screen. Change did not come quickly, but still, this was the beginning.

The Negro Sailor

Building on the success of *The Negro Soldier*, the navy released *The Negro Sailor* (1945) within months of the former's release. This subsequent film was an attempt to polish the notoriously racist reputation of the navy—made worse by the events such as the Port Chicago mutiny—among African Americans. *The Negro Sailor*, set in a black newspaper office to take advantage of respect for the black press and its community connections, was similar in plot and character development to *The Negro Soldier*. Like *The Negro Soldier*, it created a positive picture of African Americans in uniform and praised their role in military service. Although *The Negro Sailor* was not distributed as widely as its predecessor, it provided a uniquely respectful view of black Americans in a landscape of mostly degrading images. Several other films with positive themes were also produced, although, like *The Negro Sailor*, their distribution was limited. These films included *Americans All* (1943), *Close Harmony* (1943), *Don't Be a Sucker* (1943), *Henry Browne, Farmer* (1943), *Teamwork* (1942), *Negro Colleges in Wartime* (1943), *Liberty Ship* (unreleased), *The Launching of the Booker T. Washington* (unreleased), *Shoeshine Boy* (1943), and *The House I Live In* (1945). Individually, these films failed to reach the massive audiences *The Negro Soldier* enjoyed, but collectively, they represent the willingness of federal and private institutions to acknowledge African Americans in order to secure victory. Although each film was more limited in scope and purpose than *The Negro Soldier*, as a group, they indicate a crack had formed in the facade of segregation, because they recognize African American participation in key institutions of American society.

In *The Negro Sailor*, a black newspaper editor encourages patriotism among his employees, particularly a young African American man, Bill Johnson, who considers enlisting in the navy. Using the metaphor of a football game to describe teamwork, the editor argues that everyone should support the naval war. Several sequences detail career options and training that await navy recruits. Later, in the course of his basic training, Bill Johnson discovers a military museum that displays the photos and awards belonging to African Americans who served with distinction in the navy. Among those heroes is navy steward Dorie Miller, a cook who carried his wounded captain to safety during the attack on Pearl Harbor, then manned a gun to shoot down several enemy aircraft. Miller's bravery was widely acclaimed in African American communities. Through the reactions of Bill Johnson's character, the viewer is impressed with the variety of naval vessels, awed by advanced systems of navigation, and gratified by the nobility of American sailors. By the last scene, both the fictional Bill Johnson and the viewer understand that the navy operates just like a football team, with every member contributing essential skills and uniting for victory.

The Negro Sailor ends with an extended peroration that celebrates democracy and the importance of every American sailor by merging the metaphor of the football game with Bill Johnson's support for the navy. The editor's voice-over exhorts the viewer, "Bill and the boys on the DE are throwing up a lot of stuff out there but like the quarterback who has to throw the ball, the Navy. . . . depends on the men of the ordinance battalions.³ Following the logic of this metaphor leads to the conclusion that while African American sailors are allowed into the game, the navy still retains the pivotal role of quarterback.

The navy restricted black sailors' work to handling ordinance, serving as mess stewards, and other drudgery. *The Negro Sailor* does not skirt this fact, but elevates these jobs with a metaphor that taps the American institution of football. The viewer is glorified because he is part of the vast war effort. While the narrator is factual in his description of black sailors assigned to transport ordinance, he labels their units "battalions," glorifying the laborer's job and making it seem like an important part of the fighting. In another rhetorical flourish, the narrator continues,

> These are. . . . the doctors of dynamite who mix the first prescriptions. Yes, the doctors of dynamite is a good name for them and their prescriptions come in all sizes and shapes . . . . The teammates on some cruisers will welcome these eight inch projectiles and speed them on their way . . . . Yes, every sailor plays a vital position. This is the result of teamwork. On the APAs, on the ATAs, on the KAs, on the AOs, and all the other great auxiliary ships. Here serve the Negro sailors. Here serve yeomen and all the other rankings required to make up the great team. . . . So Bill Johnson made all the Navy teams. They were there at the end of the first half when these U boats surrendered in the Atlantic. Yes, they made all

the Navy teams.... Throughout our history since the first battle of the Revolution when our country was born.

The phrase "the doctors of dynamite" gives munitions handlers a more prominent and exciting place in the war. Every "Bill Johnson" is transformed into a valued navy team member in this eloquent conclusion, which pairs a quick-paced visual montage of battle scenes with a soundtrack of swelling patriotic music.

In its employment of the cinematic mode of address, an orientation emphasizing the dramatic qualities of characterization and plot structure for purposes of entertainment, *The Negro Sailor* mimics Hollywood entertainment films. The viewer participates in the excitement of navy enlistment and experiences naval training through events in Bill Johnson's life. The viewer follows Bill Johnson as he leaves his colleagues in the newsroom, undergoes naval training, and boards a ship at sea. His ordinary life in the newsroom is transformed when he volunteers for the navy. Along the way Bill expresses his admiration for former black sailors who earned silver stars and purple hearts. Background battle footage visually confirms the black sailors' critical role in the navy. Through his excitement and wonder over navy opportunities, Bill Johnson becomes a surrogate for target recruits and a witness for the African American community. This cinematic mode of address indirectly co-opts viewers by cloaking its persuasive message in a dramatic narrative whose plot intensifies at each turn.

Because it is drama, not documentary, the cinematic mode of address masks inaccuracies in reporting and exaggeration of half-truths. Fantasy is encouraged at the expense of critical questioning as the viewer experiences patriotic excitement along with Bill Johnson. The navy is transformed through the perspective of Bill Johnson into a source of exciting opportunity and comradeship. None of the government films, including *The Negro Sailor*, recognized the vast inequities that permeated American military institutions. Instead, *The Negro Soldier* blames Hitler for racism, and it implies that African Americans have not been team players in the past. Both films celebrate the moment of decision that proves African American loyalty to the nation. The problems of race are located in personal actions and attitudes rather than institutional systems. Even Hitler as an individual is blamed for the problems of race, while the Aryan ideology and sociohistorical context of racism are ignored.

What some scholars decry as the problem of historical accuracy in documentary films like *The Negro Sailor* is exactly what accounts for its effectiveness. The conscious choices of topics, camera angles, sounds, and other elements of the film medium both disguise a point of view and simultaneously engage the viewer in images scrolling across the screen.[4] Although historians denounce the inaccurate chronicle of the past that occurs when events are transposed in the drama of *The Negro Soldier* and *The Negro Sailor*, such distortion is inherent in documentary advocacy.

The authoritarian tone of the conventional documentary film is replaced by the cinematic mode of address when *The Negro Sailor* takes on a narrative form. It is more difficult to discern the film's didactic purpose when Bill Johnson communicates the message of the documentary through events and dialogue that propel the story to an exciting conclusion. In addition, the viewer is placed within the drama by virtue of identification with characters. Narrative structure may also provide coherence, inviting an apparently natural flow of images and sounds and reassuring the viewer rather than calling attention to more intrusive patterns of overt persuasion.

The documentary film that builds a story line with rudimentary characterization, plotting, and setting around a persuasive message, combines the narrative features of Hollywood movies with the persuasive purposes of the navy. Addition of narrative allows viewers to identify more personally with the message through intermediary characters and events. The ultimate effect is to reduce the distance between the viewer and the subject, encouraging an intimacy of shared experiences, and disabling critical thinking so that the message of the filmmaker is more readily received. For skeptical viewers, the narrative style makes the message more palatable because it is conveyed through likable characters and feasible plots.

Even though it highlights Bill Johnson as an individual, *The Negro Sailor* urges viewers to move from personal ambitions to collective unity. The result is preservation of the social system of segregation while praising the contributions of African Americans that support that system. This inconsistency is not raised consciously because the viewer's experience is vicarious: "The viewer associates, often subconsciously, his prior experiences and attitudes to arrive at new interpretations and conclusions."[5] *The Negro Sailor*, like *The Negro Soldier*, is visually ambiguous, allowing both white and black viewers to see opportunity and reassurance in the military. Racial tensions evaporate within the framework of the larger struggle against a common foe. Further assurance that the social order will not be overturned sometimes appears, such as when the narrator of *The Negro Sailor* cautions, "Between battles their work is rather dull but somebody has to be a waiter or a cook or a storekeeper. Everybody can't be captain on this ship." The fictional Bill Johnson replies, "I'm glad you told me all that, sir. It makes me proud just be to anywhere on the team." The power dynamic of Jim Crow segregation is reproduced within the narrative. Bill's editor takes him to a football game to reinforce the object lesson of teamwork producing victory.

The Negro Soldier and *The Negro Sailor* also promote patriotism by positing a relationship between the viewer and national duty. African Americans are represented as vital partners in the Allied war effort. They are responsible for defending their nation, represented by the members of the church and the community who appear in the films. In this way, fictional characters are encodings of ideology, or "embodiments of ideological values" that represent social codes.[6] Bill Johnson, a hard-working American newspaper reporter whose enthusiasm for reporting the news carries over into his eagerness to defend his nation, unconditionally supports his country. The paradox of disenfranchised Americans fighting for the liberty of others did not arise for Bill. Instead, he offers his nation unquestioning loyalty.

The narrative forms of *The Negro Soldier* and *The Negro Sailor* reinforce the principle of coherence. The story frame dominates *The Negro Soldier* as the individual experiences of members of the congregation are revealed. The viewer, along with members of the film congregation, receives the message of patriotism and duty from the minister, who recounts the events of history, intertwining his audience's lives in the nation's story. Likewise, *The Negro Sailor* imitates Hollywood narratives with the story of Bill Johnson. Viewers eavesdrop on conversations, follow Bill through basic training, and send him off in the country's defense. By the conclusion of the film, much as with any matinee feature, the viewer is invested in the outcome. What happens to the fictional Bill Johnson becomes important to the viewer because Bill Johnson has assumed the role of a peer. This approach is more effective than the didactic voice of documentary authority, especially for alienated or suspicious members of the audience.

For these reasons, narrative form dominated official government documentaries of the World War II era.[7] Enlistment of hundreds of talented men and women formerly employed in Hollywood making feature films for civilian distribution coincided with the rise of narrative documentary films like *The Negro Soldier* and *The Negro Sailor*. There is a parallel development in British documentary films, as seen in *Target for Tonight* (1941), *The True Story of Lili Marleen* (1944), and *A Diary for Timothy* (1945). The success of this persuasive strategy accounts for its popularity when governments attempted to influence public opinion.

Other Film Depictions

Harnessing the momentum of *The Negro Soldier*, the NAACP followed up with films about tolerance and brotherhood such as *Americans All* (1943), produced by *The March of Time*. The Department of Agriculture also produced its own film, *Henry Browne, Farmer*, urging African American farmers to increase cultivation of oil-producing crops like peanuts. Late in the war, *Teamwork* (1942) and *Don't Be a Sucker* (1942) were commissioned by the army. It is difficult to judge their impact because distribution records are missing or incomplete.

Three short films produced by Hollywood studios for African American viewers echo government's emphasis on loyalty. MGM produced *Liberty Ship* (1943), the tale of a black stevedore, an agent for Germany who meets a fellow black GI and is convinced (along with viewers) that the United States promises the best future for African Americans. Warner Brothers undertook *The Launching of the Booker T. Washington* (1943), a story about black loyalty and the activities of German agents. Neither film project was completed or distributed to theaters. Only MGM's *Shoeshine Boy* (1943) was completed and released in time to be viewed by wartime audiences. The film tells the story of an African American shoeshine boy who volunteers as an army bugler. It is highly patriotic but careful to maintain social roles demanded by segregation.

Close Harmony was produced by General Motors with the cooperation of the War Department. The film allows viewers to eavesdrop on a barbershop discussion about industrial efficiency in supplying the war effort. As might be expected, the pro-government film supports industry and attempts to dispel rumors and dissatisfaction about material output by incorporating these issues into the barbershop conversation. Custodian Sam, the only African American in the film, echoes the sentiments of white customers who support the war, vowing to do his part for victory. Sam's speaking role is substantial, but it remains clearly within the boundaries of racial expectations. Sam is known only by his first name, a familiarity that indicates his inferior status. He is employed in a menial job and only responds to white customers when directly addressed. He does not initiate conversations. Sam is the source of comic homespun counterpoint that reveals his basic ignorance of complex monetary problems in a discussion of national economics. His simplistic questions require elementary responses. During a break from sweeping floors, Sam telephones his girlfriend to discuss their plans for the evening, suggesting that he is mostly concerned with immediate gratification. The couple's conversation also hints at sexual promiscuity, evoking another stereotype. Sam's role is nonthreatening, respectful of his place in the social microcosm of the barbershop and supportive of the war. In deference to Sam, white customers elucidate basic economic principles of supply and demand and describe the government's role in the war economy.

Henry Browne, Farmer was produced and released by the Department of Agriculture. The story reflects the title: Henry Browne is a black farmer who works forty acres somewhere in the South and has a son in the all-black 99th Pursuit Squadron. As the narrator reveals during the film, Browne appreciates the importance of his peanut crop to the war effort and is eager to do his best to grow what the government needs in poor, rocky soil, without modern mechanized farm equipment. In one scene the Browne family visits their son at a local air base, parking their mule drawn farm wagon proudly among automobiles. The visibly lower economic status of the Browne family does not dampen their enthusiasm for the war. The film employs an all-black cast, an unusual feature, probably indicating that *Henry Browne, Farmer* was intended only for African American audiences.

Sponsors of these films—General Motors, the Department of Agriculture, and the War Department—achieved high quality aesthetic and technical effects with state of the art cameras, film stock, lighting, and sound equipment, in order to captivate viewers. High production values characterize each film, with sophisticated visual and sound effects research proved could affect attitudes and instill democratic values.[8] These features were especially potent for African American viewers, whose segregated theaters usually screened poor quality productions lacking technical refinement.

Despite their glorification of African Americans in the war effort and the appeal of their superior production quality, these films portray African Americans in their traditional relationship with the white majority. Rather than emphasizing justice, integration, and equal opportunity, the films show African Americans eager to fight under conditions of injustice. Although Sam the custodian interacts with white characters in *Close Harmony*, it is clear that the relationship is not equal. In spite of the predominantly black cast in *Henry Browne, Farmer*, the viewer is addressed by a white narrator who praises Henry Browne for producing good crops without the modern farm machinery available to other (probably white) farmers. Questions of inequity are not raised.

Both films privilege conventionally subordinate images of African Americans, the loyal buffoon in *Close Harmony* and the faithful servant in *Henry*

Browne, Farmer. Each film creates a cinematic relationship that makes African American servitude seem natural and perpetuates traditional media stereotypes that normalize the childlike behavior of these characters. As a result, paternalism in the films' narration seems justified. Inequitable social and military practices are left unexamined, and both films ignore the pervasive discrimination and racism in military and civilian institutions. Instead, the films avoid controversial issues by projecting the picture of a harmonious nation in which everyone unquestioningly does his part for the war effort. Thus, the appearance of black characters in respectable roles does not alter their servile relationship within the dominant culture. The films reflect a fundamentally unchanged system of social inequality.

Viewers do not see black characters in military uniform or combat in either *Close Harmony* or *Henry Browne, Farmer*. References to military duty are either comic, such as when Sam the custodian gives a goofy salute to a white customer or indirect, as when Henry Browne's son in the all-black 99th Pursuit Squadron is referenced but never seen. This oversight may ease the anxiety of some viewers about the courage of black soldiers under fire, or about the potential for racial mixing within the ranks. In both films, African Americans cooperate in expediting victory under the guidance of whites. Both films also place African Americans within their families and communities, assuming that freeing captive nations from Axis domination is a goal for all Americans. These depictions are consistent with other popular Hollywood portrayals of African Americans, where encountering a black soldier in a positive role, uniformed and eager to fight, was "a rare sight."[9] Similarly, *Teamwork* and *Negro Colleges in Wartime* use white narrative voice-overs to instruct viewers about their roles in a nation at war.

Neither film was well received by African American viewers. Because it was simultaneously dull and excessively patriotic, *Teamwork* failed to engage viewers. Its tedious narrator drones in a hypnotic cadence, extolling the virtue of Americans united for victory. *Negro Colleges in Wartime* tends to heap praise upon black educational institutions in a manner perceived as condescending, almost as though the narrator is astonished at black achievements. Viewers dismissed both efforts as "insipid" and "patronizing."[10]

Another rather unusual film addressing the subject of African Americans in uniform deserves brief mention. The film, a sixty-minute introduction to British culture called *A Welcome to Britain*, was commissioned by the British Ministry of Information and directed by Anthony Asquith, son of former prime minister Herbert Asquith.[11] It was released in Britain in

December 1943 and shown to newly-arrived American military personnel in order to ease the transition to British behaviors and attitudes. Production of the film was intended to alleviate tensions prompted by the influx of American servicemen. One set of problems involved racial issues that resulted when British Africans and West Indians, sometimes mistaken for African Americans, were evicted from restaurants, heckled for being in the company of their white wives, and subjected to other forms of harassment by American GIs. American military officials supported production of the film because they were afraid African Americans would fraternize with white British women and otherwise become accustomed to treatment as equals by British citizens who did not practice Jim Crow segregation. Billeting of American troops close to English villages and towns made social interaction of all American soldiers, including black troops, inevitable. The resulting complications ranged from marriage requests between black soldiers and white British women to allegations of rape.[12]

A sequence on race was included in *A Welcome to Britain*. It features a black soldier, a white soldier played by Burgess Meredith, and a British woman, all of who engage in conversation during a train ride. At the end of the conversation, the woman invites the two servicemen to tea at her Birmingham home. At this point, Meredith turns to the camera and addresses the film audience, noting that this sort of conversation is common in Britain, but also warning, "There are coloured soldiers as well as white here and there are less social restrictions in this country . . . that might not happen at home but the . . . point is, we're not at home, and the point is too, if we bring a lot of prejudices here what are we gonna do about 'em?"[13] Meredith's direct question is followed by a comment from General J. C. Lee, a well-respected American officer who urges, "When the Army needs Americans to fight for the country it takes Negroes along with whites. Everyone's treated the same when it comes to dying." Most British viewers responded positively to General Lee's statement, interpreting it as encouragement for "US soldiers to take a fresh look at their racist attitudes."[14] The British Ministry of Information had urged Britons in a public campaign just a few months earlier to respect American segregation practices, or at least tolerate different cultural attitudes. The responses of American servicemen were not recorded, but it is likely that they varied depending on race, origin, and previous levels of prejudice. The ambiguity of Meredith's question and Lee's answer make the film sequence palatable for most viewers. The film made no demonstrable impact, but it does clearly indicate recognition of the differences in racial attitudes between the allies.

At the end of the war, surplus government films were donated to trade unions, schools, churches, and political organizations that requested them from federal agencies. Groups such as the NAACP and the Educational Film Library Association included some government films on their distribution lists. Following the war RKO studios produced a one-reel award winning short, *The House I Live In*, which addressed the issue of bigotry.[15] The film featured the talents of Albert Maltz, Frank Ross, and popular singer Frank Sinatra, another victim of ethnic intolerance and sometimes called a "dirty guinea" because of his Italian heritage. Although no African Americans appeared in this plea for tolerance, it appealed to democracy as the foundation of American life. The lyrics of Sinatra's song, "The House I Live In," included a variety of marginalized groups–"nigger or kike or mick or polack or dago."[16] The film skirted the issue of racial prejudice by addressing religious bigotry through the plot device of a juvenile gang that attacked a boy who practiced a different faith. Stuart Hiesler, director of *The Negro Soldier*, went on to make *Storm Warning* (1950), a harsh indictment of the Ku Klux Klan.

Although these films were available upon request for screening in classrooms and by civic groups, their distribution was not widespread, and their influence is difficult to discover.

Inconsistent Messages: *The Navy Steward*

The first glimpse of dignified and competent African Americans in uniform coexisted with the overwhelming presence of images of plantation servitude, which flourished throughout the war and afterward, both in government documentaries and in Hollywood entertainment films. Denigrating and dignified images overlapped through the end of the twentieth century, although more positive images of African Americans eventually replaced the plantation caricatures. While African American soldiers and sailors graced the screen in government-sponsored films, military institutions preserved the social hierarchy of race through strict segregation, sustaining the values of a racially divided nation. Perhaps the most blatant instance of this paradox can be seen in *The Navy Steward*, which upholds the principle of African American inferiority. Ironically, at the same time the navy was bolstering its reputation with *The Negro Sailor*, during orientation black recruits saw a contradictory message in *The Navy Steward*.

The Navy Steward is an obvious departure in other ways. It is patently a training film. There is no pretense of characterization or plot. A navy steward is shown performing typical tasks that include cleaning officers' quarters, serving coffee, and laundering uniforms, while a narrator describes each task. The African American stewards are not personalized by name, they appear onscreen only to demonstrate tasks the viewer is encouraged to imitate. There is no plot or chronology of events, instead the viewer is expected to learn the tasks that are presented topically. The narrator speaks to the viewer in a role of undisguised authority. By contrast, the viewer is clearly assumed to be a passive, subordinate African American.

The Navy Steward directly contrasts with *The Negro Sailor* because the former uses the rhetorical mode of address, which provides instruction and direction. The authoritative off-screen voice provides guidelines for the completion of duties, gives advice about professional conduct, and draws boundaries for performance. The steward is passive and robotic, never speaking or looking at the camera. He completes jobs as they are described to the viewer. It is clear that the steward is inferior to the narrator, who is the source of authority. The viewer is not co-opted via dramatic devices, but is expected to complete tasks within the parameters described by the narrator. The role of the viewer is dictated by the mode of address, which is didactic rather than entertaining. His role is passive, anonymous, subordinate, and interpersonally disengaged, as he is transformed from civilian to serviceman. The relationship between the steward performing on screen and the viewer is impersonal. The vast majority of government films used this rhetorical mode of address to train servicemen on topics ranging from aircraft identification to preventing trench foot. Their purpose was to impart information efficiently rather than to persuade viewers to adopt particular attitudes.

Contrasting constructions of race exist in the modes of address employed in these two films. In *The Negro Sailor*, the African American sailor appears in the context of battle, touring the naval museum, which memorializes the heroism of black sailors. *The Negro Sailor* inspires and encourages the viewer with an implicit suggestion that the navy offers opportunity and equality. In reality, no more than 3 percent of America's black population served aboard naval vessels, where they worked exclusively as stewards, cooks, or mess men. Segregation in the navy was more stringent than in any other branch of the military service—except the marines, which excluded blacks. The navy restricted training of black enlistees to menial labor or servant chores. Employing a cinematic mode of address that engaged fantasy, exploited para-social relationships between the narrator and viewer, and posited social equality, *The Negro Sailor* set up unrealistic expectations.

Unlike *The Negro Sailor*, *The Navy Steward* offers a realistic picture of naval life for African Americans, who would be assigned to steward duties. The steward serves coffee and sandwiches during general quarters, rather then firing guns from battle stations. *The Navy Steward* exhorts the steward to do his best to perform the duties required of his station, recognizing that they are often repetitious. The film counsels the steward that every job is important, and that he should adjust his expectations to his rank. He is warned not to steal or to shirk his duties, not to disrupt those he serves, and to perform his job efficiently without backsliding into undesirable habits.[17] At the same time, the film mentions limited opportunities for advancement even within the restricted realm of stewardship. *The Navy Steward* sets up military authority that repeats Jim Crow segregation by stressing hierarchy and inequity. Unlike Bill Johnson, who functions as the trope by which the viewer assumes equality in *The Negro Sailor*, the narrator in *The Navy Steward* negates individuality with training film directives. The steward is anonymous, establishing a distant, impersonal relationship with the viewer.

Change Comes to Hollywood

The images of African Americans depicted in *The Negro Soldier* and *The Negro Sailor* contrast sharply with other popular images that were prevalent during the war.[18] African American viewers saw themselves for the first time cast in military roles. For thousands of African Americans, their contributions to their nation were crystallized in images of black men going to war, even as mainstream films offered only occasional, usually unflattering glimpses of African American in uniform.

For the most part, however, Hollywood films developed a paradigm of exclusion with relation to black themes, black actors, and black images. African Americans were invisible to most white American audiences. While black viewers had access to race films, most of these were produced by white investors and reflected the prejudices and ideologies of the dominant society. As a result, African Americans were surrounded by images of the black experience that reinforced racial definitions provided by white Americans. The power to destroy these negative images "could have only come from the ability to provide the definitions of one's past, present and future. Since blacks have always, until recently, been defined by the majority group, that group's characterization was the one that was predominant."[19] In this context, *The Negro Soldier* and *The Negro Sailor* offered revolutionary images of African Americans.

The first positive images of African Americans in uniform legitimated their claims to equal civil rights. In *The Negro Soldier* and *The Negro Sailor*, for example, the common man became the uncommon soldier, and with that transformation, conditions for citizenship were fulfilled as everyday African Americans earned rights guaranteed by American democracy. In a study of all Hollywood movies released during the war years, Dorothy B. Jones observed "certain noticeable changes in the content of films generally," including "a more constructive portrayal of minority groups."[20] She predicted, "The changes taking place in Hollywood will be accelerated by the return of film makers who have been in the Armed Services making day-to-day use of film as a dynamic weapon of war."[21] The acceleration was slow but discernible in the decades following the war.

Hollywood's wartime treatment of race relations, highly attuned to box office appeal, generally followed conservative social norms. Like other capitalist ventures, filmmaking is "so sensitive to economic risks that it all but automatically shrinks from touching on anything controversial."[22] Yet the enormous social and economic transformations of the Great Depression and World War II finally destroyed the monopoly of conservative racial attitudes, and Hollywood directors made tentative forays into the subject of racial relationships. A number of popular films showed individual blacks fighting alongside white soldiers before the end of WW II, in spite of the military policy of strict segregation. According to Thomas Cripps, "The next twenty-five years or so allowed blacks the opportunity to reshape and define a new black image still in progress."[23] Hollywood's view of the war was more relaxed and displayed artistic license with respect to facts. Some films employed mixed casts, although the limited number of African American roles was always secondary and servile. For example, films like *The Fighting 69th* (1940), *Yankee Doodle Dandy* (1942), *This Is the Army* (1943), *Sahara* (1943), *The Fighting Seebees* (1944), *They Were Expendable* (1945), *A Walk in the Sun* (1945), and *Back to Bataan* (1945) showed white military units that included at least one black enlisted man who fought alongside his white comrades. These tentative attempts showed racial cooperation but stopped short of integration.

Hollywood images of racial diversity operated at the platoon level and never challenged systemic institutional racism. Need for commercial success contributed to the ambiguity of most films. In order to avoid offending white viewers, films did not challenge the status quo, but some films projected palatable images of African Americans as soldiers bonding in the heat of battle, thus offering a liberal metaphor for social change. Films like *Crime School* (1938), *Girls on Probation* (1938), *Hell's Kitchen* (1939), *Lifeboat* (1944), *Till the End of Time* (1946), *He Walked by Night* (1948), *Intruder in the Dust* (1949), and *The Phoenix City Story* (1955) include several minor African American characters and indirectly address racism. But they glide over broad social issues with happy endings—or they sacrifice the black character, thus eliminating the problem. Throughout Hollywood films, unreflective repetition of the message that America is the land of opportunity pushes the problem of racism into the background. Films like *Pinky* (1949), *Lost Boundaries* (1949), *No Way Out* (1950), and *Intruder in the Dust* (1949) allude to the integrated platoon by including a solitary black character, typified by Sidney Poitier, creating compromise on the issue of racial equality.

But even Hollywood couldn't create a fantasy world where black officers commanded white troops or black soldiers fraternized with white civilians. That story would not be told until the end of the twentieth century. Following World War II, a reconstituted black male image emerged more strongly in Hollywood film.[24] Sidney Poitier appeared a decade later, a conservative compromise acceptable to both black and white audiences. Whether or not white audiences were ready, African Americans demanded a greater presence in public life, and their growing economic clout added force to these demands. The war had altered the racial equation dramatically. Charles E. Silberman captures the essence of the shift: "Men who had been decorated for 'outstanding courage and resourcefulness' at Bastogne, who had built the Lido Road in Southeast Asia or manned the 'Red Ball Express' in France or landed in the first invasion wave at Okinawa were not likely to be quite as afraid of white authority as their fathers. What Negroes discovered during the war . . . was their power to intimidate—not by violence, but by their very presence."[25] This presence slowly began to include positive Hollywood images. Eventually, the shift culminated in the overthrow of segregation and recognition of civil rights.

Although it is beyond the scope of this analysis, it is interesting to note that radio showed similar shifts in the representing African Americans, moving from universal stereotypical illiterates to fewer racist representations. The tremendous pressures of war influenced radio broadcasts. As a study of the Alabama Negro Extension Service discovered, "Messages were transformed as the hegemonic needs of a wartime government changed."²⁶ While radio programs were used by the federal government to influence public attitudes, accounting for some of this shift, radio did not play the same direct role film had in indoctrinating new troops.²⁷

CHAPTER SIX

Military Conditions during World War II

The world's greatest democracy fought the world's greatest racist with a segregated army.
—STEPHEN AMBROSE[1]

An overview of United States military history quickly reveals the discrepancy between the principle of harmony touted in *The Negro Soldier* and the reality of military exclusion. With few exceptions, white Americans in uniform have separated themselves from black Americans since the founding of the nation, mimicking the racial divide of the larger society.[2] The armed forces have followed this racial division, generally discouraging or outlawing black participation. Only under the dire circumstances of war, when manpower shortages dictated that blacks be allowed into military service in order to avert defeat, were blacks allowed to serve their country. The conditions in which African American troops served during World War II were multilayered and complex, involving historical traditions of racial segregation, white and black attitudes, eruptions of civilian and military violence, and the realities of wartime. This chapter examines the evolution of military enlistment practices and the structural barriers that blocked African Americans from unconditional participation in military service.

Evolution of Military Enlistment Policy

According to the earliest records, both enslaved and free blacks participated in North American military actions starting with the 1528 ill-fated expedition of Panfilo de Narvaez, whose slave Estebanico traveled though northern Mexico sending back reports of golden cities, and continuing to the current conflicts in Afghanistan and Iraq. The first law sanctioning a militia group was passed in 1607, as colonies organized for self-defense against the Native American threat. This original legislation made no reference to race, but by 1639 Virginia had enacted a bill excluding blacks from acquiring arms or ammunition as part of their militia participation. This ban was possibly adopted in response to the increasing number of slaves who, it was feared, would slaughter their masters if armed. The Militia Act of 1792 required every able-bodied citizen to defend the nation. Because militias were controlled by the colonies and later by the states, the practice of raising, training, and supporting militias continued to be patchwork at best. One condition was commonplace, regardless of otherwise inconsistent policies: There was widespread discrimination. The bottom stratum of society was over-represented in the lowest ranks, while sons of wealthy families populated the highest ranks and officer corps.[3] Without exception, slaves and free black men congregated on the lowest rungs.

The limitations of the militia system were proven during the Whiskey Rebellion of 1794. Local militias in western Pennsylvania, objecting to centralized control of revenue, refused to obey federal laws. President George Washington was forced to negotiate with neighboring counties to obtain the troops necessary to quell the insurrection, clearly demonstrating the drawbacks of the militia system. Other handicaps included poor training, erratic provisioning, and the dismal performance of local militias under combat conditions. However, divisive factions prevented the establishment of a federal militia or a national army as a viable alternative. Passage of the Provisional Army Act in 1798, the New Army Act, and the establishment of the Navy Department, mostly to counter the growing marine threat that followed the French Revolution, were initial steps in centralizing federal control of the military and wresting reliance on independent militias from the states. Later, in the face of increasing British hostility on the North American continent, in 1808 Congress made recruiting, arming, and training of the militia a federal responsibility. During the War of 1812, various Indian Wars, and the Mexican War, the militia system, however inadequate, persisted despite the federal government's centralized control.

Despite repeated failures, the militia system of defense remained intact throughout the nineteenth century. Under their militia systems, both the Union and the Confederacy experienced acute problems supplying soldiers during the Civil War. Recruiting soldiers often caused controversy. For example, the institution of the draft to fill Union ranks sparked riots in Northern cities, spawned widespread graft and favoritism, and created a division along class lines, as rich men paid for others who were less fortunate to fight in their stead. In spite of the institution of the draft, the Union army was a mostly volunteer force. Along with other impacts, the United

States Supreme Court decision in the *Dred Scott* case institutionalized the inferiority of African Americans for purposes of military service, thereby limiting their participation in subsequent conflicts.[4] The Indian Wars and the Spanish-American War also utilized volunteers to fill quotas, but unemployment owing to financial recessions and high immigration meant sufficient manpower was available without instituting a draft. The demand for servicemen during the world wars of the twentieth century exacerbated the issue of raising sufficient numbers of men and indirectly contributed to racial problems in the ranks. World War I and World War II gave rise to often haphazard and inefficient military policies on race, reflecting the attitudes of black and white, citizens and politicians. The 1944 German counterattack in the Ardennes forest (popularly known as the Battle of the Bulge) brought decision-makers to the realization that the United States could not win a two-front war without including African American soldiers in the front lines.

There has always been a black presence in US military ranks. Although numbers were usually small, African Americans served with distinction in every American military conflict. Throughout American history, African Americans have served with distinction in every facet of warfare, including: the 54th Massachusetts Volunteer Infantry in the Civil War; the 9th and 10th United States Colored Cavalry regiments during the Indian and Spanish-American wars; and the 369th Infantry Regiment during World War I. But the number of African Americans in military units was limited. Four all black units had been in existence since their formation during the Civil War: the 9th and 10th Cavalry, the 24th and 25th Infantry. Of the 380,000 African American men mobilized for military service in World War I, two hundred thousand were deployed to France. Most repaired roads, unloaded ships, dug trenches, cooked food, built military installations, and buried corpses under the direction of white officers. Still, forty-two thousand served as combat troops, although without the equipment generally given white troops. They were sent clothing cartons specifically labeled "For Colored Only," filled with rejected and previously used uniforms and poor quality boots in random sizes. In some cases underwear, overcoats, uniforms, and boots arrived months after the troops did. A report of the executive committee of the General Wartime Commission of the Churches concluded that deplorable conditions would "make it more difficult to sustain among the colored people as a whole an adequate recognition of our democratic ideals in the war and the largest devotion to our cause."[5]

World War I created the need for the first real draft since the Civil War, as branches of the military service sought to fill manpower quotas. The Dick Act (also known as the Militia Act of 1903) repealed the Militia Act of 1792 and was passed after the Spanish-American War of 1898 demonstrated weaknesses in the command structure of the American military. It had the long-term effect of lifting the conscription obligation from the individual states and placing the federal government in charge of the military. The postwar Defense Act of 1920 returned the United States to an all-volunteer military force during peacetime, and military service ranks were severely reduced during the interim between the wars.

Strict segregation and limited enlistment opportunities for African Americans existed at the beginning of World War I, but the branches of military service were not consistent in their policies regarding African Americans. Starting in 1798, the navy banned anyone of African heritage as "Persons whose Characters are Suspicious" and did not enlist black sailors.[6] Only the all-black mess man's units were open to African American men, and most were stationed ashore. The corps was so segregated that few white marines were aware that African American companies supplied their munitions. In the army, only a few vacancies among the four regular Negro units, maintained at drastically reduced strength, were available to enlistees. No new units had been created since these four were established after the Civil War.

Official policies prohibited discrimination, but social and military practices upheld segregation on grounds that segregation was not discrimination because both races had access to "separate but equal" facilities within institutions in accordance with the 1896 Supreme Court ruling in *Plessey v. Ferguson*. The segregation of black servicemen was operationalized in two ways: First, black servicemen did not train or join units with white servicemen, and second, black servicemen were restricted as much as possible to menial jobs and living quarters that were well away from white soldiers. Segregation was justified as part of American military and civilian traditions. Furthermore, the isolation of black troops would discourage their aspirations toward higher achievement, and it mitigated the influence of more militant black servicemen. Military commanders claimed that the accommodations and jobs for blacks were appropriate to their military status.

When separate facilities were not available or inefficient to maintain, the military simply did not recruit blacks. Discrimination was rampant within the separate military units. And in segregated ranks, African American men were dealt with more harshly than were European Americans. For example, twenty-nine of the thirty-five US soldiers executed during World War I were African American, as were fifty-five of the seventy men executed during World War II. Roughly 10 percent of all troops in both world wars were African American, but they received disproportionately harsher penalties than whites.[7]

More than 380,000 African Americans served in the armed forces during World War I. Many branches of the service—including the artillery, the aviation corps, and the navy—refused to allow blacks to enter their ranks. Draft registration cards were dog-eared to indicate the African ancestry of their holders, and most who entered the service found themselves assigned as laborers in quartermaster or construction battalions. For the most part, the approximately twenty-one thousand who saw combat did so as part of the French army. Overall, African Americans made up less than 3 percent of the combat strength of the army and less than 1 percent of the navy. Many African American servicemen were put to work on farms in the United States to meet agricultural labor shortages. Jim Crow laws prevailed at home, and even when African Americans were serving abroad, the British and French governments imposed sanctions that prevented blacks from socializing with local populations. Segregated quarters, from barbershops to barracks, prevented unwanted intimacies between African Americans and other, white soldiers. White American officers feared that special treatment would spoil African Americans, who would expect such privileges when they returned stateside.[8]

In spite of these barriers, African American soldiers often performed beyond the expectations of their superiors. Several African American infantry regiments serving with the French—the 367th, the 369th, the 370th, the 371st, and the 372nd—were awarded the Croix de Guerre for bravery by the French government. Two African American privates, Henry Johnson and Needham Roberts, were cited for bravery. These achievements were not recognized by the US government; neither were they reported in the white press. On the other hand, the collapse of the all-black 368th Infantry Regiment during the Argonne offensive in France received much negative publicity in mainstream newspapers and provided fodder for many military officers' arguments about the ineffectiveness of black combat troops.[9] As a result, perceptions of incompetence plagued African American soldiers throughout World War I. Aware that re-entry into American society could prove difficult after positive treatment abroad, President Woodrow Wilson charged Major Moton with suppressing hostilities. Judging by the domestic upheaval in 1919, that mission failed. Race riots broke out in twenty-nine American cities; more than one hundred African Americans died in street fighting, and seventy-seven were lynched. The cities of Chicago, Washington, DC, and Elaine, Arkansas, saw the most serious violence.

In the interim between world wars, about 3,700 blacks served in segregated units in an army of 188,000 men. In 1939, two all-black quartermaster or service units were added. And a year later, several more segregated units were added, probably as part of a campaign to expand military preparedness in anticipation of America's entry into the European conflict. These units included more quartermaster detachments, as well as field artillery, anti-aircraft, engineer, and chemical warfare units. All enlistments were strictly voluntary, made through recruitment offices across the nation.

Overall, American military commanders were reluctant to utilize black troops, even though there was support in some quarters for black enlistments. Lewis Hershey, for example, recalled how African Americans fit the American military profile because they "have been notably a loyal and patriotic group. One of their outstanding characteristics is the single-mindedness of their patriotism," having no ties to other cultures or countries.[10] Perhaps Hershey was implying a comparison to potential Japanese recruits. More often, however, the government view was that "blacks were not motivated enough or aggressive enough to fight."[11] This attitude explains why, of the almost one million black Americans selected for military duty, only one black division, the 92nd Infantry Division, saw combat in Europe.

Segregation as an Entrenched Tradition

Completed by the Army War College in 1925, a pivotal study of US participation in World War I reinforced segregationist attitudes toward African American troops. The study defended racial separation of troops as the most efficient way to configure military structure. Authors of the study did not question traditional attitudes about race, but rather underscored established white views. As Alan Osur summarizes, "It was held that the black man was physically unqualified for combat duty; was by nature subservient, mentally inferior, and believed himself to be inferior to the white man; was susceptible to the influence of crowd psychology; could not control himself in the face of danger; and did not have the initiative and resourcefulness of the white man."[12] The immorality of the African American, commonly believed to be expressed in his inability to control his sexual impulses, was also noted. Higher rates of sexually transmitted diseases among African American soldiers served as tacit proof of licentiousness. No allowance was made for the differences between black and white access to medical treatment, a result of poverty and geography, not morality.

In addition to sexual promiscuity, the report found petty thievery and lying were more common among Negroes than among whites.[13] Without question, leadership qualities were lacking among African Americans, whose secretive, superstitious, docile, yet unruly natures required strong white commanders. To support its conclusions, the report offered performance records as evidence. They were considered credible science at the time and for a decade after their release, even though these records have been criticized as misinterpreted by various contemporary scholars.[14]

Another study, completed by the War Department Personnel Division in 1937, supported the 1925 findings. Following its conclusions, the War Department study recommended that African American soldiers be restricted to segregated units, and that they comprise no more than 9 percent of the total mobilized military forces, reflecting the size of their presence in the civilian population. This percentage was significant in determining recruitment ceilings during World War II.

The importance that the War Department ascribed to these studies is indicated by the structural development of military forces in the years between world wars, as well as the construction of military units during much of the war. Secretary of War Henry L. Stimson, used army studies from 1925 and 1937 to justify continued segregation of military troops. Partly supported by this evidence and partly resulting from Jim Crow customs, a pattern of racial segregation that amounted to exclusion of African Americans from all but limited service areas persisted throughout World War II.[15] Newer service branches like the US Army Air Corps adopted an official policy of racial segregation similar to that in force in other military units in 1941. Overall, military policies formed along traditional lines of segregation in order to maintain military units separated by color in a way that mirrored American society. African Americans were assigned to duties that the studies indicated best fit their limited intellectual abilities and other inherent weaknesses. Owing to their promiscuous sexual tendencies, whenever possible they were isolated from local civilian populations. Without exception they were commanded by white officers, who often resented this assignment, viewing it as a demotion in rank.

African Americans were increasingly radicalized by their limited participation in World War I and its disappointing aftermath whereby their military contributions were ignored. In 1937 Charles H. Houston, spokesperson for the NAACP, demanded an executive order eliminating segregation in the armed forces. The Selective Service Act, which President Franklin D. Roosevelt signed into law in 1940 on the eve of war, opposed integration of the black and white races because "for practical reasons it would be impossible to put into operation."[16] In spite of shrill protests in the black press, telegrams to the president from prominent leaders like A. Phillip Randolph of the Brotherhood of Sleeping Car Porters, and public outcries of hypocrisy across the country, all branches of the armed forces would remain segregated until the end of the Korean War, in spite of policies against discrimination and President Harry S. Truman's executive order abolishing racial discrimination in the armed forces.

The 1940 Selective Service Bill, Public Law 783, allowed for recruitment of African Americans in proportion to their percentage of the total civilian population. In 1940, black Americans numbered thirteen million, approximately 10 percent of the total population. By the end of the war, more than 2.5 million African Americans, mostly men, had volunteered for military service; about 650,000 were accepted. Of these, only fifty thousand were officially registered as combat troops, although they mostly served in labor battalions. But the front lines were often tangled in combat, and black service units mingled with regular white infantry under conditions of attack such as pertained in the Battle of the Bulge. Strict segregation was often impossible to enforce under battle conditions.

The Army Plan for Mobilization, developed in anticipation of America's entry into World War II, appeared to be more inclusive than the Selective Service Bill. It gave black soldiers equal access to many units of the army, with a 10 percent goal for enlistments. In reality, the army used less than 5 percent of the black units in the first years of the war; by 1944, when the manpower crisis reached a critical stage, black units were closer to the 10 percent goal. Throughout the war, inter-service as well as intra-service squabbles occurred over which service units were absorbing their fair share of African Americans. Eventually, the War Department was forced to expand opportunities for blacks by presidential directive. Subsequently, many branches of the military services had to accept and utilize blacks at the rate of 10.6 percent of their total forces. Unfortunately, the problems that resulted were not anticipated, nor often dealt with effectively. The War Department was obliged to reevaluate its policies to accommodate demands from civilians and protests from military units themselves. This process of evolution—instituting procedures and reacting to their failure—often lead to confusing practices. The climate of ambiguity left military field commanders to their own devises, and the result was a checkerboard of implementation.

The Office of the Civilian Aide to the Secretary of War was established November 1, 1940, to facilitate the orderly introduction of African Americans into the army. Judge William H. Hastie was appointed first civilian aide; Truman Gibson was appointed his assistant. All policy matters pertaining to African Americans were to be referred to the civilian aide for comment or concurrence before final actions were taken. Hastie served from 1941, but resigned on January 15, 1943, to protest policies of segregation within the military. His reasons, published in *The Crisis*, were cited as examples of the "reactionary policies and discriminatory practices" of the United States military forces.[17] Many historians have concluded that Hastie was ineffective in his role. However, the War Department often ignored, excluded, or circumvented his office in its decision-making, and Hastie was delegated little actual power or authority. After his resignation, Hastie conducted a civilian campaign in leading black newspapers in which he detailed racial problems in the military. He also wrote a pamphlet, *On Clipped Wings: The Story of Jim Crow in the Army Air Corps*, published by the NAACP on July 1, 1943.

Following the Japanese attack on Pearl Harbor, the size of Selective Service quotas for black men dictated that all branches of the military accommodate larger numbers. The navy was exempt because it relied on volunteers rather than draftees, in effect making that branch exclusively white except for limited service areas, such as mess men or dock laborers, where blacks were allowed to enlist. Total numbers of African American service personnel across all branches of the military were less than 5 percent in 1940. By September 1944, black troops constituted 8.7% of all servicemen or 701,678. by the end of the war, the number had risen slightly, although the distribution of black soldiers throughout the services was still unbalanced. With few exceptions, they clustered together in the bottom ranks of the labor corps. Chaplains and doctors, without military authority over white troops, were the most common high ranks achieved by black soldiers.

Among the black labor units was the famed Red Ball Express, which operated in the European theater in the summer and fall of 1944, supplying desperately needed gasoline, fuel, food, and ammunition to American troops rapidly advancing on the German border. More than six thousand trucks delivered more than four hundred thousand pounds of supplies per day, driving thousands of miles to do so. The quartermaster corps, more than 75 percent of which consisted of African Americans, unloaded the supplies, drove the trucks, and worked as mechanics to keep to the express rolling.[18] Racial segregation had proven to be effective. David Colley writes, "The races were sufficiently separated that even today some white veterans of the Express are unaware that most of the drivers on the Red Ball were African Americans."[19]

The final version of the Selective Training and Service Act of 1940 granted "within the limits of the quota determined . . . an opportunity to volunteer for induction" of any person of color.[20] Nevertheless, each branch of the armed forces maintained the right to deliver final decisions about the eligibility of any man to serve. In effect, each branch of the armed forces could use its eligibility standards to control the number of African Americans enlisted within its ranks. In October 1940 the army had two black units of regimental size, and the navy was exclusively white. The army air force, known as the air corps until it officially changed its name in 1942, did not willingly accept black soldiers. In spite of the attention paid the Tuskegee Airmen by contemporary society, the army air force made only limited opportunities available to blacks during the war. And those doors were opened solely to appease demands by outside forces, "including vocal black organizations, an increasingly pressured President Roosevelt, and liberal members of Congress who pushed for greater opportunities for African Americans within the military services."[21] The marine corps, under the direct command of General Thomas Holcomb, unconditionally refused to accept African American recruits. The elite nature and small size of the corps meant that it could easily fill its manpower needs with white volunteers. Overall, it was clear that the practice of Jim Crow would continue throughout the war across all military units; integration was secondary to victory.

Adding to the military rebuffs, industry and civilian war programs turned away African Americans eager to contribute on the home front. The American Red Cross refused to accept black volunteers into its ranks because its services were restricted to whites. On the recommendation of the US surgeon general, the Red Cross turned away black blood donors to avoid indiscriminate mixing of Caucasian and African American blood.[22] Blacks were also turned away from draft board duty, local war support organizations, and most other war-related opportunities for national service.

The Defense of Military Segregation

A recurring theme within the War Department was that segregation was the most efficient system of race relations. Leadership accepted the "separate but equal" doctrine.[23] Established as law with the 1896 Supreme Court ruling in *Plessey v. Ferguson*, in practice separate but equal had resulted in two societies—black and white, separate and assumed to be equal—across the landscape of American life. Schools, churches, sporting organizations, and countless other institutions— including all branches of military service—were segregated. The establishment of "equal institutions" was almost universally unrealized, even in military services. Most reports observed that military training, facilities, equipment, and officers were all completely inadequate for African American soldiers. The military faced the colossal problems that accompanied absorption of large numbers of African Americans into a system forced to construct and maintain two separate facilities for training, housing, administration, and supporting military units divided by color. Separate buses, barbershops, blood banks, basketball courts, post offices, PXs, laundries, toilets, hospitals, and kitchens were required in all military facilities—the task was enormous.[24]

Several considerations limited the use of black troops in all branches of the military during the early months of the war. First, War Department policy forbid race mixing within military units. This policy reflected the attitudes of most senior military officers. Second, there was widespread evidence that African Americans could not perform up to the standards required by the War Department. Little latitude was given for the social, educational, and economic obstacles under which they lived in the United States. The average score for blacks on the Army General Classification Test (AGCT), given to all recruits to identify their aptitudes, was 79. Whites averaged 107. Blacks also suffered from all of the medical and dental problems that afflict those who have limited access to health care. Third, the unwieldy apparatus for enforcing segregation limited the total number of black troops that could be accommodated. Separate facilities for training and supporting black troops were insufficient for large numbers of enlistees. The same argument was made for limiting the jobs blacks could take. Since there were few African American pilots or radar operators, for example, it was impractical to create an all-black unit for them. And, there was little incentive or money for constructing new facilities. Given the social and educational disadvantages plaguing potential African American recruits, proponents of black combat forces had difficulty convincing others to use them.

For instance, the AGCT and the Mechanical Aptitude Test were administered to all enlistees and used as bases for assignment to units. Both tests relied on a certain expectation of educational preparation and cultural background, which African American recruits often did not have. It is not surprising that black inductees fell into the bottom quartiles on both tests. Their performance was dismal, especially compared to that of white inductees, who formed the standard bell curve. Unsurprisingly, it often took twice as long to train black troops. Discrimination had forced them into poor schools and into the ranks of unskilled labor to an extent not found among white inductees. In addition, lack of access to health care, inadequate basic education, and limited financial resources meant that black Americans were more often victims of socially alarming diseases such as syphilis and gonorrhea.[25]

White leaders also believed that African Americans lacked inherent mechanical adaptability and intelligence. As a tribute to the effects of environment, IQ test scores varied dramatically among incoming recruits. The highest scores were attained by Northern whites, whose median score was 60.0. Southern whites and Northern blacks scored 40.5, while African Americans from the South scored considerably lower.[26] Black recruits were assigned to units that required primarily labor with little technical aptitude or intelligence. The high rate of illiteracy and educational deficiency among black recruits compounded problems for a modern mechanized military force. Cognizant of this fact, a War Department directive effective May 15, 1941, excluded from service any man with less than a fourth-grade education or its equivalent. As a result, black registrants were rejected for failure to meet minimum standards in numbers far greater than their proportion of the population.

Another argument against the employment of black troops concerned their performance in the field. With the exception of some units, black troops often did not function particularly well when compared with white troops. Much of this discrepancy is understandable, given the conditions under which African American troops worked. Their training was often substandard, even when they were trained for the same time period as white troops. They often required remedial work to compensate for illiteracy and lack of job skills. Black troops were sometimes lead by hostile or unsupportive white officers. They were more poorly equipped, and they were subject to discriminatory policies that sometimes affected performance. But when asked to expand the use of black units War Department administrators often overlooked these factors.

The fourth consideration that limited African American field deployment was white civilians' resistance to having black troops located nearby, particularly in Southern states. And white enlisted men did not want to associate with African Americans. In some cases, black units were relocated en masse to more tolerant or remote locations. For example, in response to racial incidents the 447th Bombardment Squadron was transferred out of Selfridge Field in Michigan shortly after arrival. There is also evidence that the attitudes of commanding officers filtered down to the troops; the ease with which African American soldiers fit into their assigned bases and surrounding communities often directly resulted from commanders' tolerance.[27] Some issues, such as the capabilities of black aviation units, remained unresolved at the end of the war. Ambiguous segregation policies, domination of the white command structure, frustration of black servicemen, and racial tensions plagued the military services throughout the war.

Finally, it was widely believed that African Americans did not make good soldiers because they did not possess the requisite physical, mental, or moral characteristics. For example, both military and medical specialists thought that African Americans did not have the proper reflexes to operate complicated aviation equipment. Others suggested that blacks were cowardly by nature, reluctant to engage in combat, lacked aggressiveness, lacked the will to set or achieve objectives, did not have sufficient stamina, and were unable to cooperate in teamwork, especially under pressure.[28] While African Americans were considered ideal for tropical climates, military leaders felt that blacks could not tolerate frigid climates. Ironically, most African Americans were sent to the colder European theater of war, rather than to the Pacific, probably because naval policy excluded most blacks.

Segregation as Military Practice

The policy of segregation was at best inefficient and unwieldy. Because various parts of the United States possessed different local customs regarding racial separation, segregation caused confusion. And segregation in military service was by no means uniform. A patchwork approach had evolved, based on local customs, geographic conditions, and installation facilities. A serviceman, either white or black, stationed in the deep South would probably have a much different experience than one stationed in Hawaii, Minnesota, or California.²⁹ Military segregation practices were often abandoned under battle conditions, as frontlines shifted and service units became intermingled. There was also race mixing when African American corpsmen transported injured and dead white soldiers, although efforts were made behind the lines to keep treatment facilities, medical staffs, and blood segregated. Some of this race mixing was tolerated, especially if it was secondary to the larger goal of winning the war.

From the white vantage point, the problem was that segregation brought African Americans together in large numbers, creating a critical mass that was difficult to ignore, especially when their services were essential. There were few effective restraints, since there were simply too many individuals to manage effectively. While difficult it is to prove, black servicemen used work slowdowns and stoppages to protest injustices. The Port Chicago mutiny, as it has been designated, is an example of the devastating impact of such tactics.³⁰

An additional predicament facing the military, and especially selective service boards, was the very definition of race. In Puerto Rico, heterogeneous racial composition made determination of race a daunting proposition. Creole applicants for military service confused draft boards in Louisiana. And in Virginia, mixtures of Indian and white or black individuals prevented easy identification of race. So as not to upset local customs, on September 10, 1941, Director Hershey ruled that 25 percent Negro blood made a person a Negro unless that person had passed for white in his community. There were incidents in which black servicemen were wrongly assigned to white units because their surnames did not sound black, or because their records did not have the "C" for colored designation, adding to the complications of racial separation.³¹ Only one serious suit regarding racial classification arose during the war, but the case of Winfred W. Lynn of New York City never received a court ruling, an eventuality that effectively gave legal sanction to existing practices of racial classification. The War Department refused to end segregation even though discrimination was technically illegal, definitions of race were far from scientific, and the apparatus supporting a segregated military was ludicrously inefficient. Regardless, an army board convened at the end of the war recommended continuation both of racial segregation and of the quota system, as well as the use of blacks exclusively in support, rather than combat functions.³²

The Advisory Committee on Negro Troop Policies, more commonly known as the McCloy committee, was created in 1942 by army air force colonel Elliot D. Cooke, who noted a lack of consistency in the practices and policies affecting black troops during an inspection tour. The committee's purpose was to develop a consistent War Department policy regarding African Americans with respect to social questions and personnel training problems. Perhaps its most notable contribution was to influence General Marshall to spell out their responsibilities to all major commanders when racial tensions escalated in 1943.[33] The committee had identified commanders as the key to a healthy racial environment, noting that dissatisfaction with white officers among black soldiers constituted a significant problem in some military units. Some commanders did not appreciate the seriousness of the situation, or their inherent responsibility in mitigating the tension. On July 13, 1943, Chief of Staff George Marshall circulated a memo to his generals warning, "Disaffection among Negro troops continues to constitute an immediate and serious problem." Furthermore, he indicated, "Failure on the part of any commander to concern himself personally and vigorously with this problem will be considered as evidence of lack of capacity and cause for reclassification and removal from assignment."[34] The committee also issued a pamphlet, "Command of Negro Troops" (1943), that gave white officers advice on how to deal with sullen and intellectually inferior black troops.

Prominent political and military leaders continued to support segregation in the face of serious inefficiencies of implementation. In spite of their awareness of increasingly vocal factions that protested those policies, Secretary of War Henry Stimson and Secretary of the Navy Frank Knox had no intention of integrating African American servicemen into white units. Many groups sought greater inclusion and representation of African Americans. James Rowe and Edward J. Flynn, prominent Democratic politicians, warned that black protests would escalate if policies of racial discrimination continued. Other prominent leaders within the black community, such as Walter White and Dr. Channing H. Tobias, protested to President Roosevelt that few blacks were appointed to local draft boards, even within largely black communities. Out of a total twenty-five thousand men serving on draft boards throughout the country, a mere 250 were African American. In the first few months of the draft, no blacks were called. As protests and pressure to reach quotas for African Americans mounted, more blacks were called to serve. However, the branches of the military could delay the induction of blacks until they had openings in black units or separate facilities for training. Military scholar George Q. Flynn concluded, "According to this game, selection would remain theoretically nondiscriminatory, but induction would be by race."³⁵ Except for a short period of integration under extreme battle conditions in the Ardennes, blacks served in segregated units, performing primarily quartermaster, construction, and transportation jobs. Even the relatively few black combat units were used mostly as unskilled labor. The "right to fight" became a key slogan for black organizations that wanted to demonstrate the willingness of the black community to fulfill citizenship obligations on the front lines.

The chronic problems of implementing the Selective Service Act for a segregated military continued. By early 1943, approximately three hundred thousand African American men had been drafted but not inducted. The marines refused to accept any African Americans, and the navy limited their service to mess duty, mostly serving officers or as kitchen and laundry help, since mixed crews on ships were inconceivable. The army absorbed 375,059 blacks, primarily into labor battalions.³⁶ In contrast, whites were disproportionately called and inducted into military units, creating frustration for African American men who wanted to fight and for whites who risked their lives in far greater numbers. Influential black leaders called public attention to these discrepancies. Among many others, P. L. Prattis, editor of the *Pittsburgh Courier*, gained attention when he published his letter to President Roosevelt accusing the Selective Service of racism.

In spite of resistance to African American enlistments, wartime practices shifted subtly. The navy was highly resistant to black sailors, but even in this service branch, three stages can be identified in the evolution of racial policies during the course of World War II.³⁷ First, the navy excluded all African Americans except as mess men. Then, as manpower shortages developed and criticism by black leaders mounted, the navy grudgingly accepted African Americans for general service in segregated training camps and unit assignments. As a result, African Americans were assigned as laborers and workers in navy installations and shore facilities primarily loading munitions, such as the infamous Port Chicago base. Finally, continued external pressure led the navy to announce that it was abolishing segregated training camps and unit assignments. Since this action occurred in the final months of the war, there is some question about its sincerity. Overall, changes in navy policies were motivated by manpower shortages as much as by external pressure from the press and civil rights groups. But however slowly, the direction of change had been established.

The confusing patchwork of policies that vexed most military services was evident in the army air force. On October 9, 1940, for example, the War Department announced, that African Americans could train as pilots, mechanics, and technical specialists, although military aviation training would not be available to them. They could participate in the latter, but only in civil groups that received no military support. No blacks were in training in any branch of the military services as pilots or ground crew. As General Henry H. Arnold, chief of the air corps, commented, "Negro pilots cannot be used in our present Air Corps units since this would result in having Negro officers serving over white enlisted men. This would create an impossible social problem."[38] This attitude was widely shared, although justifications varied. Often, the reason for exclusion cited was innate racial inferiority. For example, Robert A. Lovett, assistant secretary of war for air, resisted black service in any form, even in the civilian pilot training program, because he believed that African Americans lacked the physical and emotional ability to fly aircraft. The final result was that basic issues affecting black aviators went unresolved throughout the war.

Four black fighter squadrons and one medium bomber group represented the total involvement of black airmen in army air corps combat during World War II. The War Department and the army air force spent considerable time, money, and effort to assure employment of black troops with a minimum of racial tension. They circulated surveys to collect data for official studies, wrote pamphlets and manuals, produced films and radio broadcasts, and issued a stream of memoranda instructing officers on leading black troops. But the results were disheartening. As Alan M. Osur concluded, "It is difficult to assess the effectiveness of this activity, but it is clear that racial tensions did not subside as the war progressed and the AAF's most explosive racial disturbance took place in April 1945."[39]

In addition, the War Department made it clear that it would not interfere with local communities or businesses as long as the war effort remained the primary goal. As a result, the limited, mostly symbolic actions by President Roosevelt affirming African American civil rights and the protests of civilian groups, had little practical impact on the Jim Crow system. Communities continued to follow rigid codes of racial separation for both civilians and military personnel stationed nearby. Local transportation companies and railroads, for example, maintained strict segregation practices. Military police enforced these policies in order to keep the peace.

Fractures in the Practice of Segregation

The first signs of the growing influence of African Americans came in the political sphere. In the 1940 presidential election, the black vote was needed to ensure a victory for President Roosevelt, who made a number of concessions close to election day to build support in the black community. He ordered the formation of black aviation and army combat units. He added an anti-discrimination clause to the 1940 Selective Service Act. He promoted Colonel Benjamin O. Davis Sr., to brigadier general, making him the highest-ranking black officer in military history. And he appointed William Hastie as advisor for Negro affairs and assistant to the Secretary of War. These gestures were successful in mustering black voters and allowed Roosevelt to skirt the issue of military integration, which, if implemented, would probably have driven white voters to the Republican camp. Later in 1942, Roosevelt ordered an increase in the recruitment of black officers to further appease black protesters. But African American officers were still restricted to commanding only black troops, thus blunting the impact of the presidential order.

As the war dragged into its third year, increasing black manpower in the military services became inevitable. As George Q. Flynn explains,

> Simple numbers told the story. In staffing an armed force the United States would have to rely upon the 66 million males over the age of 18. This pool would have to be cut further to eliminate men over the age of 35, who would prove physically incapable of modern war. Blacks represented some 10 percent (12,865,518) out of a total U.S. population in 1940 of 132 million. In the groups most likely to be needed in the armed forces (20 to 35 and male) blacks made up 9 percent of the total population. In the age group 20 to 35 there were some 16,213,366 males. Of this group over 14.5 million were white males and over 1.5 million were black males. Clearly War Department planners had to anticipate the use of this black population in the event of American entry into the war.[40]

As combat claimed more and more white soldiers, the pressure to include black soldiers in frontline combat roles increased.

The tipping point occurred in 1943, when domestic violence, coupled with a closely contested presidential election, forced President Roosevelt as commander-in-chief to seek a greater role for African Americans in all branches of military service. His strategy alienated Dixiecrats in the South, but it garnered enough Northern black votes to offset the loss. This tactic realigned major factions in the Democratic Party and set in motion symbolic inclusion of African Americans that, combined with the increased need for black manpower, set the stage for postwar military integration. By the end of 1943, there was a cautious, but obvious shift from traditionally ingrained racist attitudes toward alleviating the problem of race, signaled by the actions of President Roosevelt himself.

The German counteroffensive in the Ardennes a few months later contributed to the urgency of the manpower crisis. African American units, recruited and trained for combat, but stationed stateside, were needed to turn back the Nazi attack. Responding to surprise German advances in the Ardennes, frontline generals called for replacement troops, regardless of color. General Eisenhower deployed black infantry units to the front and allowed black soldiers to replace casualties in white infantry units desperately trying to repel German attackers.[41]

These changes did not automatically mean that African Americans were accepted by their white peers and officers. The records indicate that they were not. Change was slow because racial attitudes were entrenched. Some officials, however, realized that military reorganization to integrate the service units was inevitable if the United States were to maintain an effective fighting force. In addition, "Washington sought to utilize black soldiers fairly rather than to view them merely as embarrassments and problems."[42] Change met with resistance and often did not filter down through the ranks. As history indicates, final integration of the armed forces was a lengthy process that was not completed until after the Korean War. In a critique of the Selective Service, Campbell Johnson praised its impartial record for recruitment, but called for a "maximum use of manpower" in future emergencies, a recommendation that required addressing the problem of racial quotas.[43] To limit African Americans to segregated units would only perpetuate the inefficiencies experienced during World War II.

Throughout the war, "the Negro problem"—that is, the use of black volunteers without compromising the morale and efficiency of the mostly white military services—was addressed through "segregation without discrimination." Segregation acknowledged the widely held belief in distinct inherent differences in capabilities without, it was felt, putting either race at a disadvantage. It was, as War Department records attest, a practical solution that did not interfere with ultimate military objectives. This thinking pervaded the command structure as well as the ranks of both white and black servicemen. The *Army Service Forces Manual M5* elaborated: "War

Department concern with the Negro is focused directly and solely on the problem of the most effective military use of colored troops. It is essential that there be a clear understanding that the Army has no authority or intention to participate in social reform as such, but does view the problem as a matter of efficient troop utilization."[44] It is clear that the armed services did not question civilian social practices. As a reflection of the general prejudices of society, the military maintained its conservative tradition of segregation.

In hindsight, it is easy to detect the emotional and economic burden of maintaining segregation: the cost of maintaining separate facilities, the cost of discouraging thousands of citizen soldiers, and the cost of greater military effectiveness. The structural challenges of fighting a world war with a segregated military force strained the Jim Crow system and, along with attitude shifts, eventually resulted in integration of the armed services. Those attitude shifts were perhaps foreshadowed by the eight films commissioned by the War Department between 1943 and 1945 in a bid to address the issue of African Americans in military service.

CHAPTER SEVEN

Attitudinal Barriers to Change

A crisis is nearing in racial affairs here in America because the younger Negro knows no slavery like his forefathers and he refuses to accept any. The type of Negro that these white race baiters have to cope with in the future are [sic] fellows like me.
—LETTER TO THE EDITOR FROM AN ANONYMOUS SOLDIER[1]

A 1944 public opinion poll conducted by the army revealed extraordinary support for the national cause. However, only 66 percent of black respondents thought the war was their concern, compared to 89 percent of whites. Even though the majority of Americans supported the role of the United States, the attitudinal gap between blacks and whites remained virtually unaffected throughout the war. Many things undoubtedly account for these different perceptions of the war. Segregation and rampant discrimination in both civilian and military arenas affected black perceptions. And whites, convinced of the innate inferiority of blacks, did not want to work or fight with them. Ultimately, the racial frustration of blacks and whites erupted in violence that punctuated periods of apparent calm.

In addition to the structural problems bedeviling a completely segregated military, serious barriers existed on both sides of the color line, from the lowest ranks to highest decision-makers in the War Department. White Americans dominated political and military leadership, and they were often skeptical about the quality of the African American soldier.[2] In addition, black community leaders, citizens, and soldiers were increasingly unwilling to accept the degrading status they had always been obliged to carry. The military became an arena for the opinions of both constituencies. At times frustration spilled over into violence, jeopardizing victory.

However, the social upheaval initially brought on by the great migration north, then by wartime movement of millions of Americans, also introduced the conditions for attitude change. Racial experiences had diverse, unpredictable, and sometimes profound effects on American soldiers. A white soldier from Mississippi wrote to *Yank* magazine about his changing attitudes toward African Americans, and similar letters appeared in domestic newspapers.[3] But overall, white attitudes solidified and poor conditions continued for African American throughout the war, probably contributing to their lackluster support for a victory that extended freedom to others but not themselves.[4]

Several factors played into the quagmire of racial attitudes. Military leadership and attitudes toward African Americans overseas provided different perspectives that altered the attitudes of black enlisted men, along with a heightened sense of racial consciousness. The explosion of violence among citizens and on military bases demanded a response. *The Negro Soldier* was, in part, an attempt to promote harmony in the midst of racial turmoil.

Leadership

In his analysis of the use of African American troops during the war, E. T. Hall observed that the quality of military leadership was an important factor in the satisfaction of black troops, along with attitudes of commanders, individual adjustment to military life, civilian attitudes, and personal interrelationships.[5] In the absence of positive leadership, tensions rose and violence erupted.

Since white officers set the tone for their troops, leadership attitudes were critical in establishing the racial climate in the ranks. Pre-existing stereotypes regarding African American abilities to perform the tasks required of a soldier proved enervating, and some white officers flatly refused to work with black troops. They persistently viewed black soldiers as wretched fighters and a source of trouble, but "never bothered to look seriously at any causes for such poor results, contenting themselves with cracker-barrel Darwinian philosophizing and half-baked conclusions about 'innate characteristics' and 'observed facts.'"[6] When tensions rose, violent outbursts occurred, probably hardening opinions on both sides.

The strict military hierarchy replicated the racial divide in American society. Forced to take African American enlistees, military leaders responded by reverting to the racial conventions of civilian life. Directives, statements, and orders issued by the War Department were only as effective as the determination of commanders to enforce them. Even if the War Department encouraged tolerance and unity to win the war, it was up to officers to make those things happen. But many officers agreed with Major General Frank

Hunger, First Air Force commander, who stated, "Negroes can't be expected to obtain equality in 200 years and probably won't, except in some distant future."[7] Similar prejudices were reflected throughout the white military ranks. Even Attorney General Francis Biddle drew a vivid comparison: "Negroes should be chained to their places of abode as were the serfs in the medieval days."[8] Like Biddle, many commanders resisted War Department initiatives. As a whole, the military service tended to react conservatively, mirroring American society's largely conventional attitudes about race.

Staff Sergeant Bill Stevens, 48th Quartermaster Regiment, explained how the attitudes of officers affected troop behavior:

> White officers in general, conceding the exceptions like my original officers, have solidified false ideas about black troops. Their attitude toward black soldiers is entirely different from that shown whites and these attitudes are immediately picked up by white enlisted men. You might not be able to deck an officer for his snide remarks and racial slurs, but you can sure lay on white enlisted personnel. This is why there is so much fighting between black and white enlisted men. White commanders in the Pacific theater were notoriously prejudiced. As I have pointed out this kind of thing starts at the top and goes down, so anybody who thinks General MacArthur had any use for black troops had better take a second look at the treatment and use of black soldiers in that area. Black troops were just naturally suspected of cowardice, stealing, rape, the whole racial-stereotype lie.[9]

Other servicemen identified prejudices among officers that condemned black units to labor battalions and prevented any chance for them to demonstrated their combat abilities.[10] The propensity toward violence as a response to racial tension was borne out in the rising tide of racial strife as the war progressed, reaching a record number of violent incidents and riots in 1943.

Secretary of War Henry L. Stimson did not hide his feelings about black demands for inclusion. He was convinced that African Americans' lack of innate intelligence limited their ability to master modern weaponry.[11] In particular, he believed that they could neither function well under battle conditions, nor lead troops, because "leadership is not imbedded in the Negro race yet."[12] Stimson resisted intermingling of races in military units and was adamant that including African Americans in the army air force would be especially destructive to white troops, a view shared by General

Henry Arnold, chief of the air corps. They feared that fighting morale and efficiency would suffer if white airmen were forced to work with African Americans, because the emotional makeup of African Americans made them unsuitable for combat duty or any form of decision-making. Thus, blacks could only serve effectively under the direction of superior white officers. But whites would not willingly work with African Americans. Separate facilities for training black aviators did not exist, rendering African American applications for aviation training futile unless they found a civilian willing to instruct them.

As a result, the effective use of black troops was left mostly in the hands of white officers. Many, such as Major General Edward M. Almond, reflected the attitudes of a segregated society: "I do not agree that integration improves military efficiency. I believe it weakens it . . . There is no question in my mind of the inherent differences in races. This is not racism—it is common sense. Those who ignore these differences merely interfere with the combat effectiveness of battle units."[13] Such views held sway until the crisis of manpower in 1944 demanded additional men of any color for the final battles in Europe. Then, black troops were used in combat more often and in greater numbers than at any previous time in the war.

General Thomas Holcomb shared the belief of many military officers that African Americans had no place in the military. He said, "If it were a question of having a Marine Corps of 5,000 whites or 250,000 Negroes, I would rather have the whites."[14] Based on his opinion that black servicemen were inferior to whites and incapable of command, in his Letter of Instruction 421 Holcomb ordered, "In no case shall there be colored noncommissioned officers senior to white men in the same unit, and it is desirable that few, if any, be of the same rank."[15] This document, and others like it, reflected the structural barriers imposed on African Americans as a direct result of officers' attitudes. Similarly, Secretary of the Navy Frank Knox refused to consider the use of African American men, other than as mess stewards. He argued that black recruits could not possibly succeed in competition with whites for other military roles, so restricting their service was actually a benefit to them.[16]

The conviction that African Americans were inferior troops permeated the ranks from generals to privates. In his memoir of the war, General George S. Patton reported his remarks to the 761st Tank Battalion prior to an attack: "Individually they were good soldiers, but I expressed my belief at that time, and have never found the necessity of changing it, that a colored soldier cannot think fast enough to fight in armor."[17] White troops held a widespread belief that their performance far exceeded that of black troops, although there was some appreciation for the efforts of black companies such as the Red Ball express, the Marseilles black MPs, and fighter escort squadrons.[18]

White officers often considered it disgraceful to be assigned a black unit; it is not surprising that African American morale would suffer under white commanders who felt they were penalized. Through classroom instruction and a manual entitled *Leadership and the Negro Soldier* (1944), army officers were given specific instructions about dealing with black troops. The manual supports the policy of racial segregation, while sidestepping the social debate on civil rights by claiming that the task of the army "is to utilize its men on their individual merits in the achievement of final victory."[19] The manual assumes that individual merit rewarded individuals, but the book itself was based on social stereotypes about racial limitations. For instance, white officers are cautioned to be vigilant about the inherent tendency of black men to gossip, to shirk their duties, and to steal.[20] Together with lectures, discussion, and a screening of *The Negro Soldier*, the manual was at the center of a program for officers intended to mitigate the racial problems in the army.

Military services did not make use of black officers, since it was believed that blacks did not have leadership qualities. It was felt that whites naturally did a better job of commanding, and blacks preferred white commanders to those of their own race. Such paternalism reinforced unquestioned assumptions of white superiority and black inferiority, as decades of social attitudes derived from segregation carried over into military ranks. An Office of War information poll in July 1943 found that 90 percent of white Americans, but only 18 percent of African Americans, favored military segregation based on race. Even in the Northern regions of the nation, where civilian segregation was not as rigorously enforced, half of those surveyed believed in racial segregation. Most white Americans thought that any shortcomings in the accomplishments of African Americans were the fault of the black race.

Another theme that filtered through branches of the military, particularly the army and army air force, was the thought that African Americans were the source of fifth column Nazi and communist plots. It is likely that the "Double V" campaign, which encouraged African Americans to conduct a second front to secure equal right at home, reinforced this conviction about African American subversion. Frequent articles about traitorous activity appeared in military publications such as the *AAF Intelligencer*.[21]

Carlton Moss, who was instrumental in the production of the film, also played the preacher. He is shown here reading from *Mein Kampf* and warning his congregation about the dangers of the enemy. (*The Negro Soldier*)

During his sermon, the preacher recognizes members of the congregation, including this WAC in uniform. (*The Negro Soldier*)

A flashback captures the boxing match in which Joe Louis is victorious. (*The Negro Soldier*)

In an effort to enhance the appeal of the film to a broad American audience, advisors to the film demanded that members of the congregation represent respectable black men and women. (*The Negro Soldier*)

A soldier's mother reads a letter from her son describing his experiences in boot camp. (*The Negro Soldier*)

African American and white civilians arrive at the army induction center. (*The Negro Soldier*)

Bill Johnson tells his employer, Mr. Morgan, that he has just received his induction papers. (*The Negro Sailor*)

Bill Johnson, his editor, and a sports columnist attend a football game to see "teamwork in action." Teamwork becomes the central metaphor for the film. (*The Negro Sailor*)

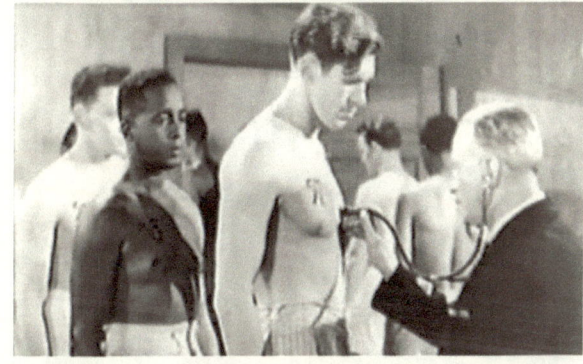

African American and white men appear in an integrated film scene as they undergo physical examinations prior to induction into the navy. The actual induction facilities were segregated. (*The Negro Sailor*)

Bill Johnson appears among white navy recruits during basic rifle training. This scene does not show the segregated training camps that actually housed recruits. (*The Negro Sailor*)

Off duty, Bill Johnson dances with an African American woman. (*The Negro Sailor*)

Bill Johnson learns the history of black contributions to the navy, including the heroism of Dorie Miller, commemorated in this portrait. (*The Negro Sailor*)

Sam the custodian reads his induction notice. (*Close Harmony*)

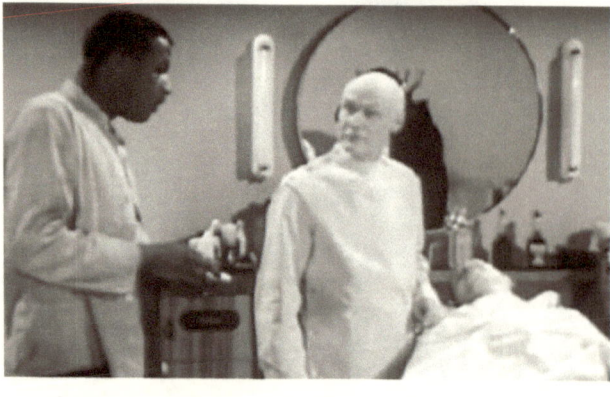

Sam tells Eli, a barber who is his employer, that he's leaving to join the army. (*Close Harmony*)

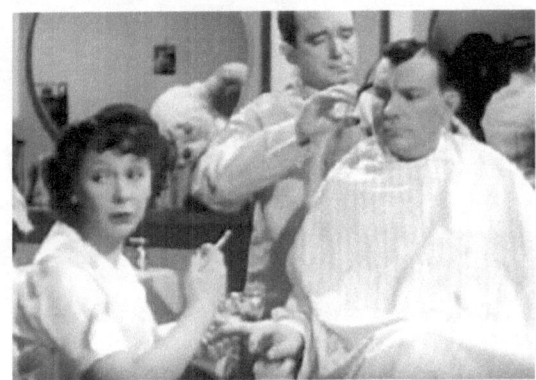

Barbershop employees and patrons discuss the need for everyone to pitch in to help the military win the war. (*Close Harmony*)

Sam talks with his girlfriend and mimics a soldier's salute. (*Close Harmony*)

The navy steward serves coffee. (*The Navy Steward*)

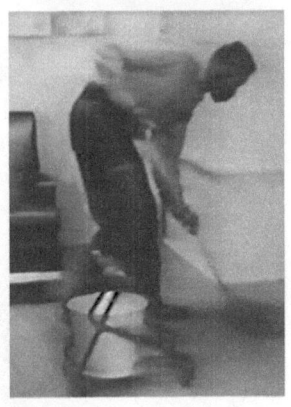

The navy steward mops the floor in the officer's mess after breakfast. (*The Navy Steward*)

Navy stewards clean an officer's personal quarters. The narrator warns the recruits viewing this training film to leave everything in place and not to steal any items. (*The Navy Steward*)

Henry Browne's family parks their mule drawn wagon in a row of automobiles at the air base, where they visit their oldest son. (*Henry Browne, Farmer*)

The oldest Browne son, in uniform, gives his family a tour of the air base where he is stationed. (*Henry Browne, Farmer*)

The Browne family watches the aircraft carrying their son take flight. (*Henry Browne, Farmer*)

One proposal to deal with the menace was the formation of a special unit of colored agents to isolate the agitators.

While disavowing bigotry, the overall pattern of the military services was to channel African Americans away from combat and technical specialties and into service corps as stewards, mess attendants, munitions handlers, cook and bakers, and truck drivers. In effect, the practice of racial segregation remained intact throughout the services. For example, rail travel, the primary means of transporting troops in the United States, observed a "black line," south of which railroad cars were segregated. The Jim Crow cars were mostly hot, dirty, crowded, and noisy. White military police were armed, but African American military police were prohibited from carrying arms and could not arrest white soldiers. They primarily supervised the transport of black troops. The social attitudes of civilian life transferred, almost unaltered, into military practices.

The rhetoric of discrimination accompanied an unquestioned conviction about the inferiority of African American soldiers. For example, during the October 1942 area commanders' conference, the air service command issued instructions for dealing with black enlisted men by exploiting the "Sambo" personality. That is, officers were urged to give blacks a chance to "show off," exploiting their natural showmanship and love of frequent praise, especially in front of others. Because of blacks' childlike natures, officers were reminded to keep them from feeling frightened and to give them little material rewards. Such instructions recall the conviction that African Americans are inferior, probably making any commitment to improve race relations a useless endeavor.[22]

The depth of ingrained acceptance of black inferiority is assumed in a statement from the War Department adjutant general's office in 1941. In part, the statement concluded, "The Army then cannot be made the means of engendering conflict among the mass of the people because of a stand with respect to Negroes which is not compatible with the position attained by the Negro in civilian life.... The Army is not a sociological laboratory; to be effective it must be organized and trained according to principles which will insure success."[23] The War Department did not question the assumption that separate facilities based on race were the most effective means of organizing the military. Remembering the attitudes in the military hierarchy with which he came into contact, Judge Hastie, civilian aide to the secretary of war, commented, "The basic resistance of field commanders and of many persons in the general staff in the War Department, never let down."[24] A few commanders, such as General Marshall, were supportive of change, but many more, such as General Henry H. Arnold, head of the army air force, were "unalterably opposed" to any proposals for change.[25] Lacking entrenched military traditions, the newly formed army air force could have adopted a progressive posture, but General Arnold supported his case for exclusion of African Americans by arguing that the relationship between ground and plane crews was personal, based on "confidence and intimacy far greater than in the other services."[26] The introduction of African Americans into this equation would be disastrous for flying crews who could not, according to Arnold, be confident that African Americans would keep their planes in top flying condition. Considering this attitude, it is obvious that black ground crews would operate under an unreasonable burden of blame if there were any mechanical failures. Arnold also kept segregated units from flying into bases where white personnel were stationed.

In the absence of well-defined policies, practices were at the discretion of commanders of subordinate units. For black troops, morale deteriorated whenever racial harassment was condoned among white troops. The basic issue of discrimination was not addressed, much less resolved. Instead, it was intensified or lessened, depending on the choices made at the level of the unit commanders, who could inflame or temper racial prejudices. In his report on the performance of African American troops following the war, E. T. Hall noted that African American enlisted men would often bring up the subject of race, blaming their performance on discrimination encouraged by their commanding officers.[27] When situations became intolerable, racial violence exploded on military bases and in surrounding communities.

While some white American members of the War Department were well intentioned regarding the treatment of African American servicemen, many, like Secretary of War Henry L. Stimson, "had no feel for, no real perception of the problems of race in America, or their impact, or the relation of the military to them. . . . He was basically uncomprehending as to the realities of the problems of race in the Army and in the American society generally."[28] Even when they faced receptive audiences, African Americans needed to educate them to understand that blacks were more than farmers, more than service personnel and unskilled labor. Sympathetic members of the War Department were often frustrated by the obstinate refusal to change adopted by the branches of the military. To that extent, well-intentioned decision-makers were captives of the military hierarchy.

As the war demand for increased manpower grew, top War Department officials began to entertain the broader use of black soldiers. But these attitudes were not uniformly shared. As a result, inconsistently administered military policies lead many in the black community to question government commitment to change. Alan M. Osur describes the situation:

> As the war progressed, attitudes at the highest levels within the War Department underwent a major and significant change. From 1940 to early 1943, officials generally believed in the inferiority of blacks, were afraid to incorporate them into the armed forces, and were certain that conspirators, inspired by Communists, Japanese spies, or other un-American groups, were responsible for racial strife.... However, beginning in 1943, the War Department began to reflect a changed attitude. There was an increasing acceptance of the notion that the black was not racially inferior, but was a victim of environment, racism, prejudice, and segregation.[29]

Evidence mounted against assumptions that literacy and white skin were prerequisites for good combat soldiers. The contrast between African American soldiers who were expert marksmen with a rifle or a sub-Thompson, but could not dot an *i* with a pencil, proved that limited educational background was not a military liability. Gradually, the realization that the resilient Soviet armies of the Eastern Front and that black troops consisted of mostly illiterate men who fought well for colonial governments in Africa, began to overcome the obstacles imposed by prejudices of US military officers.

To some extent the army especially, and the army air corps recognized that lack of education and other social restrictions, rather than biological inferiority, accounted for the more limited preparation of African Americans for military duty. Both branches provided corrective medical care, special training, and other remedial programs for African Americans, as well as disadvantaged white Americans, to bring them up to military standards. This attitude is evident in a number of training films and pamphlets, such as *Wings for This Man* (1945) narrated by then Hollywood actor Ronald Reagan. The film chronicles the achievements of the all-black 99th Pursuit Squadron.

American Military Attitudes Overseas

When African Americans were posted abroad, the racial attitudes of American society went with them—with several effects. The instances of harassment that followed black servicemen abroad varied but were widespread.

For example, the British commander of the Ministry of Information, on advice of US officials, ordered that all references to black GIs that might stimulate racial prejudice be referred to a censorship officer. Despite such strictures, the British press reported extensively on the problems of African American soldiers. Reporters especially focused in detail on court-martial proceedings involving black soldiers. Since British newspapers were not invested in the Jim Crow system, the British press often questioned American racial discrimination.[30]

Axis propaganda experts made good use of the contradiction between the professed ideal of American democracy and its treatment of black troops.[31] Axis propagandists aimed special messages at African American troops in order to undermine their willingness to fight. As Graham Smith concludes,

> German propaganda aimed at black soldiers asked whether they enjoyed the same rights as the white people do in America, the land of freedom and democracy, or are you not rather treated over there as second-class citizens? Can you go into a restaurant where white people dine? Can you get a seat in the theater where white people sit? . . . Is lynching . . . a lawful proceeding in a democratic country? Now all this is entirely different in Germany, where they do like coloured people.[32]

Effects of these messages on black troops were not documented, but American officials worried that they would exacerbate the low morale already present in their ranks.

The official policy of the War Department was to caution foreign governments and civilian populations that treating African Americans differently from what they experienced in the segregated United States would not only raise expectations unrealistically about postwar conditions, but would also embarrass US military officers. The War Department and many American civilians were anxious about the status African Americans expected in a postwar America. Among local residents of both American and foreign bases, there was also concern about black Americans in uniform stationed in their midst, partially because of racial mixing, but also because American soldiers had ready cash that created friction among local populations in places like Panama and Trinidad.

Care was taken in the assignment of black troops abroad. For example, in the Pacific theater, General Charles F. B. Price resisted the assignment of the 51st Defense Battalion to Samoa, arguing that the light-skinned Polynesian and Chinese inhabitants produced very desirable offspring with the white soldiers already stationed there. The introduction of African Americans would "infuse enough Negro blood into the population to make the island predominately Negro," producing "a very undesirable citizen."[33] Price recommended stationing the 51st Defense Battalion in Melanesia, where the islanders were already dark skinned and, in Price's estimation, of lower intelligence. Racial intermingling might "actually raise the level of physical and mental standards" of Melanesian natives.[34]

It seems that race concerns clashed with military objectives at multiple junctures. Alaskan officers were worried that black servicemen could not stand the cold climate, and Australia did not allow black immigrants, including African American servicemen.[35] Caught between the shortage of servicemen and the pressures from local commanders, the War Department made victory the primary goal and, despite continued objections from local authorities, assigned black service units in areas where they were not welcome. The men were broken up into smaller units before shipping out, presumably to minimize the impact of their deployment on local communities. Still, racial tensions arose.

Black soldiers forced civilians to assess their attitudes. Eric John Dingwall, coauthor of the 1942 ABCA pamphlet on black soldiers, summarized the tension introduced with black soldiers: "There is little doubt that many people in Great Britain, especially those who came into close contact with the Negro troops, were awakened to a wider appreciation of a problem which up to that time few of them had ever considered seriously."[36] The dissonance introduced among Britons required rethinking unexamined social attitudes and, subsequently, social interactions. While the reception of the British population was mostly positive, some Britons did not appreciate having African American troops on English soil. Cecil Roberts of the British Information Services expressed an opinion that was probably shared many others, and certainly echoed the stereotypes common among Americans: "The Negroes are a kind, easy-going people. Soft-voiced, sensual, they shuffle through life with laughter always near the surface, and have a religious emotional nature easily exploited . . . I would call them a happy race. They sing, they laugh, they dance and they doze in a manner that rebukes the pushy over-organized white folk."[37] Roberts asserted that owing to their essentially laid-back nature, African Americans should pose little threat to the British.

Attitudes of Black Enlisted Men and Civilians

The reasons blacks volunteered for military service were as varied as those of white volunteers. Many wanted to serve because of national loyalty, others wanted to find jobs and a steady income, still others thought that their lives would be improved by military service. Some probably sought adventure, and others exercised some degree of free choice in the face of an inevitable draft. Civilian opinions were equally varied. Some urged mobilization of energy against a racist government, others sought accommodation, and some argued that the quest for civil rights should be delayed until the war was won. The National Association for the Advancement of Colored People (NAACP) and the Congress of Racial Equality (CORE), as well as the more conservative Urban League, often equated the defense of the country with full citizenship rights.

The assumption that military service constituted citizenship went unquestioned as an undercurrent in many arguments made by African American civic leaders, organizations, and newspapers for military service. Leaders were positioned at both ends of the spectrum, as well as in the middle, and surveys of enlisted black personnel revealed a similar inability to come to a consensus.[38] Perhaps the fragmentation of black political voices encouraged military and government institutions to ignore demands for change. A member of the Office of War Information justified inaction on integration with this statement: "As anyone in this field soon discovers, there is no little political pulling and hauling between the various factions of Negro leadership in the government. . . . It would be a mistake [for the War Department] to align itself even implicitly with any one group."[39] While the prickly question of how best to utilize black troops created multiple views, the War Department was pressured by all black advocates, government and civilian, to recruit more African Americans.

More than a decade after the war, Mary Motley interviewed servicemen and noted the difference in attitudes between white and black servicemen reminiscing about their wartime experiences. Both races were largely unaware of the experiences of the other. Black servicemen did not understand that white soldiers were also disenchanted with the military, while white soldiers were largely ignorant of the contributions of black servicemen. Most of the interviewees recalled incidents of humiliation and frustration induced by racial separateness, although friendships also developed. Colonel Howard Donovan Queen summed up the most likely experience of black soldiers when he said, "The Negro soldier's first taste of warfare in

World War II was on army posts right here in his own country. This in its turn caused considerable confusion in the minds of the draftees as to who the enemy really was."[40]

Expectations for many soldiers, both black and white, were altered in their new environment of armed conflict, but this development was quickly followed by relapse into traditional discrimination. Technical Sergeant Willie Lawton, 369th Infantry Regiment, clarified the reality of military service: "I found throughout my military career that the Negro of some intelligence and freedom of thought definitely was not wanted and wasn't going very far. These things you expected in the states and particularly in the South but not after you are some thousand and more miles away from the United States."[41] Sergeant Eddie Donald, 761st Tank Battalion, remembered white stereotypes of African American soldiers as cowards and thieves, something he had heard many times before while still stateside.[42]

Mirroring the differences between civilian communities, the rigidity and enforcement of Jim Crow practices for African Americans in uniform varied. The inconsistent application of segregation was noted by 2nd Lieutenant Harry Duplessis, 758th Tank Battalion, who contrasted two of his training camps: "The prejudice and discrimination at Camp Hood made Fort Knox seem ultra liberal in its attitude. Camp Hood was frightening and made you wonder if you were still in the same army. Segregation there was so complete I even saw outhouses marked *White, Colored,* and *Mexican.*"[43] Contradictory military policies, along with dramatic variations in leadership, resulted in a patchwork of practices across the military services. In many ways, this inconsistency may have contributed to the wider variation in support for the war that existed among African Americans.

Rise in African American Racial Consciousness

Compared to whites, who signed up in astonishing numbers immediately after the Pearl Harbor attack and continued to join all branches of the service at a steady pace, African American enlistments were spotty and sluggish, owing to a pattern of overall distrust of the military on the part of black civilians.[44] Rates of military service exceeded 75 percent for white Americans, while no more than 50 percent of African Americans entered military service. Rejection rates were especially high in the South, where more than 75 percent of all black Americans still lived in mostly rural areas. African American volunteers were rejected for service because of educational and other deficiencies at a much higher rate than in other regions of the country.[45]

The War Department Advisory Committee on Negro Troop Policies reviewed countless incidents of African American volunteers being refused attention by white draft boards, particularly in the Southern regions of the nation.[46] It is surprising that many black men were still eager to join the service. But Master Sergeant Floyd Jones of the 578th Field Artillery Battalion recalled, "I am an American... I served because it was my job and I don't dodge jobs I feel I must do whether I like them or not."[47]

Tales of humiliation, ranging from military to social, endured by the black men who were inducted were widely shared with the black community. There was often not enough gasoline to transport black troops to training grounds or enough bullets for their rifles. They lived in tents, while white soldiers had permanent barracks. And often, black troops drilled in their civilian clothes because uniforms were not available for them. At times, the indignities included lineups so white women could pick out alleged African American rapists. African Americans who encountered white German prisoners of war noticed that the POWs were enjoyed more respect and better facilities than Negro servicemen. This difference in treatment soured many African American soldiers. Civilian Aide to the Secretary of War Judge William H. Hastie noted, "There was tremendous bitterness and vocal expression of dissatisfaction in the black community as to the result of the exclusion of blacks both from rapidly developing defense industrial mobilization, and from the rapidly expanding Army."[48] The viewpoint of the enlisted man was recorded by navy steward Ray Carter, who enlisted the day after the attack on Pearl Harbor: "If I had it to do all over again, or if I had to do it today, for what 'they' call 'our democracy' I would not go in, I would go to jail first.... I can find no reason to make me want to take up arms to save 'democracy.' What democracy?"[49]

Despite the dangers of retaliation, African American soldiers were vocal about the conditions of segregation. For example, before the well-known explosion at Port Chicago, African American munitions workers sent a letter detailing their grievances through an attorney to NAACP headquarters. Morale among the men was alarmingly low. Herbert Garfinkel pointed out, "In many respects, the discriminatory practices against Negroes which characterized the military programs... cut deeper into Negro feelings than did employment discrimination."[50] African Americans facilities ranging from movie theaters to barbershops were substantially substandard. African American troops often slept on the ground and used buckets as latrines.

Except for cleaning details for white officers' quarters, they were restricted from entering white training camps.[51]

Judge William Hastie recalled an incident in which army and navy staff members were reputedly discussing the increasing number of complaints submitted by blacks. When someone asked the navy staffer what happened to the protest, the person supposedly replied, "We file them in the wastebasket."[52] While the story may be apocryphal, it reflects the extent of the barriers facing blacks who sought equal treatment in the services. In June 1943, the NAACP issued a statement to the nation protesting the ill treatment of black soldiers. The statement concluded, "Negroes in the uniform of the nation have been beaten, mobbed, killed, and lynched."[53] The hypocrisy of the four freedoms proclaimed by President Roosevelt was evident in the nation's treatment of its black soldiers. The supreme irony was readily apparent to black Americans. Living in a wartime situation that called for unity in the face of a common enemy, they were separated by the same civilian and military institutions that called for the common effort.

One of the most sinister results of segregation and low expectations for individuals was the continual surveillance blacks endured. African Americans were continually subject to white scrutiny, having to prove repeatedly that the expectations of poor performance were unwarranted. Anticipation of failure undoubtedly corroded the effectiveness of many black servicemen. While large numbers undoubtedly gave up, Brooks E. Gray, preservationist with the Montford Point Marine Association, remembered that for him, "The injustices . . . in those segregated units sparked a fierce determination to excel."[54] Mostly, however, expectations of failure were enervating and explosive. Walter White, secretary for the National Association for the Advancement of Colored People, who participated in a fact-finding tour of the Pacific theater in 1944 after a race riot on Guam, found "a pattern of pervasive racial harassment—unofficial, spontaneous, but nonetheless cruel—may have helped bring about convictions, not of the black rioters alone, but also of some of the whites who tormented them."[55]

There were institutional barriers against any potential for change. Black servicemen who exhibited the qualities of leadership and inquired about officer candidate school were ignored; most ended up in segregated service units. Corporal Horace Evans, 761st Tank Battalion, was angered that the Patton Museum did not in any way acknowledge the participation of black troops. He also remembered the hostility of white troops toward his unit: "While we are speaking of Negro soldiers being cowards in World War II; that wasn't so. It was we had fought so much at home in those southern camps to survive that by the time we got overseas we were just plain exhausted."[56]

Altogether, the oppression wrought by both attitudinal and structural barriers imposed by segregation muted the enthusiasm of African Americans for the war effort. As prominent wartime correspondent Roi Ottley warned, there was "considerable doubt in the minds of Negro civilian and military populations, which seriously hampers the war effort."[57] Dramatic events such as the Port Chicago munitions explosion that killed 202 black troops (more than 15 percent of all black naval casualties for the entire war) hardened feelings. More damaging, however, was the court-martial and imprisonment of black strikers who refused to go back to work in unsafe conditions following the explosion.[58] The result of such incidents was to raise racial consciousness. As Nelson Perry said, "We were no longer a conglomeration of men; we were soldiers in a military organization. We sensed the growth of our consciousness, unity, and strength, a unified consciousness."[59] The budding self-respect carried over as a bargaining chip when negotiating with government and society for civil rights. Jack Crittenden remembers what he said regarding African American military service: "Give them a chance! Let previous conditions of servitude be no hold back. A man is still a man! All our men are facing the same enemy under the same flag. America owes it to them to see that they come back to the same opportunity."[60]

The Explosion of Civilian Violence

The violence of whites directed at blacks has a long history. Although for obvious reasons record keeping was casual, it is estimated that five thousand African American men, women, and children were lynched by whites in the nineteenth and twentieth centuries. Conviction of white superiority was embedded in the laws of every Southern state, and in several Western and Northern states, and echoed at all levels in American society. In the early part of the twentieth century, President Woodrow Wilson feared a mongrelized America would result if racial boundaries were crossed. This thinking carried through to 1921, when soon-to-be vice president Calvin Coolidge unabashedly echoed the common belief in the popular *Good Housekeeping* magazine: "Biological laws tell us that certain divergent people will not mix or blend. The Nordics propagate themselves successfully. With other races, the outcome shows deterioration on both sides."[61]

Between 1890 and 1910, nearly two hundred thousand Southern blacks moved north, and more than seven hundred thousand blacks migrated north during the World War I in search of better jobs and a better life. In 1910 there were ten million blacks living in the United States, 90 percent of them in the South, and three quarters of them working for white landowners.[62] Racial violence continued into the early decades of the twentieth century. While certainly not reflecting the vast extent of the problem, records show that more than one thousand African Americans were lynched between 1900 and 1915, mostly in the South. And this statistic does not capture the horrors of countless other brutalities, including beatings, rape, torture, and mutilation.[63]

World War I brought with it social and military tensions that exacerbated violence against blacks. Forty-four lynchings were reported in 1917, including instances like that in Waco, Texas, where an African American man was burned alive in the public square. During a riot in East St. Louis in early July, mobs destroyed three hundred African American homes and killed 125 African American men, women, and children. Violence erupted in the South as well as in the Northern and Western parts of the nation. In Houston, on August 23rd, 1917, two blacks, seventeen whites, and five policemen were killed in armed clashes. In their aftermath, ninety-nine African Americans were sent to prison, and thirteen were hung. By 1919, reported lynchings jumped to sixty-four. And riots broke out in smaller cities and towns across the country, from Youngstown, Ohio, and Chester, Pennsylvania, to Wrightsville, Georgia.

In response, African Americans joined militant organizations. In December 1917, the NAACP had 9,200 members in eighty branches. Within a year, membership jumped to 45,000 in 165 branches. The organization's official journal, the *Crisis*, averaged 41,289 copies per month in 1917. By 1918, the *Crisis* sold 74,187 copies every month. Other, more militant newspapers began publication, such as the *Boston Guardian*, the *Chicago Defender*, the *New York Messenger*, and the *New York Crusader*. Groups were organized to protest injustice and seek better conditions for African Americans. These included: the National Liberty Congress of Colored Americans, the African Blood Brotherhood, the National Brotherhood Workers of America, and local African American chapters of the Industrial Workers of the World, as well as the American Federation of Labor. Thousands of African Americans joined protest marches throughout the country. President Woodrow Wilson remained silent during this public unrest until July 26th, 1918, when he issued a statement against lynching. Still, he offered no support for two anti-lynching bills in Congress.

The violence that accompanied World War II outpaced anything experienced during the First World War. The Social Science Institute at Fisk University reported 242 race riots in forty-seven cities in 1943 alone.[64] Other reports document that violence swept through military ranks as well, although the War Department did not publicize those clashes. There were also many violent encounters between civilians and enlisted men that claimed hundreds of victims. Popularly known as the zoot suit riots, racial demonstrations that occurred in Los Angeles from June 3 to June 13, 1943, were by standards of the day relatively nonviolent. Yet they pitted servicemen and civilians against mostly minority Mexican and African American zoot suiters.[65] According to one study, it was the mentality of home front patriotism versus the betrayal of patriotic ideals by racial minorities. The violence resulted from the uncompromising demands of war in which citizens "succumbed to the psychological totalism of the time calling for the imperatives of either total patriotism or total disloyalty."[66] It was also a time when many ethnic groups such as Mexican Americans remained virtually unknown except through stereotypes, contributing to the hysteria. The larger worldwide conflict was reduced to a microcosm, as visions of enemy attackers became a powerful rallying symbol for citizen and soldier counterattacks.

As Mauricio Mazon concluded after his study of social unrest, "The damage to American propaganda and the morale of the nation from news or rumor of internal social conflict was incalculable. In May 1943 it appeared that the country was on the verge of serious domestic discord."[67] Outbreaks of mass violence occurred in Detroit, New York, Philadelphia, Evansville, Indiana, Beaumont, Texas, and Klamath Falls, Oregon. Hundreds of smaller skirmishes were reported across the nation, both on military bases and in civilian communities. German propaganda addressed directly to African Americans in combat zones urged them to desert and return home. And the violence provided evidence to support the propaganda: "Each lynching, race riot, and manifestation of Jim Crow during the war was publicized by the Axis as proof of the hypocrisy of President Franklin Roosevelt's Four Freedoms."[68] Propagandists asserted that Germany was more liberal and would welcome African American soldiers, unlike the segregated United States. African American soldiers were reminded that they were reduced to doing dirty work and serving as cannon fodder in a white man's war. Germany was not segregated, and German mobs did not lynch blacks.

Violence in the Military

The incidence of violence involving African American men in uniform has only been partially documented, because it was military policy to suppress such information. However, between 1941 and the end of the war, approximately twenty clashes occurred between African American soldiers, their white counterparts, and/or civilians. During the same time period, there were no instances of disruption among white troops. As Stanley Sandler concludes, this violence "presaged by at least a decade the black assertiveness that would lead eventually to the dismantling of legal racial segregation, first in the armed forces and, a full decade later, in US civil society."[69] The military uniform transformed white civilians into soldiers, respected as symbols of national pride, but a similar transformation did not occur for the African American soldier. His uniform was secondary to his race.

In April 1941, the first documented instance of racially spurred military violence during World War II was recorded at Fort Jackson, South Carolina. It was not the last. Violence that included gun battles, lynchings, beatings, and mob actions continued throughout the war. Prior to 1943, the most turbulent year in military history, hundreds of soldiers were caught up in racially motivated clashes. Many were wounded, and some were killed.[70] Racial problems enmeshed thousands of people. In 1943, major race riots took place on military bases and in neighboring cities. Riots broke out at Camp Van Dorn (Mississippi), Lake Charles (Louisiana), Camp San Luis Obispo (California), Freeman Field (Indiana), Bamber Bridge (England), Fort Bliss (Texas), and MacDill Field (Florida). Army records show at least fifty African American soldiers were killed in race riots, although these reports also contain a suspiciously high number of motor vehicle casualties among black troops, a common method of disguising deaths resulting from racial violence. Occasionally, however, records reveal details of brutalization, such as the lynching of a black private at Fort Benning in 1941, or the shooting of twenty-eight black soldiers in Alexandria, Louisiana, during rioting several months later.[71] These disturbances are a microcosm of the greater violence being acted out in American cities.

Additional reports of racial friction flowed into the War Department from across the spectrum of military service: from Camps Claiborne, Livingston, and Plauche (near Alexandria, Louisiana), Vellejo, Camp Stoneman, Camp Beale, Drew Field, Port Jackson, New Orleans, Flagstaff, Phoenix, Florence (South Carolina), Fort Dix (New Jersey), Tuskegee (Alabama), Beaumont (Texas), Prescott (Arizona), Fayetteville (North Carolina), Fort

Bragg, Camp Davis, Camp Gibbon, Jackson Barracks, Camp Stewart, Shelby, Fort Bliss, March Field, and the notorious Port Chicago. Perceived or real, racial injustices became flash points for blasts of violence. Government reports probably do not reveal the full extent of racial friction or the abuse of local black populations near military bases. Some instances were not recorded, such as the burning of black churches or other arson. The spiral of attack and retaliation lead to an increased level of militancy among black soldiers, further fueled by injustices experienced on base and in the surrounding communities.

It was difficult to avoid placing Northern blacks in the South, because most of the training facilities were on Southern soil. But the geographical relocation of less submissive black men from Northern or Western regions into the Jim Crow system of the South was a combustible blend. Weekly summaries of the racial situation in the United States, compiled by the Army Service Forces, hint at the scope of the problem. The summaries revealed that protests occurred frequently in the South, as well as across broad swaths of the United States.[72] Several especially fierce riots, such as those at Bamber Bridge, MacDill, and Fort Huachuca, stirred concern among top-ranking military and government officials.

Some unrest can be attributed to specific causes. For example, the MacDill race riot, also called a mutiny, was the direct result of leadership's failure to deal with escalating racial tension. While underlying factors such as assignment of large numbers of Northern African American men, combined with condescending treatment in bussing and venereal disease checks of blacks but not whites, may have triggered the resentment. But disregard for the black point of view probably tipped the balance in favor of violence. African American grievances did not get recognition until major outbreaks of violence brought the attention of the War Department to the situation.

At Fort Huachuca, the inspector general of the army noted racial hostility and pockets of violence. He assigned Brigadier General Benjamin O. Davis Sr., the first black general, to investigate. Davis reported that the lack of professional contact between black and white officers created inadequate cooperation that filtered down to the enlisted men.[73] When the situation was not sufficiently resolved, fighting broke out between black and white soldiers.

The most noteworthy disturbance resulted from exceedingly dangerous circumstances. An explosion at the munitions loading dock at Port Chicago, and the subsequent mutiny by Port Chicago African American seamen, cost more lives and good will than any other single incident during the war. Protests by African American sailors, following the refusal of black servicemen to continue working under hazardous conditions, reverberated through military ranks and civilians. While notorious, the Port Chicago events were not isolated. In the navy alone, one thousand black construction battalion workers staged a two-day hunger strike in March 1945 to protest Jim Crow practices. Black sailors revolted on Guam in December 1944, and black SeaBees who spoke out against navy discrimination were dishonorably discharged. The army, too, was racked with frequent racial conflict.

Different branches of the military service experienced different levels of unrest. The historically harsh treatment and outright exclusion of blacks in the navy invited backlash. The newly formed army air force, on the other hand, had no such traditions of mistreatment, but their commanding officers still did not pursue equal opportunities for African Americans. The numbers of African American service personnel absorbed by each branch of the military also contributed to the equation. The army air force, for instance, utilized smaller numbers of African Americans, and as a result, experienced fewer incidents early in the war. The army, by contrast, enlisted large numbers of black servicemen and experienced major unrest as early as 1941. For all branches of the military service, disturbances escalated throughout 1942 and reached a peak in the summer of 1943. Racial unrest continued in every branch of the military service through the end of the war.

In 1943, following riots at Selfridge Field, the air force hired consultant Dr. Lawrence Kubie to discover the causes of the disturbances. Kubie conducted psychological tests of African Americans at several air bases. His conclusions noted that morale suffered in direct proportion to the severity of segregation on base and that, over time, emotions intensified over the discrimination that attended segregation of units. It light of the psychology of discrimination, it was not surprising that as the war progressed, the propensity for racial violence also increased. Responses among commanders were piecemeal and tended to suppress, rather than correct, the underlying causes.

In addition to outright violence, another form of protest occurred. Many black service personnel did not closely identify with the war effort; it reflected the system of oppression endorsed by the nation. As a result, there was little incentive to perform at optimum levels. The sullenness and indifference among black units were often noted by their commanders and the War Department, although efforts to address the problem were not effective.[74] So, while perhaps not an overt expression of hostility, lack of enthusiasm, in and of itself, undermined national military goals. The commonly cited phrase, "Here lies a black man killed fighting a yellow man for the glory of a white man," captures the conundrum of the African American wartime experience.

Public Responses to Racial Violence

President Roosevelt, preoccupied with military strategy, did not intervene to control the violence plaguing cities, even during the peak of unrest in the summer of 1943. His Democratic party was dominated by Southern factions, and Roosevelt avoided interfering with states' rights to control issues of race. It was probably a political decision necessary to retaining control of his party and expedite legislation needed to run the country. To conduct the war and negotiate postwar policy, he was entirely dependent on Southern support in Congress. Roosevelt largely delegated the handling of racial matters to his aides, Mobilization Director James Byrnes and political secretary Marvin McIntyre, both Southerners.[75]

The issues of civil rights and race riots were distinct threats to the fragile Democratic coalition built upon the cooperation of Southern congressmen. In this sense, the push for civil rights was an impediment to the war effort; from the Roosevelt administration's perspective, there was no room for compromise. The congressional elections of 1942 increased presidential dependence on Southern Democrats because, for the first time since 1932, Democrats received less than half vote. Republicans gained forty-seven seats in the House of Representatives and urged the president to stall or renege on his promises for racial reform.

No government or military agency considered abandoning segregation as official policy, although military segregation was criticized in many quarters of the black community. While President Roosevelt recognized the difficulties introduced by military segregation, he was subject to outside influences regarding the amount of change he could force as commander in chief. According to Civilian Aide to the Secretary of War Judge Hastie, Roosevelt

> made a calculated determination that in foreign affairs, in the prosecution of the war, he considered it crucial to hold the support of the southern Democratic leadership, including the most reactionary and prejudiced of that leadership; and that he was, himself, going to take no action that

would so alienate that part of the Party and the congressional leadership that he would jeopardize essential support from foreign affairs and other domestic affairs. So the result of that was that Roosevelt would move only very cautiously, almost marginally, in this whole area.[76]

As a result, Roosevelt's actions on behalf of segregation were mostly symbolic.

In spite of the Roosevelt administration's view that equality was secondary to the main objective of winning the war, there were noteworthy individuals and groups who took up the "Double V" campaign to secure equal rights for African Americans. But many of these advocates did not have the political power base to dramatically challenge the government or elicit a broad political response. Only A. Philip Randall, president of the Brotherhood of Sleeping Car Porters, was able to capture the administration's attention by threatening a national strike. By means of executive order, Roosevelt acceded to demands for greater opportunities in war industries, but even then, the status quo remained intact. Change did not occur until manpower shortages opened greater numbers of defense jobs to black workers. When pressed by civil rights advocates, Roosevelt turned to African American community leaders for advice on racial issues: Lester Granger of the National Urban League, Dr. James Shepard, president of the North Carolina College for Negroes, and Lester Walton, minister to Liberia Prominent Southern white leaders like Jonathan Daniels, Mark Ethridge, Frank Graham, and John Temple Graves also served as advisors. These opinion leaders reflected a more moderate, gradual approach to civil rights than the majority of African Americans embraced.[77] Some scholars speculate that Eleanor Roosevelt was particularly effective at appeasing black demands for inclusion.

As a result, federal responses to racial tensions ran the gamut, from ineffective to absurd, most completely missing the target. Marshall Fields asked citizens to sign pledges not to spread rumors. Government press releases praised recent gains of African Americans. Procedures for calling in military troops to quell disturbances were reviewed and updated. FBI Director J. Edgar Hoover developed a plan to identify and imprison communist agitators who, he argued, were the source of racial unrest. Among whites, fears abounded that violence would not abate, but escalate, and among African Americans, anxiety persisted that they would lose what marginal gains had been made during the war.[78] For the most part, the War Department, aware of the cost of violence to military efficiency, urged white officers to take care in their treatment of African American soldiers. The War Department also acknowledged the serious morale problem among black troops and instituted training programs to help officers to deal more effectively with black servicemen. One temporary measure was to order up several signal corps films, most prominently *The Negro Soldier*, to foster greater racial unity. However, like most of the Roosevelt administration, the War Department hoped to avoid any measure that would divert energy or resources from the goal of victory.

President Roosevelt faced difficult choices: White voters and military leaders overwhelmingly favored a segregated military, while black voters who were crucial to his chances of reelection pressed for more opportunities for military service. As a result, Roosevelt suggested that each branch of the military offer greater opportunities for African Americans within the boundaries of segregation. On April 7, 1942, Secretary Knox advised the navy, marine corps, and coast guard that they would have to accept African Americans in general service. Beginning in January 1943, African Americans trained at Montford Point, a segregated camp, were allowed to enter the marine corps at a rate of one thousand each month. As General Ray A. Robinson disclosed later, the policy of expanding the role of African Americans "just scared us to death."[79]

Conditions for Change

In many ways, Americans fought two wars from 1941 to 1945, one on battlefields facing a foreign enemy, and one within its own military ranks and in American cities. Attitudes that fostered racial tensions also provoked the racial violence that flared intermittently but persistently throughout the war. The impact of this violence was to threaten military victory and provide a source of propaganda for the Axis.

While endangering the ultimate goal of victory over the Axis powers, mass public protests and violence proved to be powerful techniques for mobilizing African American resistance to Jim Crow segregation. In addition, these demonstrations helped to destroy white images of black passivity, demonstrating black solidarity and attracting national attention to discrimination. The increasing militancy of African Americans stimulated a new racial consciousness and awareness of their public identity. African Americans engaged in the exercise of power stood in contradiction to the old vaudeville stereotypes. They signaled to the white hierarchy as well as to black observers that African Americans were poised on the brink of new activism.

Faced with increasing domestic violence rooted in racial inequality and the demand for black soldiers and laborers created by wartime conditions, Arthur I. Waskow recognized the prevailing sentiment among decision-makers: "The authorities whose job it was to cope with such clashes of power were deeply ambivalent."[80] This federal reluctance to interfere stemmed in part from an entrenched allegiance to segregation, as well as reluctance to engage in social experimentation. This attitude partially accounts for the failure of government agencies to end military segregation.[81]

The war was a turning point for African Americans. They dreamed of having better lives with good jobs on their return to civilian life. African American servicemen reported at a much higher rate than their white counterparts that they were positive about the impact of military service on their lives. This optimistic outlook on postwar life was highest among Southern African Americans. Scholars speculate, "Ill-educated blacks facing a racist job market could hardly see it in this fashion; instead, military service reoriented them from a more collective perspective, in which group gains seemed a plausible outcome of a war for democracy, to one in which their own disadvantages as individuals was [sic] closer to the focus of their concerns."[82] Not surprisingly, many African Americans derived their identities from their communities, the source of social, financial, and religious support in an otherwise precarious environment of overt discrimination.[83] Ironically, the ambivalent message of federally produced films like *The Negro Soldier*, intended to promote wartime unity, also energized the African American push for greater inclusion in American democracy.[84]

CHAPTER EIGHT

Social Conditions for Change

Yet, in the nation of twenty-nine million, three million African Americans had been excised from the public memory of a war in which many of their fathers and grandfathers had fought and some had died. At mid-century, neither the myth of the remembered past nor the lived reality of daily life acknowledged the vital presence of African Americans in a nation they had helped to create.
—ELIZABETH RAUH BETHEL[1]

The first quarter of the twentieth century brought both hope and frustration for African Americans. After a decade of the Great Depression, the Second World War led blacks to expect increasing participation in the American way of life. In the popular "Double V" campaign, civil rights agitators joined with leaders of the highly influential black press and church to demand victory at home, along with victory overseas. This new belligerence found widespread support at all levels of the black community, creating a potent context for social change, as well as endangering the war effort.[2] Several factors generally contributed to this context for transformation of race in American society: migration of large segments of American society from the rural South to urban settings in the West and North; disappointment and resentment after African American contributions to World War I went unrecognized; and the influence of the black press. So, long before *The Negro Soldier* and other films provided a positive depiction of African Americans, conditions for change had been created.

These factors—migration, resentment, and press advocacy—interacted to exacerbate the low morale of African Americans on the eve of World War II. Migration to urban centers had destabilized traditionally black communities, increasing pressure on everything from adequate housing to basic service to jobs. In turn, blacks' resentment at their treatment during World War I, stoked by a hostile black press, added to the uniformly negative opinion of African Americans about their role, even as American involvement in another European war became inevitable. Bitterness rankled African Americans well into the 1930s.[3] Their resentment resulted from the conviction that black soldiers and civilians had proven themselves and earned respect.[4] In 1938, for example, a letter to the editor of the prominent *Pittsburgh Courier* warned President Roosevelt, "We are expecting a more dignified place in our armed forces during the next war than we occupied during the World War."[5]

This residual resentment was pressurized by the gap separating segregated African Americans from opportunities available to whites. Frustration was stoked by inferior living conditions and lingering economic effects of the Great Depression. The escalating hostility of the black press, combined with first-hand experiences in crowded urban resettlement communities, reinforced awareness of their disadvantaged circumstances for most African Americans. These attitudes created the conditions for activism during and following World War II. And, it was within these exigencies that the federal government was forced by the increasing demand for military manpower to redirect African American hostility while at the same time mollifying whites. Even though only limited gains were made during the war, the dogged determination that African Americans displayed would shape the course of the civil rights struggle for the next two decades.

Paradoxically, African Americans simultaneously supported and rejected the war; their morale was both high and low. As military historian Richard Dalfiume concludes, "Cynicism and hope existed side by side in the Negro mind."[6] Generally, African Americans were positive about their racial identity and determined to win improved social circumstances. However, their morale plummeted when they appraised the lack of opportunities in industry and the military. Perhaps paradoxically, African Americans both resisted and sought out military service.[7] They lived with the hope that military service would earn them recognition, despite the overwhelming evidence from past wars that such optimism was unwarranted. This reservoir of hope was eventually tapped by the positive images in government films.

Resentment Following World War I

There was extensive opposition to African American service in World War I, mirroring the conviction that African Americans were predisposed to be ineffective on the battlefield, although well-suited in menial roles as laborers.[8] The administration's encouraged African American support for the war effort, while remaining passive on domestic issues of equality. In one case, President Woodrow Wilson told African Americans, "With thousands of your sons in the camps and in France, out of this conflict you must expect nothing less than the enjoyment of full citizenship rights—the same as are enjoyed by every other citizen."[9] Yet Wilson remained silent during the riots that raged across the nation protesting existing inequities, and he failed to support legislation that might have addressed the complaints of African Americans.

In an attempt to gather African American support, Woodrow Wilson sent William G. Willcox, resident of the New York City Board of Education and Chairman of the Board of Trustees of Tuskegee Institute, as an emissary to boost African American morale in the Southern states. According to Willcox, African Americans would, "prove their right to stand shoulder to shoulder with their white brothers in answer to their country's call, and, if the supreme test must come, prove that their blood is as red, their hearts as true, their courage as steadfast to do and die in service."[10] These sentiments echo those of W. E. B. Du Bois, who in his famous 1917 editorial, "Close Ranks," urged, "Let us not hesitate. Let us, while this war lasts, forget our special grievances and close our ranks shoulder to shoulder with our own white fellow citizens and the allied nations that are fighting for democracy."[11] Prominent black leaders like Dr. Hollis B. Frissell, principal of Hampton Institute in Virginia, became alarmed at charges of African American disloyalty, assuring the nation, "The colored man is going to secure recognition, not by demanding his rights, but by deserving them."[12] Other African American leaders added their voices, agreeing with Wilson that equal rights could wait until they had been earned. In effect, key African American leaders sided with the Wilson administration.

To pacify African Americans, President Wilson also appointed Emmett J. Scott, private secretary to Booker T. Washington, as special assistant to the secretary of war during World War I. But public statements like this one reveal that Scott shared the viewpoint of the Wilson administration: "This is not the time to discuss race problems. Our first duty is to fight, and to continue to fight until this war is won. Then we can adjust the problems that remain in the life of the colored man."[13] The Wilson administration prioritized victory and dismissed the need to end segregation, ignoring civil rights for African Americans.

Underpinning black elites' support for the war effort during the First World War was their belief that their loyalty would be amply repaid at the war's conclusion.[14] Black leaders urged young men to join the armed forces to prove their worthiness for citizenship. They urged support for liberty loan drives, loyalty day parades, food and resource conservation, contributions to the Red Cross, and home front volunteerism. As NAACP cofounder Mary White Ovington concluded in 1917, "Wearing the uniform of a Federal soldier is prima facie evidence of citizenship."[15] And the editor of the *Chicago Defender* promised his readers, "The colored soldier who fights side by side with the white American in the titanic struggle now raging across the sea will hardly be begrudged a fair chance when the victorious armies return."[16]

In response to government inaction, membership in African American advocacy organizations exploded. In December 1917, the NAACP had 9,200 members in eighty branches. Within a year, membership jumped to forty-five thousand in 165 branches. The organization's official journal, the *Crisis*, averaged 41,289 copies per month in 1917. By 1918, the *Crisis* was selling 74,187 copies every month. Other, more militant newspapers surfaced, such as the *Boston Guardian*, the *Chicago Defender*, the *New York Messenger*, and the *New York Crusader*. Groups like the National Liberty Congress of Colored Americans, the African Blood Brotherhood, the National Brotherhood Workers of America, and local African American chapters of the Industrial Workers of the World as well as the American Federation of Labor organized to protest injustices and seek better conditions for African Americans. The Congress of Racial Equality grew rapidly in numbers and established an agenda for action. Rising hopes among black members helped fill coffers of these organizations. Thousands of African Americans joined protest marches and demonstrated throughout the country. But President Woodrow Wilson remained silent. Finally, on July 26, 1918, worried about the continuation of protests, he issued a statement against lynching but offered no support for two anti-lynching bills then before Congress.

The morale of African Americans at the end of World War I was unusually high, buoyed by pride in their contributions toward victory. As a result of the nation's triumph, African Americans thought their conditions would improve. The military victory requiring sacrifices was a "victory not merely ... for white Americans but ... a victory for the rights of oppressed humanity."[17] But triumph on the battlefield did not translate into equality at home. Expectations of improved circumstances quickly met with disappointment as social, economic, and political restrictions remained intact and then worsened during the Great Depression.

African American hopes were dashed almost as soon as the armistice was signed. Following the intense patriotic fever that embraced a fundamental belief in democratic equality for all Americans, the reality of civilian life in post-World War I America struck African Americans particularly hard. The feeling that patriotic actions during the war would carry over to break down racial barriers was crushed. W. E. B. Du Bois captured the tenor of postwar attitudes in his 1919 editorial, "Returning Soldiers":

> For the America that represents and gloats in lynching, disenfranchisement, caste, brutality and devilish insult—for this, and the hateful upturning and mixing of things, we were forced by vindictive fate to fight also. But today we return! We return from the slavery of uniform which the world's madness demanded us to don to the freedom of civil garb. We stand again to look America squarely in the face and call a spade a spade. We sing: This country of ours, despite all its better souls have done and dreamed, is yet a shameful land.[18]

Du Bois cataloged the shame of white America—lynching, disfranchisement, encouragement of ignorance, and racial insults—ending with a cry for true democracy. As one of their most eloquent leaders, he gave voice to the despair felt by African Americans across the nation.

Federal efforts to address postwar inequity were almost nonexistent, in spite of signs that racial attitudes had changed. At the end of World War I, President Woodrow Wilson dispatched Major Robert Moton, who had replaced Booker T. Washington as head of the Tuskegee Institute, to France to quell any tendency toward hostility among African American troops returning to the states, fearing that their experiences abroad would lead them to expect better treatment at home. Judging by the domestic upheaval in 1919, Moton's mission failed. There were outbreaks against African Americans in twenty-nine cities, resulting in the deaths of at least one hundred African Americans. An estimated seventy-seven African Americans, among them eleven soldiers in uniform, were lynched. Chicago, Washington, DC, and Elaine, Arkansas, were sites of the most serious violence. In the wake of the disturbances, African Americans were convicted and executed on charges of insurrection. No whites were charged.

Among the factors that contributed to the postwar violence was a tenacious unwillingness among whites to accept the wartime sacrifices of African American soldiers as legitimate. At the same time, race consciousness had increased among African Americans. Reflecting on the civil unrest in 1919–20, Kenneth B. Clark explained, "The evidence is overwhelming that Negroes as a whole were disappointed and disillusioned at the turn of events after the last War. The postwar riots, lynchings, and continuation of Jim-Crow practices seemed tragically incompatible with the slogan of 'fighting to make the world safe for democracy.' The Negroes' hope in a better future as a consequence of an allied victory dissipated soon after the war and gave way to latent cynicism and overt despair."[19] Clark further argued that African Americans began to understand the complicity of the federal government in the discrimination they encountered daily. The failure of the Wilson administration to support African American rights, the discrimination of military organizations against black soldiers, and the unrelenting oppression of Jim Crow segregation at home resulted from lack of political support for reform. The ideal of democracy became personalized in a way that had not previously occurred, as black Americans questioned their exclusion from educational, governmental, military, and social institutions. Their anger at this situation provided the basis for the attitudinal shift that informed the civil rights movement in subsequent decades, as resentment smoldered and attitudes soured.

In the period between the wars, African American lost ground politically, economically, and socially. The Great Depression had a disproportionately negative effect on African Americans, hitting them hardest of all Americans. They were among the first to lose jobs and homes and the last to be rescued by government aid programs. African American leaders like Lester Granger, executive secretary of the National Urban League, observed, "It is like kicking a man who is down, and congratulating him because he is not yet dead."[20] Black Americans held on through the grim years of the 1930s, but the optimism that followed victory in the Great War did not survive.

The initial wave of patriotism that swept black communities after the attack on Pearl Harbor in 1941 rapidly subsided and was replaced by suspicion, apathy, or both. By the middle of the war, Robert E. Park observed striking changes in African American opinions and behaviors. He wrote, "They are not so cordial as they were. In the movement and changes which the national emergency has occasioned, the racial structure of society seems to be cracking."[21] One thing seemed certain to Park, the struggle for racial equality had shifted and now required that the United States bring its racial policies into conformity with its national ideology. The problem was complicated, however, because "the war has changed the nature of the race problem, but it has not changed fundamentally the mind of the American people." Issues that were regional had become national and could not longer be ignored.

Arthur Davis, writing in the popular *Negro Digest*, addressed the question of whether a prolonged world conflict would aid the civil rights cause of black Americans. He suggested that the war made possible new opportunities in industry and industrial institutions. For example, "Trade union and plants, not out of decency but because of the emergency, [could] let down a few of their 'black' bars."[22] The reason for change was clear to Davis: "It is only through emergencies like the present that the Negro can make any appreciable progress in his journey towards American citizenship."[23] The crisis warranted continued action for reform to erase "the last vestige of American feudalism."[24] This window of opportunity eased the calls for immediate equality but, at the same time, added to the cynicism frequently expressed among African Americans.

The war was a contested issue among African Americans whose opinions spanned a continuum from pro-isolationism to prolonging the war to intensify the pressure for civil rights. The *Chicago Defender* printed an editorial arguing, "The Negro's hope for integration into American life is to identify himself with, rather than against, the best interests of the people as a whole. His loyalty to the American ideal, to democracy is his test. To seek to 'cash in' on a long war is an un-American doctrine that would give his worst enemies just and full cause to brand him as subversive of our native land. Negroes must be in the forefront of the battle against Hitlerism."[25] In contrast, many African Americans were so skeptical that they expressed pro-Axis sentiments.[26] The black press reported these leanings, and their allegations were followed by federal arrests of members of pro-Japanese underground organizations working on the Eastern Seaboard.[27]

Contributing to African American indifference to the war was a reconfigured understanding of self and community within the larger nation. Previous emphasis on personal relationships and community, encouraged in the largely agricultural South, was disrupted by the requirements of military service and employment in defense industries located mostly in Northern urban settings.[28] As African Americans from the rural South migrated North and West, they encountered new opportunities, but suffered the disruption of traditional community support. The racial inequality that infused every aspect of military life served to exacerbate these experiences.

Overall, a comparison of African Americans' attitudes toward World War I and World War II yields startling differences. A greater range of black attitudes emerged in World War II, with a tendency to cluster at the negative end of the scale. W. E. B. Du Bois modeled the dominant attitude toward military service and the national purpose in World War I in several editorials, in which he expressed the feeling that all Americans, black and white, should come together for the larger national purpose. Then, following victory, the battle for civil rights should continue. Later, in the early years of World War II, Du Bois suffered public censorship for this call to support the war unanimously, one indication that black sentiment had radically altered between the wars. Many African Americans' opinions were formed in the aftermath of World War I, as racial tensions escalated and patterns of exclusion continued in all aspects of American society. Despite black sacrifices, World War I had not changed America. On 1943, comparing African Americans in both wars, Kenneth B. Clark warned readers, "His morale today is not likely to be appreciably raised by concessions made within the framework of a rigid policy of racial segregation and discrimination. He is not as easily satisfied as he appeared to have been in 1917. He is more rigid in his demands. It takes more to dissipate the smoldering cumulative resentment and generalized bitterness residual of his oppression, disillusionment and disappointments."[29] The solution, Clark suggested, was for government to accept responsibility and change the pattern from negative to positive.[30] It became incumbent upon government to show African Americans their stake in the war, thus overcoming apathy, or worse, resentment kindled by decades of neglect.[31] While most black communities continued to support their sons and daughters in military uniform, they did not enthusiastically endorse the Allied cause.[32]

Massive Migration to Urban Centers

The steady trickle of African Americans who left the eleven states of the Confederacy at the end of the Civil War became a deluge by the first decade of the twentieth century. Disastrous weather in Alabama and Mississippi in 1915 decimated fields, and surviving cotton crops were infested with the boll weevil, further upsetting the precarious economic existence of black farmers. Unquestionably this was the most dramatic population shift in American history, between half and three quarters of a million African Americans migrated North between 1915 and 1918. On the eve of World War I, another 360,000 joined the armed forces, further uprooting African Americans from their established Southern communities.[33]

World War I broke the last chains that bound African Americans to the rural South. America's entry into the war stimulated more migration, as vast numbers of Americans left for European battlefields and Southerners left their farms for Northern factories. Labor shortages in the North intensified, as men entered military service and hostilities in Europe dried up the flow of cheap immigrant labor. Both whites and blacks were on the move. Forced by stark manpower shortages, industrialists with demanding deadlines and fat military contracts turned to the reserve of African Americans, sending labor agents into the South to entice farm workers northward. This shift signaled the first major redefinition of the role of African Americans in the economy since they were brought to the shores of North America in slave ships. The great migration changed the economic status of the black worker. However, along with the move north went Southern practices of segregation—white jobs and black jobs, white housing and black housing, white schools and black schools. It was to the advantage of white industrialists to exploit the large pool of African American unskilled and semi-skilled workers, making certain that this labor force worked efficiently without strikes or disruptions. Enforcement of segregation was intended to accomplish that goal.

The Immigration Exclusion Acts of the early 1920s ended immigration from eastern and southern Europe. The resulting vacuum pulled nearly eight hundred thousand African Americans from the South to replace immigrant labor. In the next decade, almost four hundred thousand left the South. The 1940 census reveals that the African American population outside the South had more than doubled in the preceding thirty years, increasing from 1.9 to four million. At the same time, white Americans were also relocating. For instance, fifty thousand Southern blacks moved into metropolitan Detroit between 1940 and 1943, and five hundred thousand Southern whites moved to Detroit in the same time period.[34] Many blacks who grew up in the South left behind the tight knit African American agricultural communities that began to break apart as people sought better paying jobs.[35] As the Great Depression gave way to the war boom of 1940 and 1941, the role of the federal government expanded, adding another strain on the Southern agricultural economy, as federal programs were cut or redirected. During these early war years, the federal government was a vital link to economic security and a decent life for white farmers, while their African American counterparts, who had been ignored in the social and economic programs of the New Deal, continued to suffer from the effects of the Great Depression.

Agriculture became more mechanized and capitalized during the 1920s and 1930s. Farm workers were dislocated. Adding to their distress, cotton prices plummeted from eighteen cents per pound in 1929 to a record low of six cents in just four years. Two-thirds of black sharecroppers and tenant farmers went broke or deeper into debt; over half of African Americans in Southern cities were unemployed.[36] Urged on by black newspapers that celebrated the opportunities of city life, they joined the ranks of Northern workers. The settlement of African American families outside the Cotton Belt left an indelible mark on American society. While reactions varied, most often the presence of African Americans in Northern communities challenged American views of national identity and the meaning of equality. As Northern cities began experiencing racial problems long attributed to the conditions particular to the South, their residents' reactions revealed that racial hatred was not confined to the South.

The decade between the wars was a time of extraordinarily rapid change for most African Americans. In comparison to whites of the same age and gender, African Americans were much more likely to migrate, to change occupations, and to move upward in their economic circumstances.[37] More than half of African American men of service age were likely to be living in a different region of the country after the war; by contrast less than 25 percent of white veterans migrated after leaving the service. Access to non-agricultural jobs and subsequent gains in income were also powerfully affected by wartime military experience, as vast numbers of African Americans left low paying seasonal agricultural jobs in rural areas for higher wages in the military industries of the North and West.[38] For large numbers of African Americans, the result was new opportunities for economic affluence, which in turn encouraged rising expectations.

Even after the great migration, African Americans continued to be a considerable presence in the South; over two-thirds of all African Americans still resided there.[39] But the rapid population displacement that brought African Americans to the North in record numbers dramatically changed their lives. More people were crowded together in cities, exacerbating existing housing shortages and competition for jobs, while adding tension to the situation of poorer whites, who were most likely to be displaced from their jobs or squeezed into poorer accommodations. Although not as systematically enforced, segregation was still part of the lives of African Americans. Theresa Lyons remembered a detail regarding those restrictions in everyday life: "You could only buy Pepsi. You could buy Pepsi, but you could not buy Coke. If you go in a store and ask for Coke, they will reach in there and give you Pepsi. They only sold Cokes to white folks."[40]

World War II intensified the population migration that had begun decades before and increased the concentration of African Americans, usually in the poorest parts of urban centers. The patterns of unbending racial exclusion that characterized the early twentieth century continued throughout the mobilization of 1940 and 1941. At first, there was high demand for white workers, while black workers were excluded from all but the most menial jobs. The new opportunities for whites did not immediately include blacks.[41] Morale at all levels in the black community plummeted as a result. Only as the manpower crisis intensified after military commitments siphoned away white laborers were African Americans considered as replacements.

A survey, reported in the October 19, 1942, issue of the *Wall Street Journal*, revealed that a "driving need for manpower in war industries is slowly wearing away the barriers against full and efficient use of Negro labor. But it is a ponderous process."[42] The same survey concluded that employment of African Americans was rising, particularly in Eastern and Pacific Coast industrial sectors. Maggie Dulin, who grew up in rural Kentucky, recalls that World War II brought opportunities never before available to women, black and white. It afforded her and her family an unexpected opportunity for financial gain and social advancement. Many African Americans traced the dramatic difference in their everyday lives to the war.[43]

Charles S. Johnson, editor of the National Urban League's *Opportunity* magazine, published a survey of three hundred industrial plants that together employed nearly half of the workers in Baltimore. The study reiterated the reasons African Americans faced discrimination in the workplace. Among those factors was the traditional definition of some jobs as Negro jobs. In addition, white laborers cost more and tended to avoid the disagreeable and physically challenging work reserved for African Americans. Results of the Baltimore survey were representative of the larger national labor problem, which relegated African Americans to poor jobs and poor working conditions, often without the protection of unions.[44]

Increasing Racial Hostility

The period prior to World War I, from 1890 to 1914, has been branded the "Vale of Tears." Unprecedented mob violence and acts of terrorism perpetrated against black citizens accompanied the vast migration of African Americans into Northern cities. Their presence impacted whites in social and economic ways that only increased hostility. Between 1885 and 1915, more than thirty-five hundred African Americans were victims of mobs;

in 1892 alone, 235 African Americans were lynched in their communities.[45] During this same period, the philosophy of social Darwinism and other pseudoscientific interpretations of race were popular. These theories confirmed the inherent inequality of the races, the superiority of Nordic blood, and the urgent need to safeguard racial purity. Books such as *The Negro a Beast* by Charles Carroll (1900); William P. Calhoun's *The Caucasian and the Negro* (1902); Thomas Dixon's *The Leopard's Spots* (1902); William B. Smith's *The Color Line* (1905); Robert Shufeldt's *The Negro: A Menace to American Civilization* (1907); Madison Grant's *The Passing of the Great Race* (1916); and *The Rising Tide of Color against White World Supremacy* (1921) by Lothorp Stoddard were widely read. These publications shared similar themes: race and heredity were the guiding determinants of history, and the dilution of the white race by darker races would result in the destruction of Western civilization.

More than twenty race riots in the "Red Summer of 1919" terrified city dwellers, both African Americans and whites, who responded with retaliatory violence. Soldiers returning from European battlefields produced new competition for jobs, housing, and urban facilities. The resulting pressures spilled over into racial violence, which foreshadowed the racially motivated violence that characterized World War II.

Racial attitudes also prompted tensions throughout World War II. In 1943, the Social Science Institute at Fisk University counted 242 riots in forty-seven cities. Sixty-eight deaths occurred in the 1943 Detroit protests alone.[46] Charles E. Silberman points out that, prompted by rising expectations and close quarters, African Americans increasingly replaced their fear of whites with anger. He states, "The turning point was World War II. A war fought in the name of the Four Freedoms, but managed so as to preserve segregation, was bound to increase the American Negro's already ample store of hate."[47] Service in the military only fueled the cynicism and discontent of African Americans, who viewed themselves as second-class soldiers. Silberman concludes, "World War II also destroyed whatever illusion American Negroes may have retained about white sincerity, about white Americans' willingness to grant them equality."[48] Proof of their second-class military status was everywhere–in separate recreation facilities, in segregated blood banks—as African American soldiers watched Nazi prisoners of war ride with white soldiers and eat with them in the same railroad dining cars.

Knowledge of racial conflict was not widespread among civilians because the military leadership systematically suppressed news of racial confrontations. Some awareness of racial tension was disclosed in the black press through eyewitness reports. Although official statistics were not available, accounts of lynchings were also reported. The general tone of black newspapers reflected an awareness of racial violence even in the absence of official details. For example, the *Chicago Defender* adopted as its wartime slogan, "Remember Pearl Harbor and Sikeston Too," with reference to the lynching of Theo Wright in Sikeston, Missouri, a few weeks after the Japanese attack at Pearl Harbor. But it was difficult to document the extent of racial violence, because all but the most flagrant riots were ignored, reclassified, or not disclosed through official sources. Race related deaths in the United States that took place under suspicious circumstances were often listed as motor vehicle accidents. Overseas, it was a simple matter to report such deaths as combat casualties.[49]

Whites, by contrast, largely felt that the social order was justified, that African Americans were at the bottom of society because they either were biologically inferior or lacked the resolve to better their condition. In either case, surveys of whites suggest that 60 percent or more believed in the social hierarchy as it existed.[50] Such attitudes absolved whites of guilt and required no action to address the inequities. African Americans, they felt, deserved their status, not because of anything white society had done, but because of black inferiority. This viewpoint left the responsibility for their plight squarely on the shoulders of African Americans. In fact, many whites, particularly in the South, felt that change was impossible because of the inherent nature of the black race.[51] They did not question the separate but equal doctrine enunciated in the *Plessey v. Ferguson* decision, although some were concerned that their naïveté made blacks easy targets for agitators demanding integration, an issue that offended many white Americans. Any sign of inclusion was considered "a cruel disillusionment, bearing the germs of strife and perhaps a tragedy."[52]

Setting the stage for the racial turmoil of the 1940s was perhaps the single biggest demographic change in American history, the migration of millions of African Americans from the South to the North, from rural to urban centers, and from agriculture to industry. While the northward migration picked up speed during the Depression, the war greatly accelerated the population shift by expanding industrial production and creating a labor shortage that gave African Americans an opportunity to move into industry.[53] Concentrated in urban centers as a consequence of migration, African Americans were well positioned to organize and protest their condition.[54] Some historians argue that their experience in the military, particularly more equal treatment abroad during World War I, allowed African

Americans to glimpse the promises of equality and organize to pursue it.[55] The crisis of World War II was the catalyst whereby race would increase its presence in American consciousness, and ultimately, transform the topography of the nation.

The roots of racial conflict lay in the wartime experiences of Americans. Some clung to the rigid segregation of Southern society reproduced in American institutions like the military, while others demanded the civil rights that military service ensured. Heralding the racial conflict of the 1960s, Gunnar Myrdal's *An American Dilemma* identified race as the issue most likely to shape and perplex future generations. His 1938 comprehensive study of sociological, economic, anthropological, and legal data in the United States characterized the problem of race relations as a dilemma, because of a perceived conflict between the high ideals of the American creed and the inadequate implementation of those ideals in everyday living. Since the end of the Civil War, fully a tenth of the population had not participated in the realization of human rights.

Rigid Segregation

Because they believed that American commitment to preserving social segregation was more important than achieving Roosevelt's four freedoms, many African Americans were demoralized. With the exception of liberty ships in the merchant marine, all branches of the armed forces remained strictly segregated from boot camp to the front lines. When African Americans inducted into the military discovered even more severe segregation than they had known as civilians, tensions escalated.[56] They were banned from most white post facilities—USOs, canteens, theaters, post exchanges, service clubs, buses, and chapels. Separate blood banks and hospital wards were established for African Americans.[57] Facilities for blacks were uniformly substandard, inadequately funded, and poorly maintained. The similarity between United States policies of racial segregation and Nazi plans for an Aryan race was clear to anyone living under restrictions.[58]

The result should not have surprised anyone: "It had become apparent to African Americans both within the military and in the general public that the government's recruitment efforts stopped far short of full inclusion in all activities of the armed forces . . . segregation on army bases exceeded that prevalent over most of the United States."[59] At the same time, white citizens and soldiers found the African American presence intolerable. Harassment, hate strikes, beatings, lynchings, and murders of African American soldiers escalated, reaching a peak in the 1943 race riots and requiring a federal response because they presaged another American civil war.

Low African American Morale

Pervasive animosity toward African Americans and lack of economic or military opportunities served as primary causes of low morale.[60] According to historian Lawrence Samuel, "African Americans' attitudes toward the war reflected the complex relationship between their national and racial identities."[61] Overall, African Americans were highly patriotic, but they grew increasingly hostile as racial violence and discrimination flourished. The black press widely disseminated articles recounting soldiers' experiences of exclusion in World War I.[62] In 1940 more than 150 black newspapers had a combined circulation of four million readers, and provided a vital alternative source of information for African Americans, who had been entirely ignored by mainstream news sources.[63] The African American press reflected readers' low morale and dissatisfaction and, at the same time, contributed to those feelings.

At the beginning of the war expectations about military service were high, but opinions changed rapidly as reports of harassment and discrimination filtered back home from those in uniform. In a letter to Secretary of War Roy Wilkins, the editor of a major black newspaper, the *Crisis*, expressed the widespread reversal in sentiment and warning, "There is a unanimity of opinion among all classes in all sections of the country," regarding abusive treatment of African Americans in the armed forces.[64] The War Department blamed the Negro press for low morale among African Americans, going so far as banning these newspapers on military posts.[65] The bans only served to reinforce the belief that complaints were justified, and black newspapers continued routinely to denounce government policies and actions.

As racial violence heightened, initial expectations for full military participation were replaced with bitterness grounded in military discrimination.[66] According to the results of army research, the majority of African American troops opposed segregation in military services. The majority of white troops, on the other hand, regarded segregation as a necessity.[67] The navy received the brunt of the black anger, possibly because navy policy regarding racial matters was particularly insulting.[68] It allowed black sailors to serve only as mess hall attendants. To compound matters, after a series of racial incidents in late 1940, the navy issued a statement upholding its treatment of black sailors. A backlash ensued, and "in practically every issue of the Negro press during 1940 there were articles or editorials condemning the Navy's racial policy."[69]

While the total number of African Americans serving in the army steadily increased, the number of black combat troops declined in spite of heavy enemy engagement and the need for frontline troops. In March 1944, Congressman Hamilton Fish asked Secretary of War Henry L. Stimson why black troops were not more suitably utilized. Stimson's reply that most African American recruits were too poorly educated to master modern weaponry provoked an outcry from African Americans. Articles in black newspapers headlined "Too Dumb to Fight" proclaimed the incredulity of the African American community, which was stunned by the secretary's comments. Stimson's comment weakened the morale of African Americans, unifying them as nothing else had previously done.[70] Subsequent Office of War Information surveys revealed, "Resentment at Negro discrimination is fairly widespread throughout the Negro population."[71] Other surveys reflected African American awareness that if they volunteered to fight, they fought to protect freedoms they did not fully share.[72] Once victory was attained, many African Americans did not foresee changes in their status, in spite of the promise that the war was being fought for freedom everywhere and the four freedoms at home articulated by President Roosevelt.

Black Leadership

Religion has always been a potent force among African Americans, from its early role as solace for slaves, to its more militant posture in the twentieth century. Between 1890 and the onset of World War II, black religion prospered in many forms.[73] Among scholars who have examined the powerful influence of the church in African American life, Stanley High explains part of the reason for its prominence: "He goes, because in church, more than anywhere else, he is in a world that uniquely and altogether belongs to him."[74] It is not surprising, then, that leadership often emerged from the African American church, as many black leaders received their activist training while sitting in pews on Sunday mornings.

There were popular heroes as well.[75] Thousands of African American men and women rallied around the heroic figures of Dorie Miller and Joe

Louis, who fought back with guns and fists. In much the same way, Frederick Douglass and A. Philip Randolph battled for African Americans with words on political fronts. And, although their progress lagged far behind whites, black factory workers who had made some economic gains during the period before World War II contributed to a swelling mass of Americans with heightened expectations. But wartime jobs were offered primarily to white workers, and African American hopes were soon dashed, deepening the feelings of frustration and relative depravation.[76] This pattern was simply a repeated earlier cycles of gains and losses by African Americans, whose progress during periods of economic prosperity was erased during the inevitable downturns. Historically, African Americans, who were mostly unskilled laborers, were more vulnerable to economic cycles than whites. Just a few years earlier, gains made during the brief period of World War I prosperity were nullified by the Great Depression. Still, African Americans entered World War II anticipating that they would benefit from wartime industrial expansion.

Lester Granger, executive secretary of the National Urban League, advocated greater job opportunities for African Americans, pointing out attitudes and policies in war industries that prevented their employment. He claimed that the African American labor force constituted a huge untapped pool of semi-skilled, skilled, and white-collar laborers. During the period between the wars, African Americans had made headway in acquiring the skills necessary to perform well in many parts of the mechanical and industrial trades, but they were not generally integrated into the general labor market. African Americans lacked sophisticated institutional protections. They were organized in separate, less powerful labor unions, they were employed locally by small firms, and they were generally paid on a lower scale than comparable white workers. In times of economic downturn, black Americans generally suffered more severe economic repercussions than whites.[77]

Impediments to employment existed at the institutional level. Federal, state, and private sector regulations prohibited the employment of African Americans. More than 75 percent of war manufacturers did not hire and blacks; 15 percent hired them but only for menial jobs. For example, North American Aviation explicitly refused to hire any African Americans, "regardless of their training as aircraft workers" because doing so is "against company policy."[78] Standard Steel Corporation took pride in its all white work force for twenty-five years, noting that it did not intend to hire any blacks. Vultee Aircraft did not have a single black employee among its work force of six thousand. And there were only ten African Americans among the thirty-three thousand workers employed by Douglas Aircraft Company. Wilma Woods reported that Northern Pump Company in Minneapolis, where she worked manufacturing field artillery and ordnance during the war, never hired a black worker despite chronic labor shortages and a ready pool of qualified African Americans.[79] Many African Americans shared their experiences, recalling that while they qualified for jobs, they were denied employment because of restrictions on hiring black workers. One man who scored highest in a group taking a postal exam, and who had prior experience as a military mail carrier, was not hired because he was black.[80] Federal jobs for African Americans were as elusive as those in the private sector.

Official employment policies in the public and private sectors usually prohibited hiring outside the Caucasian race. And, in spite of Executive Order 8802 prohibiting discrimination based on race in war industries, the federal government did not withhold contracts or otherwise penalize companies that did not comply. The executive order had limited impact until the shortage of workers became severe enough to force the defense industry to begin hiring blacks in order to maintain production.[81] At the beginning of the war, only 3 percent of defense industry workers were black; by November 1944 black workers accounted for 8.3 percent of the defense industry.[82] The impact on black women was even more dramatic, increasing employment from 6.5 percent to 18 percent by the end of the war. Concomitantly, the number of black women working as domestics declined from 60 to 45 percent. One woman concluded, "Hitler was the one that got us out of the white folks' kitchen."[83]

These racially based restrictions were replicated in the military service assignments. Henry Hooten, a black American soldier stationed at a British army base, was restricted to driving trucks and heavy labor. At best, with some education he could have been a company clerk. Segregation was so complete that he did not see white soldiers until his first leave.[84] Betty Young, who served four years in the women's army corps, never saw a black soldier during her entire enlistment.[85] Even well educated African Americans and those with specialized skills were subject to complete segregation. Surgeon General Magee of the United States told members of the National Medical Association in 1941 that African American doctors, dentists, and nurses would never be assigned to any post where they might encounter white patients. Considering this decision, the scene in *Pearl Harbor* (2001) where a white nurse treats a wounded black sailor is pure Hollywood fantasy. It reflects its contemporary context, but not the reality of World War II.

Influence of African American Organizations

In 1939 three national African American groups were prominent: the National Association for the Advancement of Colored People, the National Urban League, and the National Negro Congress. The NAACP was the largest, and consequently the most influential of the organizations, growing from eighty-five thousand to 530,000 members during the war. The NAACP focused on legal and educational activities, mainly appealing to middle-class, white collar African Americans. The National Urban League, a small social service agency generously funded by white philanthropists, relied on compromise and conciliation to achieve its objectives. The National Negro Congress began as a coalition of approximately five hundred civil rights and church groups. It gradually moved to the left during World War II.

African American organizations often held the national political parties accountable for their circumstances. Under a pen name, J. R. Johnson wrote in the *Socialist Appeal*, "I am not afraid to fight.... But the democracy that I want to fight for, Hitler is not depriving me of.... tell us why we must go on shedding our blood for something that we've never had.... But who are the aggressors against the Negroes? Hitler? Nonsense. The Southerners of the Democratic Party are the greatest aggressors against the Negroes in American history, and the North is not far behind them."[86] Others pointed out that Roosevelt's protest to Hitler over Nazi treatment of the Jews was met by Hitler's retort about American treatment of the Negro. The hypocrisy of the United States protesting on behalf of Jews while practicing racial discrimination at home was frequently cited by African American organizations.

African American organizations also championed specific causes. The horror of lynching was foremost among their grievances. The first bill providing punishment for lynching was introduced in Congress in 1919. It failed. Similar bills were repeatedly introduced in her period before World War II, but none were enacted. It was widely known among African Americans that President Roosevelt spoke out in one instance against the hanging of a fascist by irate Italian workers, but that he completely ignored the lynchings of dozens of African Americans. This duplicity was just one symptom of the insincerity of federal promises to deal with discrimination. In explaining why they should oppose the war, J. R. Johnson articulated the feelings of other blacks when he concluded, "But no, large masses of Negroes have no wish to support this war. Their memories of the last war and a great deception and fraud which were practiced on them are too vivid in their minds."[87] Envisioning victory, Albert Parker wrote in June 1943 that African Americans should think about the war and their lives "after it comes to an end."[88]

President Roosevelt was aware, at some level, of African American dissatisfaction, the latent power held by black organizations, and the potential for the enemy to exploit it. In a letter to Representative Marcantonio of New York written during the last week of July 1943, President Roosevelt stated, "The recent outbreaks of violence in widely scattered parts of the country endanger our national unity and comfort our enemies."[89] And even though many African Americans did not take part in rioting, their attitudes might contribute to stalling or collapsing the war effort. In a 1942 poll of black New Yorkers, for example, more than two thirds of the respondents thought that a Japanese victory would not substantially change their status.[90] The War Department was alarmed by the potential for African Americans to destabilize the national cause, making victory impossible. In the 1940 presidential election, the black vote was needed to ensure reelection for President Roosevelt. To build support among the black community, Roosevelt made a number of concessions close to election day. He ordered the formation of black aviation and army combat units. He added an anti-discrimination clause to the 1940 Selective Service Act. He promoted Colonel Benjamin O. Davis Sr., to brigadier general to make him the highest-ranking black officer in military history. And he appointed William Hastie advisor for Negro Affairs and assistant to the secretary of war. These gestures were successful in mustering black voters.

Roosevelt skirted concessions that would probably have driven white voters into the Republican camp. In protest, Hastie resigned in January 1943. His reasons, published in the *Crisis*, were tied to the "reactionary policies and discriminatory practices" of the United States military forces.[91] President Roosevelt reacted by adding several high profile African Americans to his staff, and signing an executive order to include African Americans in the defense industry. In addition, to encourage black Americans to support the war effort, his administration authorized the production and distribution of several films sponsored by the signal corps, Department of Agriculture, and private industry.

CHAPTER NINE

The Influence of the Black Press

At no time has the colored soldier been shown as a man.
—LESTER WALTON, *NEW YORK AGE*[1]

The black press reached the pinnacle of its influence during World War II. The themes that surfaced in black owned and operated newspapers and magazines eventually found an audience among the majority of white Americans, but only after they appeared in popular films like *The Negro Soldier* and *The Negro Sailor*. Until then, the black press was virtually the only source of support for civil rights that transcended local communities and churches. Because it gave credence to arguments favoring civil rights and revealed a national groundswell of support for integration, the black press was a critical component of change. Initially, its readership was almost exclusively black, but eventually the voices of African Americans were heard in the dominant culture through film.

From 1940 through 1945, black owned and operated newspapers and magazines were central to opinion formation in the black community.[2] They touched the lives of many Americans in one fashion or another, solidifying the newly emerged African American identity. The treatment of African American topics in the black press in the 1930s reflected dramatic changes from the accommodationist attitudes exemplified by leaders like Booker T. Washington around the turn of the century and the emerging racial consciousness and black identity of more activist black leadership in the 1920s and 1930s.[3]

There are several reasons for the escalating influence of the African American press. There were no black owned radio stations, the only other widely available news medium of the period. Newsreels and documentary shorts were distributed mainly through white theaters. Even when they were shown in black theaters, such films only reviewed a limited range of subjects, mostly representing government interests. Among white owned newspapers and radio stations, the majority of the news media, representations of African Americans were limited, and stereotyped blacks appeared as criminals, athletes, or troublemakers.[4] Most African American adults disregarded white media, reading black newspapers for information about the war that directly affected them. White editors, who considered the black press irrelevant, did not often glean stories for re-publication in the white press. As a result, black and white news sources distributed divergent reports as well as overall attitudes toward the war.

Almost without exception, black newspapers conducted a relentless crusade to insure equal participation in the armed services and zealously exposed instances of discrimination. Unlike the accommodationist position of the press during World War I urging readers to "close ranks," the black press served a gadfly function in World War II.[5] The editorial stance of most papers deviated considerably from the World War I call for closed ranks. Even William Calvin Chase, editor of the more moderate *Washington Bee*, often became impatient at the slow pace of change. Sometimes Chase's frustration with the hypocrisy of national policy erupted in editorial comments like this one: "The Negro is willing today to take up arms and defend the American flag. . . . His mother, sister, brother, and children are being burned at the stake and yet the American flag is his emblem and which he stands ready to defend."[6] There were few voices asking readers to wait patiently for future federal action to redress social wrongs until victory was secured.

Black newspapers acted as watchdogs, reporting cases of discrimination and general troop deployment, in addition to providing a unified set of policy demands. Home front segregation was less an issue than discrimination within the segregated military. Throughout the war, the black press called for an end to discrimination and the pursuit of equality in the service. As editorial writers pointed out in numerous African American newspapers, "Negro engineers" is a euphemism for labor battalions, Negro cavalry regiments muck out the stalls of officers' horses, and navy sailors are mess men who wait tables. Throughout the war, the black press echoed the refrain of previous wars, that the right to fight would determine postwar civilian rights. Caught up in the system of segregation, the black press, like much of the community it represented, denounced the effects of discrimination, but avoided demands to dismantle segregation. Military historian Lee Finkle points out the ultimate impact of this opinion leadership: "If we seek the roots of the 'black revolution' of the 1960s in the World War II era, a study must be made of the black masses, not their leaders. There were, indeed, stirrings among the black people. Anger and resentment often led to open conflict and widespread racial violence."[7] At the conclusion of the war, black editors became increasingly belligerent in their call for an end to segregated military units. The shift in grassroots attitudes among African Americans, expressed and reinforced through their newspapers, finally boiled over into the protests of the 1960s. This chapter will examine the scope of the influence exerted by the black press—especially in the formation of black identity—as well as its contributions to public attitudes, prevalent themes, and government responses.

The Scope of Influence

The power of the black press was apparent in its direct impact on behavior and in the scope of its readership. Newspapers such as the *Chicago Defender* focused on their large Southern audiences and emphasized job opportunities in the North, probably contributing substantially to the movement of blacks northward.[8] The black press also cultivated hope for the future, which drove thousands of African Americans to seek greater financial rewards and better their situations.

But circulation figures explain the potency of the black press more directly. In the period before the war, there were more than 230 papers with circulations (approximately 1,406,800) equaling about one-third of all African Americans. Circulation of black newspapers increased 40 percent during the first months of World War II, "functioning primarily to foster race solidarity and prod increasing militancy . . . by publicizing America's Jim Crow policies and practices."[9] Circulation numbers are vastly underestimated because newspapers were often read in black community settings like barbershops and church gatherings. One newspaper might circulate among five or six readers. While pockets of illiteracy still dotted black communities, the black press was respected. Groups would gather in community sites to hear papers like the *Crisis* read aloud. Heated disputes often followed.[10] And these discussions influenced other marginalized groups, such as the communist press. The communist *Daily Worker*, for example, framed many issues as a class struggle between blacks and whites, echoing the stance of black newspapers.[11]

Prior to the turn of the century, the black press was small and exerted relatively little influence among the often illiterate, rural black population. Newspapers lacked a concentrated urban audience and focused on an exclusive readership of literate African Americans. The first black newspaper, *Freedom's Journal*, published in 1827, helped to define black identity in the

Civil War era and bring the community together, but it never achieved national readership.[12] Relatively small at the beginning of World War I, black newspapers grew rapidly in circulation and influence. By 1919, increasingly strident black publications expressed cynicism about a fight for democracy that did not guarantee freedom for African American citizens after the war. Overall, the press focused its denunciations on specific issues affecting the black community, rather than attacking the system of discrimination that produced those problems. For example, black newspapers spotlighted the horrors of lynching, which increased from thirtyofive in 1917 to sixty in 1918. While mainstream publications considered it unpatriotic to make lynching an issue during wartime, black journalists saw nothing incongruous in criticizing injustice while supporting the war effort. This attitude persisted after the war, partially because postwar lynchings and other attacks on African Americans did not abate. By 1926, a rapidly growing minority press was probably the community's single greatest political force, a potent voice for African Americans and a powerful platform for black leaders.

Between 1919 and 1921, spurred by federal concerns and military complaints, the army's Military Intelligence branch, the Post Office, and the Bureau of Investigation actively investigated black journalists. From 1919 to 1921, Attorney General A. Mitchell Palmer pursued radicals and government critics, many of them African American journalists. His office harassed black editors, conducted secret surveillance of black journalists, held up second class bulk mailings of African American newspapers, interviewed subscribers, compiled reports on the content of articles, and publicly attacked the black press, claiming that it appealed to ignorant readers and openly deceived patriotic readers. This pattern of suspicion and investigation by official branches of government established a precedent that was followed during the early years of World War II.

By 1942 economic conditions had changed for black newspapers. Until that point they had predominantly depended on circulation for operating revenue. While white newspapers made money from corporate advertising, black newspapers did not attract advertisers. However, new federal taxes aimed at curtailing wartime excess profits encouraged American companies to begin advertising regularly in some of the larger black newspapers in order to protect their profit margins. So as to avoid jeopardizing this fresh source of income, black newspapers took a more conservative stance on issues. In some ways, Philip Morris, Pepsi Cola, Pabst Blue Ribbon, Esso, and Seagrams more effectively curtailed the criticism of the black press than any agency of the federal government did. With this new revenue stream, black newspapers flourished at the same time subscription numbers were skyrocketing. With an estimated 147,847 subscribers, the *Pittsburg Courier* had the largest wartime circulation of any black newspaper, followed by the *Baltimore Afro-American* (78,120), the *Chicago Defender* (46,000), and the *Norfolk (VA) Journal and Guide* (26,087).[13]

In addition, the *Negro Digest* began publishing in Chicago in late 1942, achieving one of the highest circulations of any black magazine. Modeled after *Reader's Digest*, it offered pieces condensed from other print sources. Other news sources like the *Crisis*, founded by W. E. B. Du Bois in 1910, reported activities of the National Association for the Advancement of Colored People throughout both world wars. Circulation of the *Crisis* increased dramatically, from seven thousand to forty-five thousand between 1940 and 1944 under the editorship of Roy Wilkins. *Opportunity*, sponsored by the National Urban League, began publishing in 1923, but reached much wider audiences during the war. Together, the *Crisis* and *Opportunity* boasted the highest circulations and longest life of any African American print sources. The quality of their reporting was also considered outstanding.[14]

The hunger for news about African American interests is evident from the soaring circulation figures of black newspapers. Black newspapers also expressed attitudes that were not present in mainstream newspapers. The tradition of militant reporting on issues like discriminatory employment practices and lynching "carried over to include criticism of the federal government for allowing the unfair treatment of black military personnel during World War I."[15] The *Chicago Defender* was probably the most influential newspaper during the era of the great northward migration through the end of World War I. But by the spring of 1942, its influence was overtaken by that of the *Pittsburgh Courier*, whose circulation surpassed all other Negro newspapers in the country. In the early months of the war, the *Pittsburgh Courier*, "began a militancy that propelled that newspaper to a circulation count no other black newspaper had ever before obtained."[16] Such aggressive coverage resonated with its audience.

Contributions of the African American Press

The critical contribution of the African American press during World War II was providing alternative viewpoints to counter the monolithic negative stereotypes dominating white publications. Black leaders were often featured in the black press when they could not get a hearing in the mainstream press. Adam Clayton Powell, Roi Ottley, and Charles Himes protested the Jim Crow army in the pages of black newspapers. In contrast, the white press often reported the failures of black troops, and suppressed or ignored their successes.[17] This pattern of negative representation had persisted since World War I. Possibly the most egregious example followed the heroic actions of the 367th, 369th, 370th, 371st, and 372nd black regiments, which resulted in awards of the Croix de Guerre for bravery under fire. Two privates from these regiments, Henry Johnson and Needham Roberts, were cited for bravery, yet their accomplishments went unreported by the mainstream press. With few exceptions, white media contributed to stereotypes of African American inferiority or completely ignored their presence in American culture. African American journalists were excluded from official sources of information. When news about African Americans was reported, it did not reach the white press.[18] In essence, two segregated print media operated in the United States.

When they were not neglected altogether, African Americans appearing mainstream media were represented almost entirely negatively. Maureen Honey describes the unrelenting oppression of the negative images of both black men and black women when she writes, "Racist stereotypes in film, radio, popular magazines, and other forms of white entertainment distorted African American life, when blacks were not ignored altogether."[19] At a time when African American men were largely ignored by mainstream media and political institutions, African American women were invisible. They comprised the bulk of African Americans employed in wartime industries and performed valuable support services in the military. The relatively few black men who were mentioned in mainstream media projected an image for all African Americans. Black military units were held up as examples of their race, for good or ill. As journalist Frank E. Bolden noted in his column "From the Grapevine," "I sometimes wonder if the men who are serving in this combat unit are aware of the great responsibility that rests upon their shoulders . . . the magnitude of responsibility and the opportunities that this Colored army unit affords." [20] Black newspapers and magazines provided an alternative to mainstream press coverage and, in doing so, allowed a broader range of representation. Still, white readers rarely encountered these depictions.

Perhaps the most widely known case that illustrates the racial weighting of mainstream press coverage was the story of Dorie Miller, who carried his wounded captain to safety, then shot down four enemy aircraft. Black reporters had to badger the navy for twelve weeks to get steward Dorie

Miller's name.[21] His heroism was widely reported in the black press but completely ignored by mainstream newspapers, which only reported black cowardice on the battlefield, in spite of evidence to the contrary.[22]

Dorie Miller's story added vigor to the complaint that blacks were allowed only to serve as mess boys, not as fighting men.[23] The *Pittsburgh Courier* asked, "Is it fair, honest or sensible that this country, with its fate in the balance, should continue to bar Negroes from service except in the mess department of the Navy, when at the first sign of danger they so dramatically showed their willingness to face death in defense of the Stars and Stripes?"[24] Dorie Miller became a well-known figure among African Americans because of reporters' perseverance His cause was advanced by black newspapers, which advocated for him to receive the Congressional Medal of Honor. Eventually Miller received the Navy Cross, the highest award in his service branch, but only because the black press had pressed his case.

This pattern of withholding information and obstructing access to information persisted and compounded problems for the black press. Even when they were able to obtain information, black newspapers were read almost exclusively by African Americans, and their stories were not picked up by white newspaper. Consequently, positive accounts of African Americans rarely reached whites. The black press persisted in expending energy to get even basic information to report to its readers. The dribble of information from official white sources functioned as a form of indirect control over the content of the black papers. Many papers were forced to tap readers for firsthand accounts to verify claims and provide substance for articles. Letters to the editor often complained about the lack of information about the performance of black troops. There is some evidence that, alarmed by the depth of blacks' anger about their treatment in the military, editors tempered the expressions of hatred they published.[25] Even so, government leaders accused black publications of subversion.[26]

Black newspapers and magazines consolidated their voices, thus magnifying their power by organizing nationally through the National Negro Publishing Association, which became active in 1940. The association expressed concern over a variety of issues that affected their members' readership, particularly naval recruitment (African Americans numbered only 2,807 out of 116,000 sailors at the end of 1939); the total exclusion of blacks from the marine corps and coast guard; discrimination in employment practices; and limited recognition of African American contributions to past American conflicts.[27] Under the auspices of the association, editors convened and discussed critical issues, sharing convictions and priorities.

For many editors, the government's refusal to honor its World War I promises resulted in militancy fueled by distrust and disappointment and circulated among black communities by journalists.

Hopes for greater opportunities for African Americans were high at the beginning of the war. However, as it became increasingly clear that discrimination was continuing or even worsening owing to the segregation policies of the military services and defense industries, the morale of Negroes across the country began to sag. In the first month of the war, newspapers recognized the problems that stemmed from this disillusionment and responded by calling for readers to win the home front war against inequality.[28] At the end of January 1942, the *Pittsburg Courier* published the following editorial comment by James G. Thompson: "The V for victory sign is being displayed prominently in all so-called democratic countries which are fighting for victory over aggression, slavery, and tyranny. Let we colored Americans adopt the double V for a double victory. The first V for victory over our enemies from without, the second V for victory over our enemies from within."[29] Capitalizing on Thompson's sentiments, the *Pittsburgh Courier* launched its "Double V" campaign in its next issue. The success of the campaign was staggering, and "The government once again became concerned that such a campaign might result in a refusal of Negroes to support the war effort at the very moment when support was most needed."[30] This alarm was probably exacerbated by the circulation spike occurring across the country, as black readers purchased papers to read about the campaign. The *Pittsburgh Courier* reported sales of 270,812, the *Baltimore Afro-American* 229,812, the *Chicago Defender* 161,009, and the *Norfolk (VA) Journal and Guide* 77,462. This massive circulation jump encouraged the press to initiate another round of charges about racial discrimination. Editor P. L. Prattis summarized their demands: "If the Washington gentry are eager to see Negro morale take an upturn, they have only to abolish jim crowism and lower the color bar in every field and phase of American life."[31]

The "Double V" campaign unified black leadership within the United States in principle, if not in practice. The campaign aimed at securing victory on two fronts: abroad and at home. One day after the Pearl Harbor attack, the NAACP board of directors met and pledged, "Though thirteen million American Negroes have more often than not been denied democracy, they are American citizens and will as in every war give unqualified support to the protection of their country. At the same time we shall not abate one iota our struggle for full citizenship rights here in the United States. We will fight but we demand the right to fight as equals in every branch of military, naval and aviation service."[32] Solidarity was communicated quickly in the *Crisis* and other newspapers. These sentiments captured the essence of the "Double V" campaign and the core issues facing black citizens at the beginning of the war. As Alan Osur concludes, "It is obvious that by 1942 a black consciousness had evolved and was an important factor in pressuring for social change."[33] It provided one of the most coherent responses to the socio-economic deprivation of African Americans, and the black press was critical in facilitating this campaign.

But black conservatives favoring accommodation also raised their voices, arguing that demands for racial advances should be postponed until victory was achieved abroad. John Temple Graves observed, "More and more there is growing an appreciation of the fact that domestic crusades which mean a division in the face of the enemy are suicidal and that the so-called Double V (for victory over enemies abroad and over enemies at home) is really a Double X, a double crossing of hopes for the very arena in which domestic crusades are waged."[34] This faction, represented in Graves's comments, urged restraint on domestic issues but solidarity behind national military goals.

The issue of racial equality focused, some felt, on the South, because African Americans constituted an overwhelming percentage of the population there. But if the issue of racial equality was forced, especially in the South, it might stimulate further hate, fear, and violence, ultimately dissipating the energy that could be more profitably spent pursuing military victory. These advocates pointed to advances for African Americans in education, citing the increased numbers of black high schools and colleges; in business, citing African American business assets growth; and the rapid decline in lynchings, now numbering only in single digits compared to the hundreds of lynchings that took place in the early decades of the twentieth century. To achieve both victory abroad and an easing of racial tensions domestically, Graves urged his readers to agree that "The Negro needs much and is promised much but there is no hope for him unless he gets along with the white men of the South."[35]

Within a month of the announcement of the "Double V" campaign, the *Pittsburgh Courier* was printing more than 340 column inches per issue on the campaign, about 8 percent of its available news space. Several months later, coverage of the campaign constituted 13 percent of the paper. Telegrams and letters poured in from supportive readers, who expressed their anger at their status as second-class citizens. Military officials blamed the presence of black newspapers in military camps for hostilities between black and white soldiers, which often erupted in physical confrontation and riots.³⁶

Themes in Black Newspapers

The black press was denied access to many of the official sources of information during the early years of the war, hampering coverage of news. In the face of these restrictions, reporters relied on readers for firsthand accounts and located other unorthodox sources for information. Letters from soldiers were important to the black press, which explains why this device was exploited in *The Negro Soldier*. Letters home were subject to censorship, and reports about the morale of soldiers writing these letters were filed. Government officials also tapped letters published in black newspapers to identify common complains and to monitor morale among the troops.³⁷ Morale varied, but race was a common denominator in determining it. Letters reprinted in the black press became an important source of news about the war because black journalists were barred from most government sources of war information. Private correspondence was a key feature in most newspaper reporting, and news gleaned in this fashion was considered credible by readers because it conveyed attitudes about the war and living conditions in the military, topics commonly ignored by censors. In view of government censorship and limited war news, these letters became an important source of news about the war.

The case of fifteen black sailors, all mess attendants on the USS *Philadelphia*, received considerable attention from readers who wrote letters to their newspapers. Ironically, the men were arrested, imprisoned, and faced court-martial because they wrote a letter to the *Pittsburgh Courier* complaining about Jim Crow conditions. Their mistake was to sign the letter, an act of courage heralded by some, but condemned by the navy. The letter, printed on October 5, 1940, warned others who would enlist that in the navy they would all become "sea-going bell hops, chambermaids and dishwashers."³⁸ During the following weeks, the case of the imprisoned sailors generated letters of protest, demonstrations, and general agitation by aroused African Americans. The NAACP protested to Secretary of the Navy Frank Knox. Newspapers published open letters to President Roosevelt and Secretary Knox asking for an immediate end to the confinement of the Negro sailors. Hundreds of protesters were arrested as the situation reinforced the negative image of the navy that prevailed in the African American community.

In order to maintain a veneer of unity, the federal government discouraged coverage of racial disturbances by both black and white press. Government offices believed that if information about the extent of racial disturbances reached either military or civilian readers, an increase in rioting would ensue. Their concerns were probably justified, although rioting escalated in 1943 despite their efforts. The Office of War Information, for example, attempted to suppress a *Life* magazine article covering the racial unrest during the summer of 1943. After some negotiation, the article was published. Government censorship could not control, however, the personal letters of millions of soldiers or the informal grapevine active in the black community.[39] Many of these letters found their way into black news reports or appeared as letters to the editor.

Unlike its white counterpart, the black press circulated stories of violence, abuse, and segregation.[40] Newspaper reporter Arthur Searles recalled the fear that gripped the black community after the lynching of a black man, Bobby Hall, by the sheriff of Baker County, Georgia, during World War II. Like many others, Searles was afraid to protest or even to leave his house.[41] African Americans, by direct experience and through media accounts, were acutely aware of the deprivations imposed by segregation. And black newspapers charted both the plunging morale of African American readers and their escalating demands for redress.[42] Black newspapers offered a unique point of view that often diverged from mainstream publications. For example, the Italian invasion of Ethiopia in 1935 was followed closely as a clash of races. Sports took on the character of a racial conflict, with the Joe Louis-Max Schmeling boxing match and the participation of Jesse Owens in the 1936 German Olympic games.

Arguments supporting their right to equal military service also dominated black publications, but they did not surface in mainstream print outlets. Some topics, like the segregation of black blood in military hospitals, were reported in popular mainstream magazines such as *Reader's Digest*, but they were written with an eye to reassuring readers that their white sons would not inadvertently receive black blood during medical procedures. Most stories regarding African Americans were not communicated in mainstream print sources, unlike the black press, which frequently published these. The *Pittsburg Courier* was an early supporter of the campaign for a more inclusive military. Within months, editorials in both the *Crisis*, a publication of the aggressive NAACP, and *Opportunity*, the voice of the more conservative National Urban League, were in full support of pressing for equal opportunities in all branches of the military. Increasingly, black pressure on government and military, articulated by black newspapers, was felt by both major political parties, as the 1940 election loomed.

Taxation without representation was another favored theme, appearing often in newspapers such as the weekly *Pittsburgh Courier*. Black citizens resented paying taxes to buttress a vast military buildup that neither employed nor enlisted them.[43] The July 1940 cover of the *Crisis* magazine showed air force planes flying over an aeronautics factory with the caption "For Whites Only." The bottom caption read, "Negro Americans may not help build them, repair them or fly them, but they must help pay for them."[44] They also resented their bottom rung on the ladder of economic opportunity. One avenue of employment for blacks, who had limited opportunities for good employment, was the military. The Great Depression had greater than usual effects on blacks, who experienced higher unemployment and slower recovery. Military service offered steady employment and a good income.[45]

The most pervasive theme in black newspapers was the contradiction between the American belief in the inalienable right to freedom, expressed eloquently in President Roosevelt's four freedoms, and the reality of American racial practices—what Gunnar Myrdal, the Swedish sociologist who studied the race problem in the United States, designated the "American Dilemma."[46] Attention to this issue generated suspicion among members of government that blacks might become targets of Axis propaganda. African Americans had nothing to lose if the Axis powers won.[47]

Although the position of African Americans was not often represented in the white press, occasional articles suggested their opinions. Stanley High, for example, articulated African American views in a 1942 article in *Reader's Digest*. He summarized the position of the black soldier: "He knows from experience that the Negro future cannot be left wholly to the unprodded action of the white man's conscience. He is prepared to use the war and the white man's global embarrassments to speed up his advance."[48] African Americans were, by insinuation, blamed for exploiting the national crisis for their own gains. But the opportunities afforded by war are likened to a new emancipation. As High concludes optimistically, "More deeply than ever before in his history, the Negro is sure that he has what it takes and can deliver. With such eagerness and such a faith, he does not believe that America will short-change him or let him down."[49] This declaration of good intentions was probably welcomed by most readers of the magazine.

Government Responses to the Black Press

The black press was considered traitorous because it encouraged criticism of federal policies and expression of dissatisfaction among already apathetic factions of the population. The Office of Facts and Figures (OFF), despite its innocuous title, conducted surveys and compiled reports on African American morale in order to guide government decisions. Weekly media reports in the black press made up part of the review. These were scrutinized by various federal departments. Alan Osur concludes, "For many War Department officials, the black press was conspicuous as a transmitter of alien ideas."[50] War department officials called for action against such extremists, calculating that a domestic revolution would cost the United States its overseas victory. There were attempts to indict African American editors for sedition, to prevent the sale of newsprint to black newspapers, and to prohibit these newspapers on military installations. The result was to reinforce the credibility of the newspapers in the eyes of their readers. The *Pittsburgh Courier*, arguably the most authoritative of the African American newspapers of the period because it stuck closely to the facts in its reports, was subject to extreme pressure from various federal agencies. Despite this duress, the *Pittsburgh Courier* persisted in its attack on discriminatory institutions and practices, reinforcing the trust of its readers.[51]

Adding to the suspicions, War Department investigations and subsequent reports in 1942 concluded that since discrimination was emphatically forbidden in military ranks, the racial unrest must be due to alien elements. Given the stereotypes of inadequate African American intelligence, it is not surprising that outside pressure groups, especially the communists, were blamed for inculcating in blacks aspirations for social and military positions above their capabilities. The black press, in turn, picked up these demands for advancement. Ultimately, military leaders resented the outside interference, thought to be contrary to good military procedure and effective military deployment. The black press was included as part of the conspiracy, because it encouraged un-American ideas and racial unrest. Members of the NAACP and Northern black servicemen stationed at Southern bases were on the list of potential traitors. The reports recommended that Northern blacks not be stationed in the South, because of the negative impact they had on Southern African American communities. One survey of five hundred black soldiers found that over 20 percent "admitted their sympathies were with other governments."[52] This news added direct evidence to the conspiracy theory circulating among military leaders, and further condemned black newspapers and the NAACP as nests of militants and radicals stirring up black soldiers, thereby jeopardizing the war.

There is evidence that J. Edgar Hoover, director of the FBI, suspected communists of being instigators of black agitation during World War II.[53] This belief may account for the FBI investigation of black newspapers like the *Norfolk (VA) Journal and Guide*, the *Baltimore Afro-American*, the *Atlanta Daily World*, the *Birmingham World*, and the *Oklahoma City Black Dispatch*, among others. The FBI was concerned that communist agents masquerading as staff members were releasing pro-communist views through these newspapers. To counter these allegations, black newspapers made frequent references to African American loyalties and denounced fifth columnist activity, although belligerence toward government polices continued. Among those newspapers accused of harboring communist staffers were the *Baltimore Afro-American*, the *Los Angeles California Eagle*, the *Chicago Defender*, the *Denver Colorado Statesman*, the *New York Crisis*, the *Denver Star*, the *Kansas City (MO) Call*, the *Los Angeles Sentinel*, the *Detroit Racial Digest*, the *New York People's Voice*, the *Detroit Michigan Chronicle*, the *Oklahoma City Black Dispatch*, and the *New York Opportunity*. The *Oklahoma City Black Dispatch* was cited for using phrases known to represent communist thinking, such as "civil liberties," "inalienable rights," and "freedom of speech and of the press."[54]

Not all government institutions presented obstacles to the black press. Attorney General Francis Biddle of the Justice Department was able to thwart many of the FBI attempts to drag members of the black press into court. The instinctive government reaction to criticism of its treatment of African Americans during World War II was to silence the black press. This response was practically universal, as various government agencies investigated, harassed, and attempted to shut down black newspapers. The dissident voice of the black press was in danger until June 1940, when Attorney General Biddle decided that no black publishers would be indicted for sedition during the war. Only the *Chicago Tribune* was charged with printing war secrets in 1942, but the case ended quickly when a grand jury refused to indict the publisher. After June 1942, the FBI, headed by J. Edgar Hoover, and the Post Office continued to agitate for legal action against African American newspapers. But the Justice Department stubbornly refused to act, serving effectively as a guardian of minority voices in wartime.[55] During the entire period, investigations failed to turn up enemy agents or communist backers, in spite of rampant allegations of subversion.

Debate over Second Amendment freedoms, instigated by criticism of government actions from the black press, also reflected opposing camps in the federal government. On the one hand, most officials, including President Roosevelt, subordinated the legal question of constitutionally guaranteed freedom of the press to the immediate need for military victory. Standing virtually alone, Attorney General Biddle took constitutional guarantees seriously and intervened on behalf of black papers. This position further protected African American journalists from persecution.

Pressure to muzzle the black press continued throughout the war, because black newspapers were identified as a key factor contributing to low black morale. In an effort to appease black constituencies, influence the news content, and curtail the influence of black newspapers, the War Department established the Negro section of the Bureau of Public Relations in mid-1942. The department later expanded the role of the bureau, following the recommendations of the McCloy committee by increasing access of black reporters to military stories and increasing coverage of news about black units. A common complaint from the black newspapers was that white war correspondents focused on battle activity, but tended to ignore the contributions of service units, which were often black.

Throughout the war, the army also scrutinized the black press. It was illogical to blame black journalists for racial disturbances near army installations. Racial incidents and sometimes riots occurred on posts where the newspapers were forbidden, as well as on posts where the newspapers were widely read. However, increasing outbursts of violence near army bases had drawn the attention of the War Department, and a primary culprit was the black press. A survey of five hundred black troops revealed that 76 percent of them read one of the five leading black newspapers, while 56 percent read the *Pittsburgh Courier*. In response to this finding, the army warned white commanders to avoid the stereotype of the "lazy, shiftless, no-good, slew-footed, happy-go-lucky, razor-toting, tap-dancing, vagrant" if they wanted to get any work out of their black troops.[56] Regardless of this recommendation, the racial violence continued. At the same time, an April 13, 1942, a *Life* magazine article attacked individuals, groups, and publications that sowed hatred and undermined the war effort. Its target was clearly the black press.

The persistent criticism of government policies by black journalists was remarkable, considering that various offices of the federal government were taking special notice of black newspapers. Among others things, the Post Office inspected black newspapers, focusing on those with lower circulation that were more susceptible to federal pressure. The *Boise Valley Herald* and the *New York Militant* were found to be in violation of wartime restrictions, and their second-class mailing permits were revoked. The Justice Department also investigated the black press, as did the FBI, the Office of Facts and Figures, the Office of War Information, the Office of Censorship, the White House, and the army. The War Production Board made periodic threats to cut off supplies of newsprint to some newspapers.

The belligerence of the black press was problematic from the viewpoint of government officials. Its critical tone was clear even before the United States entered the World War II. Immediately following the declaration of war, the *Crisis* published an editorial that claimed, "If all the people are called to gird and sacrifice for freedom, and the armies to march for freedom, then it must be for freedom for everyone, everywhere, not merely for those under the Hitler heel."[57] Such outspokenness was only marginally legal under existing wartime sedition statutes. Wartime sedition laws were passed and enforced vigorously throughout World War I, and the Espionage Act, the primary law, was still in force during World War II.

Overall, the black press was more critical of the federal government than any other group, except perhaps the extreme radical press. The dilemma for government officials was that in seeking sedition indictments, they might alienate the thirteen million African Americans who made up 10 percent of the population. Everyone realized that African American support was essential to winning the war. The tensions between the black press and the federal government, which began in World War I with the sedition laws, almost reached the breaking point. Then, at the end of 1943, the administration improved press relations by working more closely with black war correspondents.[58] In 1944 members of the black press were finally permitted to attend presidential press conferences.

President Roosevelt realized that African American voters had played an important part in his reelection in 1940. It is unlikely that he would have seriously attempted to close down or suppress the black press, because that action would surely alienate black voters. At the same time, however, it is likely that he wanted black editors to tone down their criticism. As was characteristic of his administration, Roosevelt did not deal directly with African Americans. Instead, he assigned Francis Biddle and Postmaster General Frank Walker to intervene. This action distanced him from the problem and reduced the risk of offending Southern white voters. However, in the vacuum created by President Roosevelt's inaction about the black press, other government agencies sought to set the public agenda.

Paranoia about potential government suppression of the black press showed up in editorials and columns throughout the war. Editors anticipated direct action in the wake of government labeling the Negro press subversive. This attitude was probably reinforced by persistent harassment by the Post Office and the Federal Bureau of Investigation, which continued even after it was clear the attorney general would not seek indictments for sedition. There was constant fear that black papers would lose their second class mailing permits, a financial blow that most newspapers probably would not survive.

The black press served to engage and mobilize African American sentiment following incidents like the kidnaping, hanging, and burning of Cleo Wright, an African American man in Sikeston, Missouri. As a result of the widespread reporting of this incident and others, African Americans quickly became bitter. The depth of their discouragement became apparent on January 10, 1942, when William Hastie, civilian aide to the secretary of war, met with fifty-six African American leaders in New York to discuss the wartime role of blacks. Overwhelmingly, they agreed that blacks did not fully support the war effort. Within months, officials from the Office of Facts and Figures met with fifty black ministers, businessmen, educators, editors, and labor leaders to discuss how to improve black morale. Almost unanimously, these black leaders similarly concluded that it would be nearly impossible to change black attitudes unless the government eliminated some of its discrimination.[59] The Office of War Information took over the duties of the Office of Facts and Figures on June 13, 1942, and began to wrestle with the problem of African American morale. As the *Pittsburgh Courier* noted, "The hysteria of Washington officialdom over negro morale is at once an astonishing, amusing and shameful spectacle."[60]

Many whites believed that African Americans offered the Axis powers a weak spot that could be exploited. Thus, the condition of black morale was a concern, not necessarily because it reflected an inherent inequality, but because it could be exploited by hostile interests. African Americans, as Assistant Secretary of War John J. McCloy was warned, were a potential source of fifth column activity.[61] This concern reflected a clear misunderstanding of the causes of black cynicism and low morale. Solutions to the problem of black apathy varied. Instead of suppressing the black press, some, including McCloy, advocated a vigorous counter-propaganda campaign to check the press's popularity, a measure never put into practice.

As a result of civic unrest, racial confrontations, and fears that domestic disturbances would threaten the success of the war effort, the federal government began an investigation of African American morale in 1942. The Office of War Information (formerly the Office of Facts and Figures) spearheaded the inquiry, which found, not surprisingly, that African Americans were well aware of their exclusion from most aspects of the national defense. Government actions had not reassured them that any change in their status would be forthcoming. As Richard Dalfiume summarizes, "Never before had Negroes been so united behind a cause: the war had served to focus their attention on their unequal status in American society. Black Americans were almost unanimous in wanting a show of good intention from the federal government that changes would be made in the racial status quo."[62] The black press was a critical factor in developing this unity.

Some War Department officials harbored a concern that African American protestors were ripe for recruitment for communist and Axis operations. While they did not examine the grounds for such protests, they did attempt to control the black press, which they felt was partially responsible for such attitudes, and they directed some propaganda at African Americans, in hopes that they could persuade blacks to rally behind the Allied cause. The primary message of such attempts was that African Americans would also lose if victory went to the Axis powers.[63] When it came to responses to discrimination and racist practices, the most significant differences between African Americans resulted from geographic origin. Only about 10 percent of blacks from the rural South felt that racist practices should be attacked during the war. Seventy percent of Northern blacks thought that such strikes should occur while war was being waged.[64]

By the summer of 1942, the black press had become in some ways less strident. The space devoted to the "Double V" campaign had shrunk. To attribute this less critical tone to government pressure is misleading. Other factors contributed to the change, including apparent economic gains for black Americans. There were also some changed in military policy. Black men were commissioned for the first time in the air corps, marines, and coast guard. Their status was upgraded in the army and navy, and black men and women were being hired in larger numbers throughout the defense industry. Because of such improvements, the fortunes of African Americans began improving in 1942, and a more positive tone crept into editorials in the black press. In addition, the United States's military prospects began to improve as it went on the offensive. Overwhelming naval victories in the Coral Sea and at Midway, accompanied by the landing at Guadalcanal, generated enthusiasm in most Americans and moderated the outlook of black newspapers.

The Black Press and African American Identity

The black press reached its pinnacle during World War II, both in national readership and in socio-political influence. African American owned and operated newspapers and magazines that had a direct and profound impact on millions of readers in the black community. The opinions expressed on editorial pages and the treatment of topics relevant to African Americans were among the only positive representations of black Americans at the time. The black press was a critical element in reworking black identity, continuing the coalescence of political power begun during World War I and forming the groundwork for the civil rights demands of the 1960s.

Throughout the war, the black press called for an end to discrimination and for the pursuit of equality at home and in the service. The popular "Double V" campaign for a two-front victory against racism dominated the first few months of the war, but then as the war industry improved the economic conditions of African Americans and branches of the armed services enlisted more black recruits, newspapers moderated their demands for immediate home front changes.

Throughout the war, the federal government tapped the black press as a barometer of African American public opinion, but simultaneously harassed black journalists. Alarmed at the expression of low morale in the black newspapers, federal agencies made minor adjustments to accommodate black interests, allowing black reporters to attend press conferences for the first time in 1944.

In spite of the dominance of mainstream publications, which represented mostly white perspectives without regard to Americans subject to Jim Crow segregation, the black press functioned effectively during the war. It could be argued that by redefining the conditions of participation in society and by encouraging a positive identity among readers, this outlet for expression of black perspectives sowed the seeds of civil rights activism in the decades that followed. As African Americans found their public voice through their own media, they also developed a political base from which to challenge Jim Crow laws and practices. The black press developed in the black community the unity necessary for resistance to oppression.

Although it often alarmed whites, the black press was still mainly isolated from mainstream America, rarely read by white Americans. Its readership was almost exclusively black and its political power restricted to encouraging hostility toward established institutions. As a voice for change, the black press did little to alter stereotypes that permeated the dominant culture. It did not challenge the conviction of black inferiority held by most whites. It would take film, a medium that engaged both white and black audiences, to challenge the fundamental contradiction posed by the idea of freedom in the land of segregation.

CHAPTER TEN

The Negotiation of Racial Identity

By examining the communication practices of a society, much can be learned about the culture itself.
—JAMES CAREY[1]

World War II initiated an innovative discourse, a new way of conceptualizing democracy. With its allies, the United States directly opposed the racism of the Third Reich, lauding the ideals of democracy over the racial oppressions of fascism. Celeste Condit and John Lucaites point to the ideological oppositions undergirding World War II and conclude that for the United States, "The war, however, revolutionized the way in which Americans talked about equality. The emphasis on 'world democracy' that had effectively justified World War I became even more potent in World War II."[2] But the practice of democracy contradicted its ideal as the United States exploited black labor and lives under a system that brutalized and excluded African Americans from the fruits of democracy.

At a time when white Americans overwhelmingly supported segregation, the federal government acknowledged African American contributions to the war effort in order to raise morale among African Americans and limit disruptions as they demanded equality. In order to accomplish this objective, the federal government produced and distributed films, particularly *The Negro Soldier*, followed by *The Negro Sailor* and others, celebrating a new image of the African American. In reconstructing the African American as citizen soldier, filmmakers plundered the past, retelling the American story and creating a new image of African Americans. This revised history generated an unmistakably positive message. It redefined African Americans as central to securing and protecting democracy, and thus deserving of the equality guaranteed by democracy. This shift in perception entirely depended upon on images that transformed the African American from the caricature of the minstrel era into a model citizen.

During World War II the images of African Americans underwent a dramatic transformation from the pre-war traditions of racial exclusion that had solidified in American culture.[3] The function of conversion narrative in identity construction is key to understanding the nature of the change. This chapter focuses on the role of narrative in the construction of racial identity, racial images, and national identity, and the impact of the reconciliation of emerging images with national identity. The black press was critical in solidifying attitudes among its largely black readership, but it would require another medium to reach white Americans. Government sanctioned films, unlike the black press, communicated new images of African Americans to vast audiences.

Narrative and the Construction of Racial Identity

American history is simultaneously at once a repository and a perpetrator of values that are directly expressed as attitudes and behaviors.[4] Through the ages, traces of those attitudes and behaviors have been preserved as various human artifacts found in cave paintings and hieroglyph carvings, more recently expressions in print and, most recently, electronic media. Films preserve the architectures of ideology that formed 1940s America, mirroring the attitudes and behaviors of the era. We can begin to reconstruct the process of social change by shifting through the detritus of history to uncover the complexities of race in the United States.

Americans flocked to theaters during World War II, and the films they watched preserve the perspectives of the nation, especially of a government that attempted to shape public perceptions. The federal government faced the difficult task of preserving segregation, as whites demanded, while appeasing African Americans who sought broader participation in American institutions. Warren Susman points out the inherent conservative tendency of media when he writes, "It is possible to suggest that the newly developed media and their special kinds of appeal helped to reinforce a social order rapidly disintegrating under economic and social pressures that were too great to endure, and helped create an environment in which the sharing of common experiences, be they of hunger, dust bowls, or war, made uniform demand of action and reform more striking and urgent."[5] It was the experience of global war, shared by all Americans, that ultimately provided a common denominator for change.

The attitudes accounting for racial identity in the United States have a complicated history that is more often influenced by social and political concerns than by any physiological or genetic characteristics. The human tendency is to create racial distinctions that divide groups and become embedded in institutions, preserved as architectures of ideology that perpetuate racial divisions so that they seem natural. This normalization of racial distinctions, in turn, is perpetuated by succeeding generations, who are unlikely to question the racial distinctions with which they have grown up. Only severe, external events can disrupt this cycle.

Narrative is a fundamental way through which human beings make sense of their worlds. Narrative expresses essential myths in origin stories and sustains society through celebrations of the feats of its heroes. As Brian Ward suggests, "The worlds of American media and culture comprised major arenas in which black and white racial identities, values, and ambitions were variously articulated, affirmed, attacked, and adjusted."[6] Wartime films served as a record of social change, witnessing the emergence of a new racial construction.

Films as cultural texts preserve images that are current at a particular point in time. They offer a window on the social negotiation of identities, as embedded images give way to alternatives. Through the images presented on screen, a black man in uniform may evoke one meaning for someone who supports segregation, while the same image offers another meaning for an African American viewer who has never seen a dignified representation of a black man. Meaning can also be evaluated by comparing films. In *The Navy Steward*, for example, blackness compels obedience to white authority. On the other hand, African Americans in *The Negro Sailor* and *The Negro Soldier* establish a more ambiguous relationship with the audience. The African American serviceman is treated with dignity, and this potential for heroism changes his relationship with viewers according to race. Ultimately, relationships established on screen expose the contradictions of their social context.[7] In this way, images are critical purveyors of ideology.

Images also provide subtle para-social persuasion. That is, they involve us by constructing our role in relationship to the subject onscreen. In essence, we become the kind of viewer we are addressed as.[8] In this process we are constructed by ideologies, as the film narrative entices us into ideological discourses and provides our place within their structures. In this light, images define us by designating the kind of viewer they intend us to be. In this construction, the representation of African Americans as fools assumes that they lack intelligence and exist neither as masters of their environments nor of their fates. At the core, the common denominator of these images is the inferiority of African Americans. By inference, white viewers are assumed to be superior. Unless we challenge these assumptions, we are usurped into the ideology that allowed their creation and become part of its supporting structure.

The black characters that shuffled, sang, danced, and played the fool in early films presented little threat to the dominant white society. Black characters were accepted within film narratives only to the extent that their roles fell within expectations of a segregated society.[9] Cued by movie stereotypes, disparaging images of African Americans dominated newsreels and other documentary films. There was little room for alternatives and, if they had been available, more dignified black images undoubtedly would have been rejected within the limited expectations of racist ideology. The consistency of the portrayals within the constraints of racist ideology accounts for the conclusion that "at no time has the colored soldier been shown as a man."[10] Black heroes were entirely absent, leaving African Americans hungry for any positive screen presence and blinding others to the possibility of black heroes.[11]

Racial Images and National Ideology

Just as in other types of film, in propaganda the relationship between the viewer and symbols of national identity is constructed through narrative that describes the role of the viewer in relationship to the story, depicting a role to be fulfilled.[12] In the traditional story of national conflict, the narrative glorifies personal sacrifice for the nation by sharing stories of heroic actions. In this way, the symbols of heroism create social control by influencing the behavior of individuals who seek to emulate heroism. The enduring images of war are not the factual records of life and death on the front lines, but rather as Michael Griffin argues, "those that most readily present themselves as symbols of cultural and national myth."[13] Films that are successful in creating this sort of social control are powerful weapons for government.[14] During hostilities, the need for social control is particularly acute, giving rise to the use of potent national symbols, as governments justify the sacrifice and death of millions of citizens. The narrative value of heroic depictions is paramount.

Creating a film that would appeal to both white and black Americans proved to be a complex undertaking, resolved by the narrative of conversion. The conversion narrative pivoted on the term "democracy," which implies equality, but many leaders in the African American community called attention to the hypocrisy of fighting a war for democracy when none existed for them at home. During World War II the racial crisis for European Americans took a back seat to the epic struggle between the forces of good and evil abroad. Conversely, for African Americans the military struggle paralleled their engagement with civil rights issues. The successful resolution of the war was only one point of contention, and perhaps not the most important one. The conflict had equality as its subtext, and the two films merged the issue of the war with the issue of race.

In this particular form, the narrative functions to restructure contradictions so that multiple audiences can participate in the same narrative. The key to participation is the multiple, simultaneous meanings in images. In effect, the message offers a layered discourse that is open to divers interpretations. In *The Negro Soldier* and *The Negro Sailor*, film becomes the ideal vehicle for the presentation of ambiguous images that imply equality and dignity for African American viewers, while preserving separation for white Americans. Simultaneously, the film brings historical events into focus and structures racial distinction in favor of a transcendent national identity through conversion of the past narrative. The resulting coherence favors national over individual identity. Thus, the ideological dimension of the narrative dominates, as individual heroism is directed toward the goal of national victory. The basic premise of nationalism is imbedded in the film, pointing to patriotic actions endorsed by family and community. In this way, the film implicates the viewer in a rewritten history that supports the socially approved framework of the war.[15] Thus, the film plays a central role in the promulgation and reproduction of dominant social ideologies, functioning as a powerful agent of socialization that communicates the values of the culture.[16]

The representation of African Americans as American heroes also imitated the fantasy elements of romantic discourse. By constructing heroes of outsized dimensions, the films constrained the opportunity for critical thought. The collective fantasy of the African American hero in uniform shoved aside the realities of contingency and difference in the practice of segregation. As Ronald Jacobs suggests, this sort of discourse encourages social solidarity, but it does so at the cost of critical dissent. Jacobs writes,

Confronted with a discursive environment dominated by romance, marginalized groups with a concern for maintaining their own cultural autonomy are forced to choose a path of either "exit" or "loyalty," where the latter implies assimilation and the loss of distinctive identity. Furthermore, romantic narratives suffer from an "excess of plot," in which the teleological power of mythically validated past origins and future destinations precludes reflexivity and the interrogation either of present or of possible destinations.[17]

The Negro Soldier and *The Negro Sailor* offer romanticized visions of military integration, subsuming African Americans as heroes in the altered national narrative. In effect, there is little room for dissent from this vision.

Reordering Racial Identity

World War II government films gave visual presence to African Americans in American life. The films' message of unity and brotherhood in the face of Aryan evil necessitated a re-examination of racial relationships. Images of African Americans as soldiers, endorsed by the federal government, helped to raise race as a national issue. African Americans followed up on their inclusion in the war effort by demanding greater roles in postwar society. They maintained that their willingness to fight entitled them to the benefits of citizenship.

World War II spurred the development of newfound pride among African Americans, as government sponsored films elevated African Americans from comedic plantation caricatures to more dignified members of the nation. Federal government films came close to constituting a national cinema during wartime. As an expression of the lifestyle, consciousness, and attitudes of the nation, they provided images that were central to this awakened identity.[18] And films such as *The Negro Soldier* became the site where old images clashed with new ones, sponsoring a revitalized vision among different interest groups.[19] Harold Cruse notes the importance of the World War II experience, adding, "But in the years right after World War II, the outlines of new factors were already clearly, visibly, coming on the scene. All at once—in a manner of speaking—a new level of protest activity, a new nationalism and a new Africa consciousness converged to transform the content and quality of black and white relations into something never before seen."[20] The sudden transformation had been building within the black community during the war and erupted with intensity at its end.

World War II, with its attendant economic and social turmoil, provided fertile ground for developing the new black identity. While it would take another decade for African American demands to elicit permanent alterations in American institutions, the roots of the civil rights movement of the 1960s lie in the new identity created through the experiences of African Americans in World War II. The conversion narrative would generate images that would reshape the collective memory of the nation, preserve fundamental ideologies, and articulate national ideologies within the evolution of institutional practices.

NEW IMAGES RESHAPE HISTORICAL MEMORY

Film is a technology of memory. Like photographs, paintings, sculptures, and other visual media, it represents particular historical events and persons through visual symbols that are not the reality, but a preservation of memory.[21] The power of visual representations derives from their ability to condense a myriad of thoughts in a single instance. They also have a profound capacity to concentrate emotions and share them simultaneously with others. For this reason, film images often subsume personal experiences, mixing them with national causes through heightened emotions. They can establish the presence of the individual within the remembered past.[22] Film engages viewers more fully, through more physical senses, than other recreations of history in print or painting or music. Film recovers the radiance of the past.[23] As Robert Rosenstone summarizes, "In the movie theater, we are, for a time, prisoners of history."[24] And while films can capture larger movements and processes as epics, "film tends to highlight individuals."[25] Viewers relive history through the experience of the individuals, placing themselves vicariously in those roles. In subtle ways, images allow the viewer to inhabit dual spaces, participate in multiple lives, and experience "a sense of fractured possibility" that reshapes their own memories while they are experiencing the collective memories of their culture.[26]

In its representations of history, film works more effectively than other media, because it recovers "all the past's liveliness–partly that of dream and memory, of time decomposed and recomposed, all corrected and interpreted."[27] These are not the aspects of the past captured in traditional histories accepted as accurate and factual. Instead, film representations offer "vicarious validations" of the world we perceive, relieving our fears of alienation and loneliness by replacing them with an "awareness of ourselves and our ability to accept our perception of the world which impinges on our consciousness."[28] Film representations provide an emotional investment in the representations of the world as we believe it to be.

Historical memory is always about the configuration of cultural power, the justification of things as they are in the present. As a result, stories are more about present conditions than past events. During periods of crisis, when external or internal dangers threaten to unravel the threads that bind the culture together, stories take on the additional function of strengthening community ties. And the historical identities shared within the cultural community "embody a perceived continuity with the past [which] may in this way function in a psychologically reassuring way for the individual in times of upheaval"[29] Periods of crisis may require a stronger connection of individuals to the group, increasing the symbolic identification of the individual within the larger group. Thus, public expressions are heightened in song, theater, and film. The goal for investigation of historical narratives then, should be the way in which they create connections between individuals and nations in symbolic expressions. It is likely that a repetitive display of cultural symbols become unquestioned truth in support of nationalism. And, as governments on both sides of the conflict discovered during World War II, film is an ideal medium for that repetitive display of cultural symbols required to reassure their citizens.

In the twentieth century, visual images have been essential to voice historical memory. As Marita Sturken suggests, "The past is not simply there in memory, but it must be articulated to become memory.... Camera images are a major factor in this traversing of memories among the realms of personal memory, cultural memory, and history."[30] Thus, the theater screen became the front line, as the federal government attempted to mitigate racial unrest and enlist the cooperation of African Americans by raising their morale during World War II. The defeat of the caricature of African American incompetence was the most important casualty on the battlefield of public memory.

IMAGES PRESERVE FUNDAMENTAL IDEOLOGIES

While the introduction of new images reshapes national memories, at the same time ideological underpinnings of the social forces of the dominant culture remain intact. *The Negro Soldier*, *The Negro Sailor*, and other federally sponsored films produced and distributed during World War II represent the dominant ideological position of the government and military. Although more dignified images of African Americans were projected, the underlying conceptions continued to serve what Michel Foucault has called the "regime of truth" by which society organizes its discourse and establishes its truths.[31] The constructions of race remained essentially unchanged even though African American soldiers were included in the apparatus of war. They continued to perform menial labor in segregated units within a hierarchy of racial discrimination. The fundamental ideology of racial inferiority remained intact, preserved through the practice of segregation. In this way, the films represented orthodox and politically conservative social conditions.[32]

Thomas Cripps argues that the very film images that raised issues of racial inequality during World War II "served as a conservative brake on racial liberalism after the war."[33] By giving African Americans a reason to fight, the images produced during the war described racial discrimination as a temporary condition, not serious enough to require attention at the conclusion of the war. Cripps notes that both Hollywood and the federal government desired to create a metaphor for national unity that was immediately satisfying, but offered no promise of disruption in society following the war. While film images helped to bring racism to national attention, the ambiguity embedded in those images allowed powerful conservative social forces to snap back to prewar racial definitions.

Images that convey fundamental ideologies forge a shared meaning that links the experiences of the individual with the goals of the nation. Through the manipulation of symbols and frames in film, "agent actions become social structure, ideas become norms, and the subjective becomes the intersubjective."[34] In short, film becomes the agent of change to the extent that it implicates people in the ideology of their nation. Rhetoric becomes the agent of change. It provides the narrative of the shared drama that catches up the viewers in mutual participation or "identification."[35] Such identification supersedes the individual experience and creates a language of the public good that is not self-interested, but becomes part of the fabric of the national tale of origins and purposes. It becomes a community discourse that derives from the values, actions, and attitudes of its adherents, slowly but constantly shifting within the web of culture and history. The national narrative is in constant flux, reacting to the events of the day, but owing to its fundamental ideology, rigid enough to provide a core for meaningful interpretation.

Because it contains the embedded values and beliefs of the culture that recorded it, the national narrative is a rich resource for understanding the past. The surface value of stories to entertain or engage viewers is only part of their function. As Teun A. van Dijk explains, "Stories are not merely to entertain the listeners, they may also have persuasive functions, and more generally, they may contribute to the reproduction of knowledge, beliefs, attitudes, ideologies, norms, or values of a group or of society as a whole. . . . They may be one of the ways to inform people or to 'tell the code' of institutions."[36] The construction of communal stories captures the essence of who people think they are, their cultural values and beliefs. The function of narrative is to model those values and beliefs as well as to perpetuate them.[37]

IMAGES ARTICULATE NATIONAL IDENTITY WITHIN EVOLVING PRACTICES

Images of war are more than mere descriptions of people and events. These images are symbols that encapsulate emotions, condensing the feelings of patriotism and nationalism in scenes of sacrifice. As such, they are "consensus narratives."[38] The images serve as metaphors for the nation as they mobilize the viewer, bearing witness to national pride as they transcend the individual to encompass the goals of the nation. The emotional valence accompanying images is referred to by Daniel Schacter: "It is now clear that we do not store judgment-free snapshots of our past experiences but rather hold onto the meaning, sense, and emotions these experiences provided us."[39] This emotional component provides the clue to the effectiveness of images. Referring to war photography, Michael Griffin argues, "The enduring images of war are not those that exhibit the most raw and genuine depictions of life and death on the battlefield, nor those that illustrate historically specific information about people, places, and things, but rather those that most readily present themselves as symbols of cultural and national myth."[40] This observation suggests that the power of the image is directly linked to its ability to transmit the national identity.

Arguably, the images disseminated by the Office of War Information that changed people's views of themselves as citizens of this nation capable of fighting to defend liberty are the most influential of the war. By altering the morale of the African American soldier and convincing others that he could fight, the films provided a vital edge, achieved at a point in the war when it was most needed, when African Americans curtailed their demands for an immediate end to racial discrimination and enabled the government to turn its full attention to pursue victory. In this way, government films like *The Negro Soldier* and *The Negro Sailor* participated in the appropriation of patriotic symbols that encouraged individual identity with the norms and values of the dominant culture, contributing to the reproduction of basic ideologies, the broad but indispensable shared set of values and beliefs through which individuals act, often in complex relationship to a range of social structures. It is through these ideologies that values, such as patriotism, freedom, democracy, and liberty came to seem like inevitable reasons to sacrifice for the nation. The images perpetuated by the culture were shorthand forms of ideologies.[41] In this way, *The Negro Soldier* and *The Negro Sailor* served as important sites of the struggle between the dominant white culture and the racial minority. On the one hand, the images of racial dignity created an opportunity for the transformation of racial ideologies, while at the same time the backdrop of the segregated military articulated the social, political, and economic constraints of ongoing practices of discrimination.[42] Thus, government films straddled the divide between constituencies through images that both changed and upheld constructions of race.[43]

CHAPTER ELEVEN

The Challenge of Change in the Aftermath of World War II

History . . . does not refer merely, or even principally, to the past. On the contrary, the great force of history comes from the fact that we carry it within us, are unconsciously controlled by it in many ways, and history is literally present in all that we do.
—JAMES BALDWIN[1]

Like other scholars, Harold Cruse identified America's entry into World War II as "the beginning of the end of Negro ethnic group insularity; an entirely new phase of American Negro life was under way."[2] As African Americans moved into Northern cities seeking greater economic advantages and established a presence in organizations like the military service, their views of their role in American society shifted. In addition, the rest of America was increasingly exposed to African Americans who worked in war industries and served in other capacities as dictated by severe labor shortages on the home front. Evidence of the shift in thinking is available in research conducted during and after the war. The army made large-scale surveys of enlisted personnel in segregated military settings in 1943 and 1951 to assess their attitudes toward racial integration in army units. The resulting studies, published as "*The American Soldier* and Project Clear," revealed enormous shifts in soldiers' attitudes toward integration during the eight-year period. By 1951, soldiers showed decidedly more positive dispositions toward racial integration. At the same time, opposition to integration declined by more than 35 percent. This remarkable change in attitudes occurred among both white and African American soldiers.

The most surprising revelation of both surveys was that increased interracial contact most often lead to more favorable attitudes toward racial integration.[3] In one study of interracial housing, investigators discovered, contrary to previous thinking, that increased contact between individuals of different races generally resulted in an increased tendency to like each other. So, white Americans were more likely to develop favorable attitudes toward African Americans if the two groups came into frequent contact, resulting in support for social change.[4]

Explanations for the shift in attitudes vary, but it is likely that increasing awareness of the contributions of African Americans in World War II and their subsequent performance in the Korean War contributed substantially to changing attitudes. Both government-sponsored films like *The Negro Soldier* and *The Negro Sailor* and commercial Hollywood fare provided more positive images of African Americans for public consumption. Charles C. Moskos links these changing African American attitudes to subsequent social changes: "Such a finding is strongly indicative of the reformation in Negro public opinion from traditional acquiescence to Jim Crow to the ground swell that laid the basis for the subsequent civil rights movement."[5] It is probable that wartime military experience contributed to a spirit of activism among African American servicemen returning to civilian life. Veterans of World War II formed the core of a new militancy. African Americans increasingly refused to be intimidated by the constraints of a system of segregation rooted in physical threat and force. Their experiences in military service emboldened black veterans to challenge the social hierarchy built on race, making World War II and the civil rights movement inextricably intertwined as two watershed events in the twentieth century American experience.

World War II had brought a million black men together. One unintended consequence was the construction of a black community with a heightened sense of American identity. As servicemen, African Americans had earned their right to full American citizenship. The war served as the precursor to the freedom movement that began less than a decade later and exploded into a full-scale demand for equal rights in the 1960s. In 1943 Nelson Perry wrote, "America will be forced to make a drastic change in policy toward the Negro in the very near future," predicting the drastic changes that would sweep the nation.[6] His prediction was based on changes he saw occurring among his fellow African American servicemen. The extent of change in racial laws and practices depended on the convergence of grassroots demands with increasing consciousness of the legacy of discrimination fostered by the experiences of World War II.

Desegregation

At the end of World War II, political pressure from various groups of African Americans prompted President Harry Truman to begin the process of unraveling segregation in the armed forces. Progress was slow at first, as entrenched military commanders resisted change, then gained momentum until by the end of the Korean War, integration had transformed the military. Breakthroughs were required on several fronts—not just structural changes initiated by Truman's executive order, but probably more important attitudinal changes, which were required across vast segments of American society, in arenas that ranged from political to economic, legal, and social.

The movement of the military toward desegregation was hampered by resistance from both officers and enlisted men, whose attitudes were shored up by social and military tradition. At the end of World War II, newly appointed Secretary of War Robert P. Patterson commissioned Lieutenant General A. C. Gillem and three other generals to review the use of black troops and make recommendations to resolve the issue of haphazard military policies. The Gillem board produced a series of conclusions recommending increased opportunities for African Americans within a continued system of segregation. In particular, it argued that up to 10 percent of the total military forces consist of African Americans, matching their percentage of the civilian population. Whenever possible, military service units should deploy black troops to take advantage of their skills and training. The report did not advise integration.

Not surprisingly, black leaders opposed the recommendations and continued to place political pressure on the War Department, the president, and Congress. A year later, in light of escalating tensions with the Soviet Union, the adjutant general's Office echoed the Gillem commission, urging the full use of 10 percent of African Americans in a segregated armed force. The presence of African Americans would help to resolve racial problems that had plagued the services since 1943, soothing racial tensions among service units.

But World War II opened up opportunities to African Americans that had previously been closed. On the civilian front, the rupture introduced by the conflict opened industrial jobs previously unattainable by African Americans. They concentrated in cities and were organized by effective leaders. They came to realize that they shared common experiences of disenfranchisement. As Bill Payne noted, "A lot of the sixties movement came from some of the veterans who came back after World War II with radical ideas. You know, they just weren't going to take it any more."[7] Jim Williams, another World War II veteran, said, "Black veterans had a certain anger. We felt as though we served our country, and we weren't going to stand for that nonsense any more." Other benefits also resulted directly from military service in the war. The GI Bill of Rights was an especially good opportunity for African Americans. Its provisions made an education and a better life realities.

In a public standoff representative of the debate in the nation as a whole, Senator James O. Eastland of Mississippi debated Lieutenant Colonel John H. Sherman several months after the war in an issue of *Negro Digest*. Eastland took the position that African Americans were poor soldiers and lazy service troops. Segregation and leadership were not to blame, he argued, because Japanese American soldiers performed admirably under similar circumstances. He concluded, "There could not be anything to the argument that segregation was responsible for the Negroes' inability to fight, and for their tendency to run when the showdown came."[8] Sherman countered by noting that disadvantaged whites and blacks shared similar undesirable character traits, the handicaps of "successive generations of poverty, not of race."[9] African Americans, especially, had little incentive to fight for a segregated place in American society. Pride, self-respect and a cohesive military unit, Sherman said, "are the things Negroes will work for, eagerly fight for, and gladly die for. I know. I have seen them do all three.... By their response they have put upon us the duty to make that Army ideal permanent."[10] The issues that complicated attitudes about segregation and the role of African Americans in society surfaced during this debate. While Eastland and Sherman voiced public concerns, they could not provide answers. Those came only with incremental political and legal steps to dismantle segregation.

In the fall of 1947, the Committee on Civil Rights appointed by President Harry Truman issued a landmark set of findings, *To Secure These Rights*, which condemned racial segregation in every aspect of American society and called for an end to segregation in every branch of the armed services. In a decisive move on July 26, 1948, Truman acted on the committee's recommendations and issued Executive Order 9981, instituting the policy of equal treatment and opportunity for all those serving in the military.[11] While it would take another six years and the Korean War to finally implement the policy, the end of military segregation was in sight.

Responses to Truman's order varied. Many African Americans hailed it as a victory, a reward for their contributions during World War II. The Southern white press mostly condemned the order and charged that Truman was disingenuously courting the black vote. Branches of the military resisted by declaring that the order would not result in integrated fighting units.[12] Some scholars have concluded that Truman envisioned that "the armed services would become a model for the nation."[13] Eventually, they did. Unwittingly, the government had delineated the case for integration much earlier. In its short-term quest for racial cooperation to achieve victory, the War Department relied upon images of equality in *The Negro Soldier* that moved the question of equal rights into the national spotlight.

Others have concluded that the mixed official signals of wartime America did not directly promise rewards of equality for sacrifices in war, but simply suppressed the immediate demand for civil rights. Some historians argue that black leaders failed to exploit "their service in the recent world war[.] African Americans in the late 1940s rarely invoked their collective sacrifice to prick white Americans' consciences."[14] In the aftermath of World War I, black leaders, especially those associated with the NAACP, argued that war sacrifices should be rewarded, but got only limited public response from the black community. Following World War II, there was mass support and an intense willingness to mobilize among African Americans. For government leaders, a lasting lesson of World War II was the looming possibility of civilian and military racial unrest that could jeopardize victory. As a practical measure to ensure more effective fighting strength in future conflicts, the first step in solving racial tension was to desegregate the armed forces.

As part of the strategy to end segregation, Truman appointed Charles Fahy of Georgia to chair the Committee on Equality and Treatment of Opportunity in the Armed Forces. Fahy worked separately with each branch of the military in a cooperative attempt to nudge the services toward integration. The army air force, so resistant to integration during the war, took the first step by ending assignments and promotions based on race. Yet, progress was slow. It took until May 1949 for the air force to outline an enlistment program that considered merit and ability rather than race.

With the army air force providing a model, ranking officers no longer constituted the primary obstacle to integration as pressures for change came from outside civilian quarters. Reluctantly, other branches of the military began slow integration of their ranks. In 1950, the army ended race-based quotas as American troops entered the Korean campaign, although leading generals opposed this action. After General Douglas MacArthur was relieved of command, Truman ordered immediate integration of American troops in Korea. The results were less than spectacular. Field commanders like General Edward M. Almond, who enthusiastically supported segregation, probably stalled the process of integration. The slowdown persisted. In 1951, United States based training centers were integrated. By the end of 1954, the army had disbanded its all black units and redistributed their personnel into regular white army units. Progress reports on the status of integration issued in 1955 reflected fresh military thinking. Integration was considered positive because it resulted in greater military efficiency.

Six years after Executive Order 9981, the army still harbored stubborn holdouts, including segregated military facilities on some Southern bases. The armed services were not considered fully integrated until 1956, after the Korean War.[15] Even though the military services were slow to end segregation, they outpaced other American institutions and society generally in creating opportunity and equal treatment. Racial integration had become official United States defense policy "far in advance of civilian America," which would take another decade to resolve basic issues of racial equality.[16]

The Pace of Social Change

There is evidence that many Americans were confused by the eruption of racial hostilities in the late 1950s and early 1960s. They found it difficult to understand such assertiveness, so entirely out of character for African Americans. In their view, blacks were clearly undermining the social order, challenging social conditions that whites found comfortable and reassuring. These confrontations created a backlash of fear that spawned escalating violence in those who were alarmed at the challenges to their social status and economic advantages and the unearned privileges of color. After reviewing violent outbursts that occurred during and after World War II, Arthur Schlesinger Jr. doubted that "black Americans would have gotten anywhere without militancy."[17] Confrontation was necessary to goad America into action, to force white Americans to react, to examine their consciences, to move beyond the status quo.

Government films like *The Negro Soldier* and *The Negro Sailor* were among the first indications of a new social order. In a sense these films are the framing devices for social change that depends on willingness to engage change. In many ways, the retrospective on military history provided by the Department of Defense documentary *The African American Soldier in World War II* (1995) reaches a similar conclusion. The central organizing story line that weaves together the racial hierarchy is maintained by the symbols that legitimize relationships, granting power to some and denying it to others.[18] *The Negro Soldier*, produced to sooth racial tensions, marks the point of fracture with its introduction of a new image of dignity and the retelling of American history so as to include African Americans.[19]

Throughout American wars, military institutions have played a vital role in the shifting definition of American citizenship. The changes brought about by combat ripple out into the larger society. In effect, the armed services have a potent impact on other social and political structures.[20] Their relationship to society seems circular, because military institutions not only affect the surrounding culture, in their daily operations they also reflect its values and practices. This relationship has necessarily influenced ideas of identity "to the extent that mass armies defined their recruits in terms of political and normative ideas of citizenship, military service functioned as an essential and necessary contribution to political institutions."[21] Throughout the more recent history of Western civilization, three dimensions of citizenship can be recognized, from civil definitions of citizenship in the eighteenth century, to a political understanding of citizenship in the nineteenth century, and finally, social dimensions of citizenship (including economic welfare) in the twentieth century.[22] This shifting understanding of citizenship has expanded the proportion of the population defined as citizens as formal citizenship becomes universal in a "mass society."[23]

For today's recruits, it is hard to conceive that until the middle of the twentieth century, the armed forces were one of America's most segregated institutions. Now the military is arguably at the forefront of practicing equal treatment along racial lines, although questions of sexual orientation and gender still provoke disagreement. Arguably, more than any other event, World War II had a profound impact on the evolution of American social issues in the twentieth century. The conflict reshaped economic, political, and social institutions in fundamental ways. Among those changes, racial conflicts radically altered America—its society, its politics and its image of itself—sowing the seeds for civil rights activism in the decades to follow. As historians Erenberg and Hirsch conclude, "The demands of war . . . required profound reworking of American national identity."[24] World War II redefined the conditions of citizenship for millions of African Americans. The World War II generation, against the grain of segregation, lay the groundwork for the civil rights movement of the 1950s and 1960s. Treated as second-class citizens, African Americans found strength in church and community. These institutions formed a political and economic base from which to challenge Jim Crow laws and practices.[25]

Notes

INTRODUCTION

1. John Blassingame et al. *The Frederick Douglass Papers: Series One–Speeches, Debates and Interviews*, Vol. 1. New Haven, CT: Yale University Press, 1979, p. 264.

2. Whenever "colored," "nigger," and "Negro" are used in primary materials, the original terms are retained. In addition, "race" and similar configurations in this study indicate only African Americans and whites, not other racial groups.

3. Although African American women who volunteered for military service were subjected to similar conditions of segregation during World War II, their numbers remained small and are difficult to substantiate through public records. For that reason, this book focuses on the experiences of African American men, with the understanding that black women were also part of the wartime effort to gain citizenship rights for African Americans.

4. Ronald R. Krebs, *Fighting for Rights: Military Service and the Politics of Citizenship*. Ithaca, NY: Cornell University Press, 2006, p. 116.

5. Reich, Elizabeth. *Militant Vision: Black Soldiers, Internationalism and the Transformation of American Cinema*. New Brunswick, NJ: Rutgers University Press, 2016.

6. John W. Dower, *War without Mercy: Race & Power in the Pacific War*. New York: Pantheon, 1986, p. 4.

7. Krebs.

8. Krebs, p. 3.

9. Michael Geyer, "War and the Context of General History in an Age of Total War." *Journal of Military History* (1993) 57: 152.

10. Leo Bogart, *Project Clear: Social Research and the Desegregation of the U.S. Army*. New Brunswick, NJ: Transaction, 1992.

11. Mayfield S. Bray and William T. Murphy, *Audiovisual Records in the National Archives of the United States Relating to World War II*. Washington: National Archives and Records Service, 1974.

12. R. C. Raack, "Historiography as Cinematography: A Prolegomenon to Film Work for Historians," *Journal of Contemporary History* (1983) 18: 411–38.

13. Robert M. Entman and Andrew Rojecki, *The Black Image in the White Mind*. Chicago: University of Chicago Press, 2000, p. 206.

14. *The Rhetoric of Aristotle*. Trans. Lane Cooper. New York: Appleton-Century-Crofts, (1932/1960).

15. John E. O'Connor, *Image as an Artifact: The Historical Analysis of Film and Television*. Malabar, FL: Robert E. Krieger Publishing Company, 1990, p. 221.

16. Krebs, p. 13.

CHAPTER ONE

1. William M. Kelso, "The Archaeology of Slavery at Thomas Jefferson's Monticello: 'A Wolf by the Ears.'" *Journal of New World Archaeology* (1986) 6: 5–20.
2. John W. Dower, *War without Mercy: Race & Power in the Pacific War.* New York: Pantheon, 1986.
3. Arthur O. Lovejoy, *The Great Chain of Being: A Study of the History of an Idea.* New Brunswick, NJ: Transition, 2009 reprint (1936).
4. Dower.
5. Karen E. Rosenblum and Toni-Michelle C. Travis, *The Meaning of Difference: American Constructions of Race, Sex and Gender, Social Class, and Sexual Orientation.* New York: McGraw-Hill, 1996, p. 12.
6. Rosenblum and Travis.
7. *Plessy v. Ferguson*, 1896.
8. Ronald Takaki, *A Different Mirror: A History of Multicultural America.* Boston: Little, Brown and Company, 1993, p. 10.
9. John Rankin, "The Question of Transfusing Blood." *Atlantic Monthly* (January 1943): 95.
10. Takaki, p. 27.
11. Takaki, p. 59.
12. Takaki, p. 67.
13. Takaki, p. 67.
14. Dower.
15. Dower, p. 8.
16. Dower.
17. "How to Tell Japs from the Chinese." *Life* (December 22, 1941) 11: 81.
18. American History Project, "How to Tell a Chinese from a Jap." 27 April 2011 <http://historymatters.gmu.edu/d/6795, Accessed April 17, 2011.>
19. Virginius Dabney, "Nearer and Nearer the Precipice." *Atlantic Monthly* (January 1943): 97.
20. Dower, p. 5.
21. Ruth Benedict, *Patterns of Culture.* New York: Houghton Mifflin, 1934; Ruth Benedict with Gene Weltfish, *The Races of Mankind: Public Affairs Pamphlet No. 85.* New York: Public Affairs Committee, Inc., 1943.
22. Beth Bailey and David Farber, "The Double V Campaign in World War II Hawaii: African Americans, Racial Identity, and Federal Power." *Journal of Social History* (1993) 13: 817–43.
23. Dower.
24. Dower.
25. John Modell, Marc Goulden, and Sigurdur Magnusson, "World War II in the Lives of Black Americans: Some Findings and an Interpretation." *The American Experience in World War II: The American People at War: Minorities and Women in the Second World War*, Vol. 10. Ed. Walter L. Hixson. New York: Routledge, 2003, p. 144.
26. Patricia A. Turner, *Ceramic Uncles & Celluloid Mammies.* New York: Anchor, 1994, p. 19.
27. Timothy E. Cook, "The Bear Market in Political Socialization and the Costs of Misunderstood Psychological Theories." *American Political Science Review* (1985) 79: 1079–93; Peter Karsten, *Soldiers and Society: The Effects of Military Service and War on American Life.* Westport, CN: Greenwood, 1978; Stanley A. Renshon, "Assumptive Frameworks in Political Socialization Theory." *Handbook of Political Socialization: Theory and Research.* Ed. Stanley A. Renshon. New York: Free Press, 1977, pp. 3–44.

28. Takaki, p. 2.
29. Turner, p. xiv.

CHAPTER TWO

1. Mary M. Cheh, "VMI Essays: An Essay on VMI and Military Service: Yes, We Do Have to be Equal Together." *Washington and Lee Law Review* (1993) 50: 57.
2. Antonio Santosuosso, *Soldiers, Citizens, and the Symbols of War: From Classical Greece to Republican Rome, 500–167 B.C.* Boulder, CO: Westview, 1997, p. 201.
3. James Burk, "Citizenship Status and Military Service: The Quest for Inclusion by Minorities and Conscientious Objectors." *Armed Forces & Society* (1995) 21: 503.
4. Reinhard Bendix, *Nation-Building and Citizenship*. New York: John Wiley & Sons, 1964; T. H. Marshall, "Citizenship and Social Class." *Class, Citizenship, and Social Development*. Ed. T. H. Marshall. Chicago: University of Chicago Press, 1977, pp. 71–134.
5. Christopher Parker, "War and African American Citizenship, 1865–1965: The Role of Military Service." *African American Citizenship*. Eds. Henry Louis Gates Jr. et al. New York: Oxford University Press, 2012, p. 428.
6. Marshall; Judith Shklar, *American Citizenship*. Cambridge: Harvard University Press, 1991.
7. James M. McPherson, *The Negro's Civil War: How American Negroes Felt and Acted during the War for the Union*. Urbana: University of Illinois Press, 1982.
8. Cheh.
9. Kenneth L. Karst, "The Supreme Court 1976 Term–Foreword: Equal Citizenship Under the Fourteenth Amendment." *Harvard Law Review* (1977): 91.
10. Santosuosso, p. 201.
11. Ronald R. Krebs, *Fighting for Rights: Military Service and the Politics of Citizenship*. Ithaca, NY: Cornell University Press, 2006.
12. Otto Hintze, "Military Organization and the Organization of the State." *The Historical Essays of Otto Hintze*. Ed. Felix Gilbert. New York: Oxford University Press, 1975, p. 211.
13. David R. Segal, *Recruiting for Uncle Sam: Citizenship and Military Manpower Policy*. Lawrence: University of Kansas Press, 1989.
14. Karen Ross, *Black and White Media: Black Images in Popular Film and Television*. Cambridge: Blackwell, 1996.
15. R. Claire Snyder, "The Citizen-Soldier Tradition and Gender Integration of the U.S. Military." *Armed Forces & Society* (2003) 29: 187.
16. Dwight D. Eisenhower, "Farewell Address to the Nation on January 17, 1961." 25 July 2013 <hrrp://www.ourdocuments.gov/doc.php?flash=true&doc=90>.
17. Samuel F. Scott, "The French Revolution and the Professionalization of the French Officer Corps, 1789–1793." *On Military Ideology*. Eds. Morris Janowitz and Jacques Van Dorrn. Rotterdam: University of Rotterdam Press, 1971, pp. 5–56.
18. Snyder, p. 186.
19. Morris Janowitz, "The All-Volunteer Military as a 'Sociopolitical' Problem." *Social Problems* (1975) 22: 435; Segal; Snyder.
20. Jack Shuler, *Calling Out Liberty: The Stono Slave Rebellion and the Universal Struggle for Human Rights*. Jackson: University Press of Mississippi, 2009.
21. Patricia Bradley, *Slavery, Propaganda, and the American Revolution*. Jackson: University Press of Mississippi, 1999.

22. Bernard C. Nalty, *Strength for the Fight: A History of Black Americans in the Military*. New York: Macmillan, 1986.

23. Nalty, p. 5.

24. William Loren Katz, *The Black West*. Garden City, NY: Anchor Press, 1973.

25. Carol Botsch et al., *African-Americans and the Palmetto State*. Columbia: South Carolina State Department of Education, 1994.

26. Charles Tilly, "Citizenship, Identity and Social History." *International Review of Social History* (1995) 40: 1–17.

27. Russell F. Weigley, *History of the United States Army*. Bloomington: Indiana University Press, 1984.

28. Parker, p. 428.

29. Nalty, p. 18.

30. Clinton Williamson, *American Suffrage: From Property to Democracy*. Princeton: Princeton University Press, 1960.

31. Shklar, p. 59.

32. Mary Patrick Motley, *The Invisible Soldier: The Experience of the Black Soldier, World War II*. Detroit: Wayne State University Press, 1975.

33. Eric Foner, *Reconstruction: America's Unfinished Revolution, 1863–1877*. New York: Harper & Row, 1988, p. 8.

34. Quoted in McPherson, p. 104.

35. Shklar, p. 17.

36. John Hope Franklin, "History of Racial Segregation in the United States." *The Making of Black America: The Black Community in Modern America*, vol. 2. Eds. August Meier and Elliott Rudwick. New York: Atheneum, 1969, p. 8.

37. William E. Griggs, *The World War II Black Regiment That Built the Alaskan Military Highway: A Photographic History*. Jackson: University Press of Mississippi, 2002.

38. Russell F. Weigley, *History of the United States Army*. Bloomington: Indiana University Press, 1984, p. 14.

39. Stanley Sandler, *Segregated Skies: All-Black Combat Squadrons of WW II*. Washington, DC: Smithsonian Institution Press, 1992, p. xi.

40. See, for example, Stephen E. Ambrose, *Citizen Soldiers: From the Normandy Beaches to the Surrender of Germany*. New York: Simon & Schuster, 2002.

41. Linda K. Kerber, *No Constitutional Right to be Ladies*. New York: Hill and Wang, 1998.

42. McPherson.

43. W. E. B. Du Bois, "Niagara Movement," *Horizon* (Sept. 1908) 4: 1–9.

44. C. L. R. James, George Breitman, Edgar Keemer, et al., *Fighting Racism in World War II*. New York: Monad, 1990, p. 256.

45. Janowitz.

46. Burk; Snyder.

47. Santosuosso, p. 206.

48. Santosuosso, p. 201.

49. In this tradition, since 1798 the Navy banned anyone of African heritage as "Persons whose Characters are Suspicious." See Nalty.

50. James Andrews, "Reflections of the National Character in American Rhetoric." *Central States Speech Journal* (1971) 42: 316–24; R. Steele and Charles Redding, "The American Value System." *Western Speech* (1962) 26: 83–91.

51. For a copy of this speech, see http://www.gdg.org/Links/everet.html.

52. Garry Wills, *Lincoln at Gettysburg: The Words that Remade America*. New York: Simon & Schuster, 2006.

53. Linda G. Tucker, *Lockstep and Dance: Images of Black Men in Popular Culture*. Jackson: University Press of Mississippi, 2007.

54. John K. Mahon, *History of the Militia and the National Guard*. New York: MacMillan Publishing Co., 1983; Allan R. Millett and Peter Maslowski, *For the Common Defense: A Military History of the United States of America*. New York: Free Press, 1984.

55. Herbert Aptheker, *Afro-American History: The Modern Era*. New York: Citadel Press, 1971.

56. Scott L. Malcomson, *One Drop of Blood: The American Misadventure of Race*. New York: Farrar Straus Giroux, 2000, p. 367.

57. Malcomson, p. 368.

58. Krebs.

59. Max Weber. "The Meaning of Discipline." *From Max Weber: Essays in Sociology*. Eds. H.H. Gerth and C. Wright Mills. New York: Oxford University Press, 1946, pp. 253–61.

60. Paul Russell Anderson. "Universal Military Training and National Security." *Annals of the Academy of Social and Political Science* (1945) 24: 1; William L. Ransom. "Military Training: Compulsory or Volunteer?" *Proceedings of the Academy of Science in the City of New York* 6 (1916) 4.

61. Mark Solomon, *The Cry Was Unity: Communists and African Americans, 1917–1936*. Jackson: University Press of Mississippi, 1998.

62. Quoted in Aptheker, p. 164.

63. Quoted in Aptheker, p. 165.

64. Burk, p. 520.

65. Burk, p. 508.

66. Burk.

67. Burk, p. 520.

68. Cheh, p. 53.

69. Motley, p. 25.

70. W. E. B. Du Bois. *The Souls of Black Folk*. Chicago: A. C. McClurg and Co., 1903. (Edition cited is Fawcett Publications, Greenwich, CT, 1961), p. 17.

71. James, Breitman, Keemer, et al., p. 60.

72. Franklin D. Roosevelt, "Statement on Peace Time Universal Selective Service on September 16, 1940." 6 June 2013. Http://www.presidency.ucsb.edu/site/docs.

73. Because they were viewed as outside colonial jurisdiction but nevertheless were engaged by both British, French, and colonists as guides, interpreters, foragers, and skirmishers during the colonial wars as well as subsequent wars, Native Americans pose a case parallel to that of African Americans. On June 2, 1924, the Indian Citizenship Act granted citizenship to all Native Americans born in the United States, along with the formal recognition of their military service obligation. But Native Americans were barred from voting until 1948 in some states because voting was regulated by state law.

74. Sandler, p. xii.

75. Robert Scarborough, "Foreigners Find Military Fast Track to Citizenship." *Washington (DC) Times* (August 22, 2002); Marjorie Valbrun, "Military Track to Citizenship: Acceptance through Service." *Wall Street Journal* (April 2, 2003); David Wood, "Pentagon Does Not Track Thousands of Foreigners in U.S. Military." 22 May 2004. http://www.newhouse.com/archive/story1a061102.html.

CHAPTER THREE

1. Pearl Bowser, "Sexual Imagery and the Black Woman in Cinema." *Black Cinema Aesthetics: Issues in Black Filmmaking*. Ed. Yearwood Gladstone. Columbus: Ohio University's Centre for Afro-American Studies, 1982, pp. 42–52.

2. The term Hollywood is used to indicate both the economic system for the production and delivery of commercial American motion pictures to theaters around the world, and a highly conventionalized system for telling stories in motion pictures.

3. Thomas Cripps, *Slow Fade to Black: The Negro in American Film, 1900–1942*. New York: Oxford University Press, 1977.

4. Jean Folkerts and Stephen Lacy, *The Media in Your Life*. Boston: Pearson, 2004.

5. Thomas Cripps and David Culbert, "The Negro Soldier (1944): Film Propaganda in Black and White." *American Quarterly* (1979) 31: 616–40.

6. Folkerts and Lacy.

7. Daniel J. Leab, *From Sambo to Superspade: The Black Experience in Motion Pictures*. Boston: Houghton Mifflin Company, 1975, p. 184.

8. Susan L. Carruthers, *The Media at War: Communication and Conflict in the Twentieth Century*. New York: St. Martin's Press, 2000.

9. Quoted in Robert Sklar and Vito Zagarrio, *Frank Capra: Authorship and the Studio System*. Philadelphia: Temple University Press, 1998, p. 192.

10. Sklar and Zagarrio, p. 183.

11. Richard Griffith, "The Use of Films by the U.S. Armed Services." *Documentary Film*. Ed. Paul Rotha. London: Faber and Faber, 2011.

12. Griffith.

13. Mayfield S. Bray and William T. Murphy, *Audiovisual Records in the National Archives of the United States Relating to World War II*. Washington, DC: National Archives and Records Service, 1974.

14. K. Short, "Hollywood: An Essential War Industry." *Historical Journal of Film, Radio and Television* (1985) 5: 90–99.

15. Carruthers, p. 97.

16. *This Is Our War: Selected Stories of Six War Correspondents–Six Who Were Sent Overseas by the Afro-American Newspapers*. Baltimore: Afro-American Company, 1945.

17. See, for example: *D-Day: 24 Hours That Saved the World*, 70th Anniversary Tribute. New York: Time Magazine, 2014.

18. John W. Dower, *War without Mercy: Race & Power in the Pacific War*. New York: Pantheon, 1986.

19. Sklar and Zagarrio, p. 192.

20. Sklar and Zagarrio, p. 171.

21. Sklar and Zagarrio, p. 178.

22. Sklar and Zagarrio, p. 179.

23. Bill Moyers, "The Propaganda Battle." A Walk Through the 20th Century television broadcast. 11 March 2009. <www.mtv.com/movies/movie/171843/moviemain.jhtml>.

24. Kathleen M. German, "Hollywood Goes to War: An Analysis of Frank Capra's 'Why We Fight' Series." *Western Journal of Speech Communication* (1990) 54: 237–48.

25. Dower, p. 24.

26. *This Is Our War*.

27. Katharine Q. Seelye, "When Hollywood's Big Guns Come Right From the Source." *New York Times* (June 10, 2002): A1.

28. C. Knoppes and G. Black, "What to Show the World: The Office of War Information and Hollywood, 1942–45." *Journal of American History* (1977) LXIV: 87–105.

29. Sklar and Zagarrio, p. 183.

30. Stephen R. Goldzwig, "Civil Rights and the Cold War: A Rhetorical History of the Truman Administration's Desegregation of the United States Army." *Doing Rhetorical History*. Ed. Kathleen J. Turner. Tuscaloosa: University of Alabama Press, 1998, pp. 143–69.

31. Jannette L. Dates and William Barlow, "A War of Images." *Split Image: African Americans in the Mass Media*. Eds. Jannette L. Dates and William Barlow. Washington, DC: Howard University Press, 1993, pp. 1–22.

32. Jim Pines, *Blacks in Films: A Survey of Racial Themes and Images in American Film*. London: Cassell & Collier Macmillan, 1975, p. 7.

33. Quoted in Leab, p. 50.

34. Robert C. Toll, *Blacking Up: The Minstrel Show in Nineteenth Century America*. New York: Oxford University Press, 1974, p. 274.

35. Cookie Lommel, *African Americans in Film and Television*. New York: Chelsea House, 2003.

36. Donald Bogle, *Prime Time Blues: African Americans on Network Television*. New York: Farrar, Straus and Giroux, 2001, p. 49.

37. Lommel, p. 34.

38. Leab, p. 104.

39. Some scholars argue that the J. J. character played by comedian Jimmy Walker on the television series *Good Times* harkens back to minstrel show characters. The widely recognized character was popular partially because he was nonthreatening. He was devoid of maturity, intelligence, or any kind of political consciousness. He was childlike in the same way African Americans had been considered childlike in earlier generations. Webster, the main character in the television series of that name, is a similar minstrel inspired character, lovable to many viewers because he reinforces their superior position in the social structure; as a black child, he requires guidance.

40. Lommel.

41. William White, "Speech to Hollywood Writer's Mobilization Congress" (October 1, 1943). Writer's Congress, Los Angeles Series II, Box A, 277; also quoted in Stephen Tuck, "African American Struggles for a New Place in Popular Culture." *Fog of War: The Second World War and the Civil Rights Movement*. Eds. Kevin M. Druse and Stephen Tuck. New York: Oxford University Press, 2012, pp. 103–25.

42. Sterling A. Brown, *The Negro in American Fiction*. Manchester, NH: Ayers Co., 1969.

43. Jesse Algeron Rhines, *Black Film/White Money*. New Brunswick, NJ: Rutgers University Press, 1996.

44. Rhines.

45. Cripps.

46. James Murray, *To Find an Image: Black Films from Uncle Tom to Super Fly*. Indianapolis: Bobbs-Merrill, 1973.

47. Leab, p. 328.

48. Toll.

49. Pines, p. 7.

50. Bogle, p. 33.

51. Murray, p. 16.
52. Bogle, p. 42.
53. Bogle, p. 56.
54. Pines, p. 7.
55. Brian Ward, *Media, Culture, and the Modern African American Freedom Struggle*. Gainesville: University Press of Florida, 2001.
56. Rhines.
57. Thomas Winter, "*The Training of Colored Troops*: A Cinematic Effort to Promote National Cohesion." *Hollywood's World War I: Motion Picture Images*. Eds. Peter C. Rollins and John E. O'Connor. Bowling Green, OH: Bowling Green State University Popular Press, 1997, pp. 3–25.
58. Leab, p. 49.
59. Winter.
60. Joseph Campbell, *The Hero with a Thousand Faces*. New York: Meridian, 1949.
61. Quoted in Leab, p. 48.
62. Winter.
63. Winter, p. 21.
64. Cripps, pp. 279–81.
65. Cripps.
66. Harold Cruse, *The Crisis of the Negro Intellectual: From Its Origins to the Present*. New York: William Morrow and Company, 1967, pp. 208–9.
67. Sklar and Zagarrio, p. 192.
68. Graham Smith, *When John Crow Met John Bull: Black American Soldiers in World War II Britain*. New York: St. Martin's Press, 1987.
69. Leab, p. 129.
70. Murray, pp. 3, 16.
71. Patricia A. Turner, *Ceramic Uncles & Celluloid Mammies*. New York: Anchor, 1994, p. xiv.
72. Turner, p. 19.
73. Murray, p. 16.
74. Lawrence D. Reddick, "The Negro in the United States Navy during World War II." *Journal of Negro History* (April 1947) XXXII.
75. Leab, p. 101.
76. Leab.
77. Leab.
78. Leab, p. 226.
79. Leab, p. 226.
80. Cripps; Entman, and Rojecki.

CHAPTER FOUR

1. Pearl Bowser, "Sexual Imagery and the Black Woman in Cinema." *Black Cinema Aesthetics: Issues in Black Filmmaking*. Ed. Gladstone Yearwood. Columbus: Ohio University's Centre for Afro-American Studies, 1982, p. 43.
2. Quoted in Thomas Cripps and David Culbert, "The Negro Soldier (1944): Film Propaganda in Black and White." *American Quarterly* (1979) 31: 637.
3. May.

4. Stephen R. Goldzwig, "Civil Rights and the Cold War: A Rhetorical History of the Truman Administration's Desegregation of the United States Army." *Doing Rhetorical History*. Ed. Kathleen J. Turner. Tuscaloosa: University of Alabama Press, 1998. 143–69.

5. G. E. Pauley, "Rhetoric and Timeliness: An Analysis of Lyndon B. Johnson's Voting Rights Address." *Western Journal of Communication* (1998) 62: 26–53.

6. Michael S. Sherry, *In the Shadow of War*. New Haven: Yale University Press, 1995, pp. 100–1.

7. A. Russell Buchanan, *Black Americans in World War II*. Santa Barbara, CA: Clio, 1977.

8. Philip Klinkner and Rogers Smith, *The Unsteady March: The Rise and Decline of Racial Equality in America*. Chicago: University of Chicago Press, 1999.

9. Maggi M. Morehouse, *Fighting in the Jim Crow Army: Black Men and Women Remember World War II*. Lanham, MD: Rowman & Littlefield, 2000, p. 239.

10. Goldzwig.

11. Quoted in Morehouse, p. 36.

12. Quoted in Morehouse, p. 115.

13. *Leadership and the Negro Soldier*, Army Service Forces Manual M5. Washington, DC: United States Government Printing Office, 1944.

14. Sonja K. Foss, "Visual Imagery as Communication." *Text & Performance Quarterly* (1992) 12: 85–96; Gronbeck.

15. Quoted in Cripps and Culbert, p. 617.

16. John Morton Blum, *V Was for Victory: Politics and American Culture during World War II*. New York: Harcourt Brace Jovanovich, 1976, p. 37; Mauricio Mazon, *The Zoot-Suit Riots: The Psychology of Symbolic Annihilation*. Austin: University of Texas Press, 1984, p. 32.

17. Mazon, p. 33.

18. Bill Moyers, "The Propaganda Battle." *A Walk through the 20th Century* television broadcast. 11 March 2009. <www.mtv.com/movies/movie/171843/moviemain.jhtml>.

19. Daniel J. Leab, *From Sambo to Superspade: The Black Experience in Motion Pictures*. Boston: Houghton Mifflin Company, 1975, p. 128; originally from James Agee, *Agee on Film: Reviews and Comments*. Boston: Beacon Press, 1958, p. 80.

20. Quoted in Cripps and Culbert, p. 631.

21. Quoted in Cripps and Culbert, p. 632.

22. Daniel Kryder, *Divided Arsenal: Race and the American State during World War II*. Cambridge: Cambridge University Press, 2000.

23. Quoted in Cripps and Culbert, p. 618.

24. Cripps and Culbert identify four primary audiences for *The Negro Soldier*: commanders in the army itself, blacks viewers, social scientists associated with the Army Information and Education Division, and the Hollywood film community.

25. NAACP Press Release. (April 27, 1944). NAACP 1940-55, General Office File, Films; *The Negro Soldier*, 1944–45, NAACP Microfilm.

26. William White, "Speech to Hollywood Writer's Mobilization Congress." October 1, 1943. Writer's Congress, Los Angeles Series II, Box A, 277.

27. Thomas Cripps, "Racial Ambiguities in American Propaganda Movies." *Film & Radio Propaganda in World War II*. Ed. K. R. M. Short. Knoxville: University of Tennessee Press, 1983, p. 130.

28. Quoted in Cripps and Culbert, p. 617.

29. Sherry, p. 100.

30. Siegfried Kracauer, *Theory of Film*. New York: Oxford University Press, 1960, p. 160.

31. Christopher Parker, "War and African American Citizenship, 1865–1965: The Role of Military Service." *African American Citizenship, 1865–Present*. Eds. Henry Louis Gates Jr. et al. New York: Oxford University Press, 2012, p. 428.

32. Quoted in Cripps and Culbert, p. 640.

33. Cripps and Culbert.

34. Clyde Taylor, "Paths of Enlightenment: Heroes, Rebels, and Thinkers." *Struggles for Representation: African American Documentary Film and Video*. Eds. Phyllis R. Klotman and Janet K. Cutler. Bloomington: Indiana University Press, 1999. 122–50.

35. Quoted in Cripps and Culbert, p. 632.

36. *The Negro Soldier*. Signal Corps, 1944. All subsequent references to the film will be noted in the text.

37. L. May, "Making the American Consensus: The Narrative of Conversion and Subversion in World War II Films." *The War in American Culture*. Eds. Lewis A. Erenberg and Susan E. Hirsch. Chicago: University of Chicago Press, 1996. 71–102,

38. Taylor, p. 123.

39. Edith Wyschogrod, *An Ethics of Remembering*. Chicago: University of Chicago Press, 1998.

40. Michael Osborn, "Rhetorical Depiction." *Form, Genre, and the Study of Political Discourse*. Eds. Herbert W. Simons and A. A. Aghazarian. Columbia: University of South Carolina Press, 1986. 79–107.

41. Quoted in Cripps and Culbert, p. 625.

42. Elizabeth Bird and R. Dardenne, "Myth, Chronicle, and Story: Exploring the Narrative Qualities of News." *Media, Myths and Narratives: Television and the Press*. Ed. James Carey. Newbury Park, CA: Sage, 1988. 67–86; Walter R. Fisher, *Human Communication as Narration*. Columbia: University of South Carolina Press, 1987; Walter R. Fisher, "Narration, Reason, and Community." *Memory, Identity, Community: The Idea of Narrative in the Human Sciences* (pp. 307–27). Eds. Lewis P. Hinchman and Sandra K. Hinchman. Albany: State University of New York Press, 1997; C. J. Griffin, "The Rhetoric of Form in Conversion Narratives." *Quarterly Journal of Speech* (1990) 76: 152–63; Stuart Hall, "The Whites of their Eyes: Racist Ideologies and the Media." *Silver Linings: Some Strategies for the Eighties*. Eds. George Bridges and Rosalind Brunt. London: Lawrence & Wishart, 1981. 28–52.

43. Osborn, p. 99.

44. Bird and Dardenne.

45. May, p. 96.

46. May.

47. Molefi K. Asante, *The Afrocentric Idea*. Philadelphia: Temple University Press, 1987; H. A. Baer, *African-American Religion in the Twentieth Century*. Knoxville: University of Tennessee Press, 1992; F. Edwords, "The Religious Character of American Patriotism." *Humanist* (1987, November/December) 47: 20–25; E. Franklin Frazier, *The Negro Church in America*. New York: Schocken Books, 1964; C. Eric Lincoln and Lawrence H. Mamiya, *The Black Church in the African-American Experience*. Durham: Duke University Press, 1990; Archie Smith Jr. and Gill G. Barnes, *Navigating the Deep River: Spirituality in African American Families*. Cleveland, OH: United Church Press, 1997; Carter G. Woodson, *The History of the Negro Church*. Washington, DC: Associated Publishers, 1921.

48. Teun A. van Dijk, "Stories and Racism." *Narrative and Social Control*. Ed. Dennis K. Mumby. Newbury Park, CA: Sage, 1993, p. 125.

49. May.

50. C. V. Hamilton, *The Black Preacher in America*. New York: William Morrow, 1972.

51. Ulysses Lee, *The Employment of Negro Troops*. Washington, DC: Office of the Chief of Military History, United States Army, 1966.

52. Gladstone L. Yearwood, *Black Film as a Signifying Practice: Cinema, Narration and the African-American Aesthetic Tradition*. Trenton, NJ: African World Press, 2000, p. 141.

53. Wyschogrod.

54. Osborn.

55. Yearwood, p. 144.

56. D. Thelen, "Memory and American History." *Journal of American History* (1989) 75: 1125.

57. M. Schudson, "The Present in the Past versus the Past in the Present." *Communication* (1989) 11: 112.

58. Lee, p. 387.

59. J. W. Chambers and D. Culbert, *World War II: Film and History*. New York: Oxford University Press, 1996, p. 133.

60. Celeste M. Condit and John L. Lucaites, *Crafting Equality: America's Anglo-African Word*. Chicago: University of Chicago Press, 1993.

61. Graeme Turner, *Film as Social Practice*. New York: Routledge, 1993, p. 173.

62. Robert A. Rosenstone, "History in Images/History in Words: Reflections on the Possibility of Really Putting History onto Film." *American Historical Review* (1988) 43: 1178–95.

63. Buchanan; Richard M. Dalfiume, *Desegregation of the Armed Forces: Fighting on Two Fronts*. Columbia: University of Missouri Press, 1969.

64. Bruce E. Gronbeck, "Reconceptualizing the Visual Expedience in Media Studies." *Communication: Views from the Helm for the 21st Century*. Ed. Judith S. Trent. Boston: Allyn and Bacon, 1998, p. 292.

65. Osborn, p. 80.

66. C. C. Moskos and J. S. Butler, *All That We Can Be: Black Leadership and Racial Integration the Army Way*. New York: HarperCollins, 1996.

67. N. A. Wynn, *The Afro-American and the Second World War*. New York: Holmes and Meier, 1975, p. 21.

68. Ian Angus and Sut Jhally, *Cultural Politics in Contemporary America*, quoted in bell hooks, *Yearning: Race, Gender, and Cultural Politics*. Boston: South End Press, 1990, p. 5.

69. Vincent F. Rocchio, *Reel Racism: Confronting Hollywood's Construction of Afro-American Culture*. Boulder, CO: Westview Press, 2000.

70. Joseph Campbell, *The Hero with a Thousand Faces*. New York: Meridian, 1949, p. 10.

71. Turner, p. 178.

72. Manthia Diawara, "Black Spectatorship: Problems of Identification and Resistance." *Black American Cinema*. Ed. Manthia Diawara. New York: Routledge, 1993, p. 215.

73. Stephen Ambrose, *Citizen Soldiers: From the Normandy Beaches to the Surrender of Germany*. New York: Simon & Schuster, 2002.

74. J. Ronald Green, "'Twoness' in the Style of Oscar Micheaux." *Black American Cinema*. Ed. Manthia Diawara. New York: Routledge, 1993, p. 27.

75. Rocchio, p. 76.

76. Rocchio, p. 77.

77. bell hooks, *Outlaw Culture: Resisting Representations*. New York: Routledge, 1994, p. 4.

78. "These Truly are the Brave," *Ebony* (August 1968) 123: 177.

CHAPTER FIVE

1. A. Philip Randolph, "Keynote Speech." *Official Proceedings of the Second National Negro Congress.* Philadelphia, PA: October 15–17, 1937.

2. Celeste Condit and John L. Lucaites, *Crafting Equality: America's Anglo-African Word.* Chicago: University of Chicago Press, 1993; D. Meckiffe, and M. Murray, "Radio and the Black Soldier during World War II." *Critical Studies in Mass Communication* (1998) 15: 337–56.

3. *The Negro Sailor*, 1945. US Department of War. National Archives. Original film transcript by author. All subsequent citations are from the author's transcription of the film.

4. Robert A. Rosenstone, "History in Images/History in Words: Reflections on the Possibility of Really Putting History onto Film." *American Historical Review* (1988) 43: 1178–95; Robert Brent Toplin, "The Filmmaker as Historian." *American Historical Review* (1988) 43: 1210–27.

5. Siegfried Kracauer, *Theory of Film*. New York: Oxford University Press, 1960, p. 160.

6. John Fiske, *Television Culture: Popular Pleasures and Politics*. London: Methuen, 1987.

7. John Corner, *A Critical Introduction to Documentary*. Manchester, UK: Manchester University Press, 1996.

8. Thomas Cripps and David Culbert, "*The Negro Soldier* (1944): Film Propaganda in Black and White." *American Quarterly* (1979) 31: 616–40.

9. Thomas Winter, "*The Training of Colored Troops*: A Cinematic Effort to Promote National Cohesion." *Hollywood's World War I: Motion Picture Images*. Eds. Peter C. Rollins and John E. O'Connor. Bowling Green, OH: Bowling Green State University Popular Press, 1997, p. 21.

10. Quoted in Cripps and Culbert, p. 619.

11. Graham Smith, *When John Crow Met John Bull: Black American Soldiers in World War II Britain*. New York: St. Martin's Press, 1987, pp. 86–88.

12. Norman Longmate, *The GIs: The Americans in Britain 1942–1945*. London: Charles Scribner, 1974; Christopher Thorne, "Britain and the Black GIs: Racial Issues and Anglo-American Relations in 1942." *New Community*, (Summer 1974): n.p.

13. *A Welcome to Britain*, 1943. British Ministry of Information film. British Imperial War Museum archives. Original film transcription by author. All subsequent citations are from the author's transcription of the film.

14. Smith, p. 89.

15. Robert J. Norrell, *The House I Live In: Race in the American Century*. New York: Oxford University Press, 2005, pp. 141–46.

16. Norrell, p. 142.

17. Winter, p. 7.

18. Gladstone L. Yearwood, *Black Film as a Signifying Practice: Cinema, Narration and the African-American Aesthetic Tradition*. Trenton, NJ: African World Press, 2000, p. 42.

19. Joyce Lardner, "Introduction to Tomorrow's Tomorrow: The Black Woman." *Feminism and Methodology*. Ed. S. Harding. Bloomington: Indiana University Press, 1972, p. 75.

20. Dorothy B. Jones, "The Hollywood Film: 1942–1945." *Hollywood Quarterly* (1945) 1: 16.

21. Jones, p. 14.

22. Kracauer, 1949, p. 59.

23. Thomas Cripps, *Slow Fade to Black: The Negro in American Film, 1900–1942*. New York: Oxford University Press, 1977, p. 383.

24. Yearwood, p. 39.

25. Charles E. Silberman, *Crisis in Black and White*. New York: Vintage, 1964, p. 64.

26. Allison M. Hattaway and Susan L. Brinson, "Race and Radio: The Alabama Negro Extension Service Broadcasts, 1940–1945." *Journal of Radio Studies* (2001) 8: 374.

27. Michelle Hilmes, *Radio Voices: American Broadcasting, 1922–1952*. Minneapolis: University of Minnesota Press, 1997.

CHAPTER SIX

1. Stephen E. Ambrose, *Citizen Soldiers: From the Normandy Beaches to the Surrender of Germany*. New York: Simon & Schuster, 2002.

2. J. Michael Martinez, *A Long Dark Night: Race in America from Jim Crow to World War II*. New York: Rowman & Littlefield, 2016.

3. David R. Segal, *Recruiting for Uncle Sam: Citizenship and Military Manpower Policy*. Lawrence: University Press of Kansas, 1989, p. 43.

4. Christopher Parker, "War and African American Citizenship, 1865–1965: The Role of Military Service." *African American Citizenship, 1865–Present*. Ed. Henry Louis Gates Jr. et al. New York: Oxford University Press, 2012, p. 421.

5. Quoted in Herbert Aptheker, *Afro-American History: The Modern Era*. New York: Citadel Press, 1971, p. 167.

6. Bernard C. Nalty, *The Right to Fight: African-American Marines in World War II*. Washington, DC: Marine Corps Historical Center, 1995.

7. Stanley Sandler, "Homefront Battlefront: Military Racial Disturbances in the Zone of the Interior, 1941–1945." *The American Experience in World War II: The American People at War: Minorities and Women in the Second World War*, Vol. 10. Ed. Walter L. Hixson. New York: Routledge, 2003, p. 132.

8. George S. Patton Jr., *War as I Knew It*. Boston: Houghton Mifflin, 1947.

9. John Hope Franklin and Alfred A. Moss, *From Slavery to Freedom*. New York: McGraw-Hill, 1994; Bernard C. Nalty, *Strength for the Fight: A History of Black Americans in the Military*. New York: Macmillan, 1986.

10. Lewis Hershey, "They're in the Army." *Negro Digest* (December 1942): 71.

11. Robert Hodges, "Buffalo Soldiers' Assault on the Gothic Line." 13 April 2012. <Http://www.military.com/Content/General >.

12. Alan M. Osur, *Blacks in the Army Air Forces during World War II: The Problem of Race Relations*. Washington, DC: Department of Defense, Department of the Air Force, Office of Air Force History. US Government Printing Office, 1977.

13. Quoted in Osur, p. 5.

14. Osur.

15. Sandler.

16. Philip McGuire, *Taps for a Jim Crow Army: Letters from Black Soldiers in World War II*. Lexington: University of Kentucky Press, 1993, p. 127.

17. Quoted in Leslie H. Fishel and Benjamin Quarles, *The Negro American: A Documentary History*. Glenview, IL: Scott, Foresman, 1967, p. 473.

18. David P. Colley, "On the Road to Victory: The Red Ball Express." 11 November 2003. <http://www.military.com/Content/MoreContent?file=PRredball>.

19. Colley.

20. Quoted in George Q. Flynn, "Selective Service and American Blacks during World War II." *Journal of Negro History* (1984) 69: 14.

21. Osur.

22. General James C. Magee, "Memo to Assistant Secretary of War John J. McCloy." September 3, 1941. ASW 291.2, Record Group 335. Washington, DC: National Archives.
23. Osur.
24. Osur, pp. 71–85.
25. Ulysses Lee, *The Employment of Negro Troops*. Washington, DC: Office of the Chief of Military History, United States Army, 1966, pp. 8–20, 239–74.
26. Charles E. Silberman, *Crisis in Black and White*. New York: Vintage, 1964, p. 260.
27. Alan M. Osur, *Separate & Unequal: Race Relations in the AAF during World War II*. Honolulu: University Press of the Pacific, 2004.
28. Osur, 2004.
29. Beth Bailey and David Farber, "The 'Double V' Campaign in World War II Hawaii: African Americans, Racial Ideology, and Federal Power." *The American Experience in World War II: The American People at War: Minorities and Women in the Second World War*, Vol. 10. Ed. Walter L. Hixson. New York: Routledge, 2003, pp. 163–88.
30. For additional information on this event, see Robert L. Allen, *The Port Chicago Mutiny: The Story of the Largest Mass Mutiny Trial in U.S. Naval History*. New York: Warner Books, 1989.
31. Maggi M. Morehouse, *Fighting in the Jim Crow Army: Black Men and Women Remember World War II*. Lanham, MD: Rowman & Littlefield, 2000, p. 105.
32. Segal, p. 10.
33. Osur, 2004.
34. Osur, 2004, p. 77.
35. Flynn, p. 19.
36. Flynn, p. 20.
37. Lawrence D. Reddick, "The Negro in the United States Navy during World War II." *Journal of Negro History* (April 1947) XXXII.
38. Sandler, p. 13.
39. Osur, 2004, p. 62.
40. Flynn, p.14.
41. Robert W. Mullen, *Blacks in America's Wars*. New York: Monad Press, 1973, p. 59.
42. Osur 1977, p. iii.
43. Quoted in Flynn, p. 23.
44. Morehouse, p. 3.

CHAPTER SEVEN

1. Quoted in Maggi M. Morehouse, *Fighting in the Jim Crow Army: Black Men and Women Remember World War II*. Lanham, MD: Rowman & Littlefield, 2000, p. 112.
2. Idus A. Newby, *Jim Crow's Defense: Anti-Negro Thought in American, 1900–1930*. Baton Rouge: University of Louisiana Press, 1965.
3. Graham Smith, *When John Crow Met John Bull: Black American Soldiers in World War II Britain*. New York: St. Martin's Press, 1987, p. 221.
4. "Oral History Interview with Judge William H. Hastie." January 5, 1972. Truman Presidential Museum & Library Online. 12 October 2011. <http://ww.trumanlibrary.org/oralhist/hastie.htm>.
5. E. T. Hall, "Race Prejudice and Negro-White Relations in the Army." *American Journal of Sociology* (1947) 52: 401–9.

6. Stanley Sandler, *Segregated Skies: All-Black Combat Squadrons of WW II.* Washington, DC: Smithsonian Institution Press, 1992, p. xii.

7. Quoted in Alan Osur, *Separate & Unequal: Race Relations in the AAF during World War II.* Honolulu: University Press of the Pacific, 2004, p. 56.

8. *Harper's*, 1943; quoted in Morehouse, p. 100.

9. Quoted in Mary Patrick Motley, *The Invisible Soldier: The Experience of the Black Soldier, World War II.* Detroit: Wayne State University Press, 1975, pp. 75–76.

10. Quoted in Motley, pp. 75–76.

11. Lee Finkle, *Forum for Protest: The Black Press during World War II.* Cranbury, NJ: Associated University Presses, 1975, p. 183.

12. Quoted in Osur, 2004, p. 15.

13. Quoted in Morehouse, p. 37.

14. Bernard C. Nalty, *The Right to Fight: African-American Marines in World War II.* Washington, DC: Marine Corps Historical Center, 1995, p. 1.

15. Cited in Nalty.

16. Nalty.

17. George S. Patton Jr., *War as I Knew It.* Boston: Houghton Mifflin, 1947, p. 160.

18. Hall.

19. *Leadership and the Negro Soldier*, Army Service Forces Manual M5, Washington, DC: United States Government Printing Office, 1944, p. iv.

20. The same assumption that black stewards needed to be managed to prevent these undesirable traits was made in the signal corps film *The Navy Steward*.

21. Stanley Sandler, "Homefront Battlefront: Military Racial Disturbances in the Zone of the Interior, 1941–1945." *The American Experience in World War II: The American People at War: Minorities and Women in the Second World War*, Vol. 10. Ed. Walter L. Hixson. New York: Routledge, 2003, p. 138.

22. Alan M. Osur, *Blacks in the Army Air Forces during World War II: The Problem of Race Relations.* Washington, DC: Department of Defense, US Government Printing Office, 1977, p. 84.

23. Quoted in Osur, 1977, p. 8.

24. "Oral History."

25. "Oral History."

26. "Oral History."

27. Hall.

28. "Oral History."

29. Osur, 2004, p. 62.

30. Robert L. Allen, *The Port Chicago Mutiny: The Story of the Largest Mass Mutiny Trial in U.S. Naval History.* New York: Warner Books, 1989, p. 173.

31. Alfred M. Lee and Norman D. Humphrey, *Race Riot.* New York: Dryden Press, 1943.

32. Smith, p. 16.

33. Quoted in Nalty, p. 12.

34. Quoted in Nalty, p. 12.

35. A. Russell Buchanan, *Black Americans in World War II.* Santa Barbara, CA: Clio, 1977; J. L. Galloway, "Last of the Buffalo Soldiers." *U.S. News & World Report* (May 6, 1996) 117: 45–46: Wallace Lee, "Are Negroes Good Soldiers? Negro Digest Poll." *Negro Digest* (December 1945): 28.

36. Quoted in Smith, p. 227.

37. Quoted in Smith, p. 226.

38. Morehouse, p. 10.
39. Morehouse, p. 10.
40. Quoted in Motley, p. 40.
41. Quoted in Motley, p. 101.
42. Quoted in Motley, p. 157.
43. Quoted in Motley, p. 328.
44. Nalty.
45. US Selective Service System, *Selective Service, 4th Report of the Director, 1944–45 and 1946–47: Selective Service and Victory*. Washington: US Government Printing, 1948.
46. Sandler 1992, p. 33.
47. Quoted in Motley, p. 177.
48. "Oral History."
49. Quoted in Motley, p. 110.
50. Herbert Garfinkel, *When Negroes March: The March on Washington Movement in the Organizational Politics for FEPC*. Glencoe, IL: Scott Foresman, 1959, p. 20.
51. Ronald Takaki, *Double Victory: A Multicultural History of America in World War II*. New York: Little, Brown and Company, 2000.
52. "Oral History."
53. Herbert Shapiro, *White Violence and Black Response: From Reconstruction to Montgomery*. Amherst: The University of Massachusetts Press, 1988, p. 308.
54. Quoted in Nalty, p. 28.
55. Quoted in Nalty, p. 23.
56. Quoted in Motley, pp. 156, 159.
57. Morehouse, p. 100.
58. Takaki.
59. Morehouse, p. 93.
60. Quoted in Allen, p. 54.
61. Quoted in Clinton Cox, "From Columbus to Hitler and Back Again." *Race & Class* (2002) 43: 47.
62. Harvard Sitkoff, *The Struggle for Black Equality 1954–1980*. Toronto: Collins Publishers, 1981.
63. Sitkoff.
64. Social Science Institute, Fiske University, *Monthly Summary of Events and Trends in Race Relations*, 1944, vol. 1. Also see Harvard Sitkoff, "Racial Militancy and Interracial Violence in the Second World War." *Journal of American History* (December 1971) 58: 661–81.
65. Mauricio Mazon, *The Zoot-Suit Riots: The Psychology of Symbolic Annihilation*. Austin: University of Texas Press, 1984.
66. Mazon, p. 14.
67. Mazon, p. 60.
68. Sitkoff 1981, p. 16.
69. Sandler 2003, p. 131.
70. Sandler 2003.
71. Ulysses Lee, *The Employment of Negro Troops*. Washington, DC: Office of the Chief of Military History, United States Army, 1966.
72. Osur 1999, p. 95.
73. Morehouse, p. 83.
74. Osur 2004, p. 93.

75. I. F. Stone, "Capital Notes." *Nation* (January 23, 1943) 156: 115.
76. "Oral History."
77. Thomas Sancton, "A Southern View of the Race Question." *Negro Quarterly: A Review of Negro Life and Culture* (1942) 1: 197–200; Sitkoff 1971.
78. James Boyd, *Nation* (June 26, 1943) 156: 884–87; Rayford W. Logan, *What the Negro Wants*. Chapel Hill: University of North Carolina Press, 1944.
79. Nalty, p. 3.
80. Arthur I. Waskow, *From Race Riot to Sit-In: 1919 and the 1960s*. New York: Doubleday, 1966, p. 3.
81. David R. Segal, *Recruiting for Uncle Sam: Citizenship and Military Manpower Policy*. Lawrence: University of Kansas Press, 1989, p. 11.
82. John Modell, Marc Goulden, and Sigurdur Magnusson, "World War II in the Lives of Black Americans: Some Findings and an Interpretation." *The American Experience in World War II: The American People at War: Minorities and Women in the Second World War*, Vol. 10. Ed. Walter L. Hixson. New York: Routledge, 2003, p. 126.
83. Jack M. Bloom, *Class, Race, and the Civil Rights Movement*. Bloomington: University of Indiana Press, 1987.
84. Nalty.

CHAPTER EIGHT

1. Elizabeth Rauh Bethel, *The Roots of African-American Identity: Memory and History in Antebellum Free Communities*. New York: St. Martin's Press, 1997, p. 3.
2. Richard M. Dalfiume, *Desegregation of the Armed Forces: Fighting on Two Fronts*. Columbia: University of Missouri Press, 1969; Charles S. Johnson, *To Stem This Tide: A Survey of Racial Tension Areas in the United States*. Boston: Publisher Unknown, 1943; Howard W. Odum, *Race and Rumors of Race: Challenge to Crisis*. Chapel Hill: University of North Carolina Press, 1943.
3. Dalfiume; Ulysses Lee, *The Employment of Negro Troops*. Washington, DC: Office of the Chief of Military History, United States Army, 1966.
4. A. Russell Buchanan, *Black American in World War II*. Santa Barbara, CA: Clio, 1977; Mary Patrick Motley, *The Invisible Soldier: The Experience of the Black Soldier, World War II*. Detroit: Wayne State University Press, 1975; Martha S. Putney, *When the Nation Was in Need: Blacks in the Women's Army Corps during World War II*. Metuchen, NJ: Scarecrow Press, 1992.
5. R. L. Vann, "Letter to the Editor." *Pittsburgh Courier* (January 19, 1939): 51.
6. Richard Dalfiume, "The 'Forgotten Years' of the Negro Revolution." *The American Experience in World War II: The American People at War: Minorities and Women in the Second World War*, Vol. 10. Ed. Walter L. Hixson. New York: Routledge 2003, p. 96.
7. Metz T. P. Lochard, "Negroes and Defense." *Nation* (June 4, 1941) 152: 14–16; Walter White, "It's Our Country, Too: The Negro Demands the Right to Be Allowed to Fight for It." *Saturday Evening Post* (December 14, 1940) 213: 27, 61–68.
8. Herbert Aptheker, *Afro-American History: The Modern Era*. New York: Citadel Press, 1971.
9. Quoted in Aptheker, p. 161.
10. Quoted in Aptheker, p. 164.
11. W. E. B. Du Bois, "Close Ranks." *Crisis*, (July 16, 1918): 111.
12. Quoted in Aptheker, p. 165.

13. Quoted in Aptheker, p. 163.

14. William G. Jordan, "The Damnable Dilemma: African American Accommodation and Protest during World War I." *Journal of American History* (1995) 81: 1562–83.

15. Quoted in Carolyn Wedin, *Inheritors of the Spirit: Mary White Ovington and the Founding of the NAACP*. New York: John Wiley, 1998, p. 47.

16. Quoted in A. D. DeSantis, "Selling the American Dream Myth to Black Southerners: The Chicago *Defender* and the Great Migration of 1915–1919." *Western Journal of Communication* (1998) 62: 478.

17. Kenneth B. Clark, "Morale of the Negro on the Home Front: World Wars I and II." *Journal of Negro Education* (Summer 1943) 12: 423.

18. W. E. B. Du Bois, "Returning Soldiers." *Crisis* (May 1919) 18: 13.

19. Clark, p. 420.

20. Quoted in Clark, p. 428.

21. Robert E. Park, "Racial Ideologies." *American Society in Wartime*. Ed. William Fielding Ogburn. Chicago: University of Chicago Press, 1943, p. 174.

22. Arthur P. Davis, "Will a Long War Aid the Negro?" *Negro Digest* (November 1943) 2: 43.

23. Davis.

24. Davis.

25. Quoted in Chas H. Thompson, "The American Negro in World War I and World War II." *Journal of Negro Education* (1943) 12: 45.

26. Clark, p. 423.

27. Dalfiume; Lester M. Jones, "The Editorial Policy of Negro Newspapers of 1917–1918 as Compared with That of 1941–1942." *Journal of Negro History* (1944) XXIX: 24–31.

28. John Modell, Marc Goulden, and Sigurdur Magnusson, "World War II in the Lives of Black Americans: Some Findings and an Interpretation." *The American Experience in World War II: The American People at War: Minorities and Women in the Second World War*, Vol. 10. Ed. Walter L. Hixson. New York: Routledge, 2003, pp. 120–30.

29. Clark, p. 426.

30. Clark, p. 427.

31. Clark, p. 427.

32. Ronald R. Krebs, *Fighting for Rights: Military Service and the Politics of Citizenship*. Ithaca, NY: Cornell University Press, 2006, p. 124.

33. Francis L. Broderick and August Meier, *Negro Protest Thought in the Twentieth Century*. Indianapolis, IN: Bobbs-Merrill Company, 1965.

34. Mary Patrick Motley, *The Invisible Soldier: The Experience of the Black Soldier, World War II*. Detroit: Wayne State University Press, 1975.

35. William H. Chafe, Raymond Gavins, and Robert Korstad, et al., *Remembering Jim Crow*. New York: Center for Documentary Studies for the Behind the Veil Project, 2001.

36. Harvard Sitkoff, *A New Deal for Blacks: The Emergence of Civil Rights as a National Issue—The Depression Decade*. New York: Oxford University Press, 2008.

37. Nathan Hare, "Recent Trends in the Occupational Mobility of Negroes, 1930–1960: An Intracohort Analysis," *Social Forces* (December 1965) 44: 166–73; Ira De A. Reid, "Special Problems of Negro Migration during the War." *Milbank Memorial Fund Quarterly* (July 1947) 23: 284–92; US Bureau of the Census, *16th Census of the United States, 1940: Population. The Labor Force*. Washington, DC: Government Printing Office, 1943. Table 1; William Edward Vickery, *The Economics of the Negro Migration, 1900–1960*. New York: Ayer Co., 1977.

38. Modell, Goulden, and Magnusson.

39. Charles E. Silberman, *Crisis in Black and White*. New York: Vintage, 1964.
40. Chafe, Gavins, and Korstad, et al., p. 26.
41. Silberman.
42. Survey reported in the *Wall Street Journal* (October 19, 1942): 73.
43. Chafe, Gavins, and Korstad, et al., p. 26.
44. Leslie H. Fishel and Benjamin Quarles, *The Negro American: A Documentary History*. Glenview, IL: Scott, Foresman, 1967.
45. Gayraud S. Wilmore, *Black Religion and Black Radicalism: An Interpretation of the Religious History of Afro-American People*. Maryknoll, NY: Orbis Books, 1994.
46. Harvard Sitkoff, "Racial Militancy and Interracial Violence in the Second World War." *Journal of American History* (1971) 58: 661–81.
47. Silberman, p. 60.
48. Silberman, p. 61.
49. Silberman.
50. "Intelligence Report: White Attitudes Toward Negroes." OWI: Bureau of Intelligence. "The Polls: Race Relations." *Public Opinion Quarterly* (August 5, 1942) XXVI: 137–48.
51. Clark Foreman, "Race Tension in the South." *New Republic* (September 21, 1942) 107: 340–42; Graves, p. 500; Carey McWilliams, "Race Tensions: Second Phase." *Common Ground* (1943) IV: 7–12; Park, p. 174.
52. Graves, p. 505.
53. A. D. DeSantis, "Selling the American Dream Myth to Black Southerners: The Chicago *Defender* and the Great Migration of 1915–1919." *Western Journal of Communication* (1998) 62: 474–511.
54. Deirdre Mullane, *Crossing the Danger Water*. New York: Doubleday, 1993.
55. Ulysses Lee, *The Employment of Negro Troops*. Washington, DC: Office of the Chief of Military History, United States Army, 1966.
56. C. Dollard and D. Young, "In the Armed Forces." *Survey Graphic* (1947) 36: 66–68, 111–16.
57. A. Russell Buchanan, *Black Americans in World War II*. Santa Barbara, CA: Clio, 1977; Richard M. Dalfiume, "Desegregation of the United States Armed Forces, 1939–1953." University of Missouri: unpublished doctoral dissertation, 1966; Michelle Hilmes, *Radio Voices: American Broadcasting, 1922–1952*. Minneapolis: University of Minnesota Press, 1977.
58. "Nazi Plan for Negroes Copies Southern U.S.A." *Crisis* (March 1941) 48: 71.
59. Hilmes, p. 262.
60. Davis; Finkle; Motley; Percival L. Prattis, "The Role of the Negro Press in Race Relations." *Phylon* (1946) 7: 273–83; L. R. Samuel, *Pledging Allegiance: American Identity and the Bond Drive of World War II*. Washington, DC: Smithsonian Institution Press, 1997; Patrick S. Washburn, *A Question of Sedition: The Federal Government's Investigation of the Black Press during World War II*. New York: Oxford University Press, 1986.
61. Samuel, p. 131.
62. "For Manhood in National Defense." *Crisis* (December 1940) 47: 375; Jones; H. H. Long, "The Negro Soldier in the Army of the United States." *Journal of Negro Education* (1943) 12: 314; W. Wilson, "Old Jim Crow in Uniform." *Crisis* (February 1939) 46: 42–44; Roy Wilkins, Letter to the Editor. *Crisis* (March 1939) 46: 71–73, 82, 93.
63. Finkle; Samuel; N. A. Wynn, *The Afro-American and the Second World War*. New York: Holmes and Meier, 1975.
64. Wilkins, p. 93.

65. Dalfiume 1969; Washburn.
66. Buchanan.
67. Finkle; Sitkoff; Wynn.
68. Buchanan.
69. Dalfiume 1969, pp. 29–30.
70. Finkle.
71. Office of War Information, "The Negro Looks at War." (May 1942). Schomburg Collection, appendixes III, IX (Typescript), p. 1.
72. Finkle; C. L. R. James. George Breitman, Edgar Keemer, et al., *Fighting Racism in World War II*. New York: Monad, 1990; Samuel; Sitkoff; Wynn.
73. Wilmore.
74. Stanley High, "How the Negro Fights for Freedom." *Reader's Digest* (July 1942) 41: 116.
75. Finkle.
76. Ted Gurr, *Why Men Rebel*. New Haven: Princeton University Press, 1970.
77. Robert C. Weaver, "Racial Employment Trends in National Defense." *Phylon* (1941) II: 337–58.
78. US Bureau of the Census. *16th Census of the United States, 1940: Population. The Labor Force*. Washington, DC: Government Printing Office, 1943. Table 1.
79. Wilma Woods, personal interview, August 12, 2007.
80. Chafe, Gavins, and Korstad, et al., p. 26.
81. Ronald Takaki, *Double Victory: A Multicultural History of America in World War II*. New York: Little, Brown and Company, 2000.
82. Karen Tucker Anderson, "Last Hired, First Fired: Black Women Workers during World War II." *Journal of American History* (1982) 69: 84–85.
83. Sherna Berger Gluck, *Rosie the Riveter Revisited: Women, the War, and Social Change*. New York: Meridian, 1987, p. 38.
84. Chafe, Gavins, and Korstad, et al.
85. Betty Young, personal interview, June 25, 1989.
86. James, Breitman, Keemer, et al., p. 28.
87. James, Breitman, Keemer, et al., p. 36.
88. James, Breitman, Keemer, et al., p. 242.
89. James, Breitman, Keemer, et al., p. 270.
90. Survey S-1.
91. Quoted in Fishel and Quarles, p. 473.

CHAPTER NINE

1. Quoted in Daniel J. Leab, *From Sambo to Superspade: The Black Experience in Motion Pictures*. Boston: Houghton Mifflin Company, 1975, p. 48.
2. The popularity of black news sources may explain why a newspaper office is the setting for *The Negro Sailor*.
3. Lee Finkle, *Forum for Protest: The Black Press during World War II*. Cranbury, NJ: Associated University Presses, 1976, p. 90.
4. Stanley Sandler, "Homefront Battlefront: Military Racial Disturbances in the Zone of the Interior, 1941–1945." *The American Experience in World War II: The American People at War: Minorities and Women in the Second World War*, Vol. 10. Ed. Walter L. Hixson. New York: Routledge, 2003, pp. 131–45.

5. In one of the most widely quoted lines of newsprint from World War I, W. E. B. Du Bois wrote in his "Close Ranks" editorial (*Crisis*, July 16, 1918, p. 111), "Let us, while this war lasts, forget our special grievances and close ranks shoulder to shoulder with our own fellow citizens." He argued that African Americans would gain more by supporting a nation where democracy was at least an ideal, even if that ideal was not realized for some of its citizens.

6. Quoted in Finkle, p. 46.

7. Finkle, p. 222.

8. Charles A. Simmons, *The African American Press: With Special Reference to Four Newspapers, 1827–1965*. Jefferson, NC: McFarland & Company, 1998, p. 29.

9. Harvard Sitkoff, "Racial Militancy and Interracial Violence in the Second World War." *Journal of American History* (1971) 58: 662.

10. Maggi M. Morehouse, *Fighting in the Jim Crow Army: Black Men and Women Remember World War II*. Lanham, MD: Rowman & Littlefield, 2000.

11. Stanley High, "How the Negro Fights for Freedom." *Reader's Digest* (July 1942) 41: 117.

12. Lerone Bennett, *The Shaping of Black America*. New York: Penguin Books, 1969.

13. Alan M. Osur, *Blacks in the Army Air Forces during World War II: The Problem of Race Relations*. Washington, DC: Department of Defense, Department of the Air Force, Office of Air Force History. US Government Printing Office, 1977, p. 146.

14. Maureen Honey, *Bitter Fruit: African American Women in World War II*. Columbia: University of Missouri Press, 1999.

15. Simmons, p. 7.

16. Simmons, p. 7.

17. Harold Martin, "How Do Our Negro Troops Measure Up?" *Saturday Evening Post* (June 16, 1951): 13.

18. N. A. Wynn, *The Afro-American and the Second World War*. New York: Holmes and Meier, 1975, p. 79.

19. Honey, p. 4.

20. Quoted in Morehouse, p. 134.

21. Finkle, 1975, p. 95.

22. Christopher Parker, "War and African American Citizenship, 1865–1965: The Role of Military Service." *African American Citizenship, 1865–Present*. Eds. Henry Louis Gates Jr. et al. New York: Oxford University Press, 2012, pp. 454, 446.

23. "Used Men as Seagoing Chambermaids, Bell Hops, Dishwashers," *Pittsburgh Courier* (October 5, 1940): 1.

24. "A Hero from the Galley," *Pittsburgh Courier* (January 3, 1942); Quoted in Patrick S. Washburn. *A Question of Sedition: The Federal Government's Investigation of the Black Press during World War II*. New York: Oxford University Press, 1986, p. 53.

25. Finkle, p. 104.

26. Wynn, p. 78.

27. Simmons, p. 70.

28. Washburn.

29. James G. Thompson, "Should I Sacrifice to Live 'Half-American?'" *Pittsburgh Courier* (January 31, 1942): 3.

30. Simmons, p. 80.

31. Quoted in Washburn, p. 101.

32. Minutes of the Meeting of the Board of Directors, NAACP, 8 December 1941; Box #38, Arthur B. Spingarn Papers, Library of Congress.

33. Alan M. Osur, *Separate & Unequal: Race Relations in the AAF during World War II.* Honolulu: University Press of the Pacific, 2004, p. 12.

34. John Temple Graves, "The Southern Negro and the War Crisis." *Virginia Quarterly Review* (1942) 18: 512.

35. Graves, p. 517.

36. Washburn.

37. Beth Bailey and David Farber, "The 'Double V' Campaign in World War II Hawaii: African Americans, Racial Ideology, and Federal Power." *The American Experience in World War II: The American People at War: Minorities and Women in the Second World War*, Vol. 10. Ed. Walter L. Hixson. New York: Routledge, 2003, p. 183.

38. C. L. R. James, George Breitman, Edgar Keemer, et al., *Fighting Racism in World War II.* New York: Monad Press, 1990, p. 66.

39. Morehouse, p. 114.

40. Ralph N. Davis, "The Negro Newspapers and the War." *Sociology and Social Research* (1943) 27: 373–80; Percival L. Prattis, "The Role of the Negro Press in Race Relations." *Phylon* (1946) 7: 273–83; Thomas Sancton, "The Negro Press." *New Republic* (April 26, 1943) 108: 557–60.

41. William H. Chafe, Raymond Gavins, and Robert Korstad, et al., *Remembering Jim Crow.* New York: Center for Documentary Studies for the Behind the Veil Project, 2001.

42. Horace R. Cayton, "Negro Morale." *Opportunity: Journal of Negro Life* (1941) 19: 371–75; Kenneth B. Clark, "Morale of the Negro on the Home Front: World Wars I and II." *Journal of Negro Education* (Summer 1943) 12: 417–28; "Jim Crow in the Camps," *Nation* (March 20, 1943) 156: 429; Lucille B. Milner, "Jim Crow in the Army." *New Republic* (March 13, 1944) 110: 429; "Negroes in the Armed Forces," *New Republic* (October 18, 1943) 109: 542–43; Howard W. Odum, *Race and Rumors of Race: Challenge to Crisis.* Chapel Hill: University of North Carolina Press, 1943; Prattis.

43. Robert W. Mullen, *Blacks in America's Wars.* New York: Monad Press, 1973.

44. *Crisis*, July 1940, cover.

45. Alan M. Osur, *Blacks in the Army Air Forces during World War II: The Problem of Race Relations.* Washington, DC: Department of Defense, Department of the Air Force, Office of Air Force History. US Government Printing Office, 1977, pp. 9–10.

46. Gunnar Myrdal, *An American Dilemma: The Negro Problem and Modern Democracy.* New York: Harper & Bros., 1944, p. 4.

47. Osur.

48. High.

49. High.

50. Osur, 2004, p. 62.

51. Simmons.

52. Quoted in Osur, 1977, p. 65.

53. Simmons, p. 106.

54. Simmons, p. 86.

55. Washburn.

56. Assistant Secretary of War, box #40, 291.2, NARG 107. Quoted in footnote 24 in Sandler (2003).

57. "Now Is the Time Not to Be Silent." *Crisis* (January 1942): 7.

58. Ulysses Lee, *The Employment of Negro Troops.* Washington, DC: Office of the Chief of Military History, United States Army, 1966.

59. Washburn.
60. Washburn, p. 102.
61. G-2 Memorandum to Assistant Secretary of War McCloy. June 27, 1942. ASW 291.2, Record Group 335.
62. Richard M. Dalfiume, "The 'Forgotten Years' of the Negro Revolution." *The American Experience in World War II: The American People at War: Minorities and Women in the Second World War*, Vol. 10. Ed. Walter L. Hixson. New York: Routledge, 2003, p. 158.
63. Osur, 1977.
64. Richard Pollenberg, *America at War: The Home Front, 1941–1945*. Englewood Cliffs, NJ: Prentice-Hall, 1968, p. 106.

CHAPTER TEN

1. James Carey, *Communication as Culture: Essays on Media and Society*. Boston: Unwin Hyman, 1989, p. 84.
2. Celeste M. Condit and John L. Lucaites, *Crafting Equality: America's Anglo-African Word*. Chicago: University of Chicago Press, 1993, p. 171.
3. Harold Cruse, *The Crisis of the Negro Intellectual: From Its Origins to the Present*. New York: William Morrow and Company, 1967, p. 14.
4. Carey.
5. Warren Susman, *Culture as History: The Transformation of American Society in the Twentieth Century*. New York: Pantheon, 1984, p. 159.
6. Brian Ward, *Media, Culture, and the Modern African American Freedom Struggle*. Gainesville: University Press of Florida, 2001, p. 3.
7. Louis Althusser, "Ideology and Ideological State Apparatuses." *Lenin and Philosophy and Other Essays*, Trans. Ben Brewster. New York: Monthly Review Press, 1971, p. 162.
8. Althusser.
9. C. Knoppes and G. Black, "What to Show the World: The Office of War Information and Hollywood, 1942–45." *Journal of American History* (1977) LXIV: 87–105.
10. Daniel J. Leab, *From Sambo to Superspade: The Black Experience in Motion Pictures*. Boston: Houghton Mifflin Company, 1975, p. 48.
11. James Murray, *To Find an Image: Black Films from Uncle Tom to Super Fly*. Indianapolis: Bobbs-Merrill, 1973.
12. Bird and Dardenne.
13. Michael Griffin, "The Great War Photographs: Constructing Myths of History and Photojournalism." *Picturing the Past: Media, History, & Photography*. Eds. Bonnie Brennen and Hanno Hardt. Urbana: University of Illinois Press, 1999, p. 129.
14. Michael Osborn, "Rhetorical Depiction." *Form, Genre, and the Study of Political Discourse*. Eds. Herbert W. Simons and A. A. Aghazarian. Columbia: University of South Carolina Press, 1986, p. 99.
15. Robert A. Rosenstone, "History in Images/History in Words: Reflections on the Possibility of Really Putting History onto Film." *American Historical Review* (1988) 43: 1178–95.
16. Yearwood, p. 11.
17. Ronald N. Jacobs, *Race, Media, and the Crisis of Civil Society*. Cambridge, UK: University of Cambridge Press, 2000, p. 149.
18. Jonathan Rosenbaum, "Multinational Pest Control: Does American Cinema Still Exist?" *Film and Nationalism*. Ed. Alan Williams. New Brunswick, NJ: Rutgers, 2002, pp. 217–29.
19. Alan Williams, "Introduction." *Film and Nationalism*. New Brunswick, NJ: Rutgers University Press, 2002.

20. Cruse, p. 455.
21. Yearwood.
22. Siegfried Kracauer, *Theory of Film*. New York: Oxford University Press, 1960, pp. 77–79.
23. R. C. Raack, "Historiography as Cinematography: A Prolegomenon to Film Work for historians." *Journal of Contemporary History* (1983) 18: p. 418.
24. Rosenstone, p. 1177.
25. Rosenstone, p. 1178.
26. Patricia A. Turner, *Ceramic Uncles & Celluloid Mammies*. New York: Anchor, 1994, p. xiv.
27. Raack, p. 416.
28. Raack, p. 416.
29. Thomas Hylland Eriksen, *Ethnicity and Nationalism: Anthropological Perspectives*. Boulder, CO: Pluto Press, 1993, p. 68.
30. Marita Sturken, "Absent Images of Memory: Remembering and Reenacting the Japanese Internment." *Perilous Memories: The Asia-Pacific War(s)*. Eds. G. T. Fujitani, M. White, and L. Yoneyama. Durham NC: Duke University Press, 2001, p. 35.
31. Michel Foucault, "The Order of Discourse." *Language and Politics*. Ed. Michael J. Shapiro. New York: New York University Press, 1984, p. 133.
32. Hayden White. "The Value of Narrativity in the Representation of Reality." *Critical Inquiry* (1980) 7: 5–27.
33. Thomas Cripps, "Racial Ambiguities in American Propaganda Movies." *Film & Radio Propaganda in World War II*. Ed. K. R. M. Short. Knoxville: University of Tennessee Press, 1983, p. 126.
34. Martha Finnemore and Kathryn Sikkink, "International Norm Dynamics and Political Change." *International Organization* (1998) 52: 914.
35. Kenneth Burke, "The Range of Rhetoric," *A Rhetoric of Motives*. Oakland: University of California Press, 1950, pp. 3–46.
36. Teun A. van Dijk, "Stories and Racism." *Narrative and Social Control*. Ed. Dennis K. Mumby. Newbury Park, CA: Sage, 1993, p. 125.
37. Walter Fisher, *Human Communication as Narration*. Columbia: University of South Carolina Press. 1987; Walter R. Fisher, "Narration, Reason, and Community." *Memory, Identity, Community: The Idea of Narrative in the Human Sciences*. Eds. Lewis P. Hinchman and Sandra K. Hinchman. Albany: State University of New York Press, 1997, pp. 307–27.
38. Griffin, 1999, p. 129.
39. Daniel Schacter, *Searching for Memory*. New York: Basic Books, 1996, p. 5.
40. Griffin, p. 123.
41. McGee.
42. Stuart Hall, "The Whites of their Eyes: Racist Ideologies and the Media." *Silver Linings: Some Strategies for the Eighties*. Eds. George Bridges and Rosalind Brunt. London, UK: Lawrence & Wishart, 1981, pp. 28–52.
43. Stuart Hall, "Gramsci's Relevance for the Study of Race and Ethnicity." *Journal of Communication Inquiry* (1986) 10: 5–27.

CHAPTER ELEVEN

1. Quoted in Scott L. Malcomson, *One Drop of Blood: The American Misadventure of Race*. New York: Farrar Straus Giroux, 2000, p. 374.
2. Harold Cruse, *The Crisis of the Negro Intellectual: From Its Origins to the Present*. New York: William Morrow and Company, 1967.

3. Charles C. Moskos, "Racial Integration in the Armed Forces." *The Making of Black America: The Black Community in Modern America*, Vol. 2. Eds. August Meier and Elliott Rudwick. New York: Atheneum, 1969, pp. 425–47.

4. Deutsch and Collins, p. 11.

5. Moskos, p. 436.

6. Quoted in Morehouse, p. 200.

7. Quoted in Morehouse, p. 222.

8. James O. Eastland, "Are Negroes Good Soldiers?" *Negro Digest* (December 1945): 30.

9. Lt. Colonel John H. Sherman, "Are Negroes Good Soldiers?" *Negro Digest* (December 1945): 32.

10. Sherman, 1945, p. 33.

11. Gerald Jaynes, "The Expansion of Economic Rights since World War II." *African American Citizenship, 1865–Present*. Eds. Henry Louis Gates Jr. et al. New York: Oxford University Press, 2012, p. 323.

12. Kimberly L. Phillips, "'Did the Battlefield Kill Jim Crow?' The Cold War Military, Civil Rights, and Black Freedom Struggles." *Fog of War: The Second World War and the Civil Rights Movement*. Eds. Kevin M. Kruse and Stephen Tuck. New York: Oxford University Press, 2012, p. 210.

13. Stephen R. Goldzwig, "Civil Rights and the Cold War: A Rhetorical History of the Truman Administration's Desegregation of the United States Army." *Doing Rhetorical History*. Ed. Kathleen J. Turner. Tuscaloosa: University of Alabama Press, 1998, p. 154.

14. Ronald R. Krebs, *Fighting for Rights: Military Service and the Politics of Citizenship*. Ithaca, NY: Cornell University Press, 2006, p. 41.

15. Stanley Sandler, "Homefront Battlefront: Military Racial Disturbances in the Zone of the Interior, 1941–1945." *The American Experience in World War II: The American People at War: Minorities and Women in the Second World War*, Vol. 10. Ed. Walter L. Hixson. New York: Routledge, 2003, pp. 131–45.

16. Stanley Sandler, *Segregated Skies: All-Black Combat Squadrons of WW II*. Washington, DC: Smithsonian Institution Press, 1992, p. xv.

17. Arthur M. Schlesinger Jr., "Political and Social Change: 1941–1968." *Interpreting American History: Conversations with Historians*. Ed. John A. Garraty. New York: Macmillan, p. 278.

18. Krebs, 2006, p. 20; also see Michel Foucault, "Film and Popular Memory." *Radical Philosophy* (1975) 11: 24–29 and Michel Foucault, "The Order of Discourse." *Language and Politics*. Ed. Michael J. Shapiro. New York: New York University Press, 1984, pp. 124–37.

19. Foucault.

20. Morris Janowitz, "The All-Volunteer Military as a 'Sociopolitical' Problem." *Social Problems* (1975) 22:188.

21. Janowitz, 1975, p. 189.

22. From T. H. Marshall, 1950. Cited in Morris Janowitz, "Military Institutions and Citizenship in Western Societies." *Armed Forces and Society* (1976) 2: 186.

23. Janowitz, 1976, p. 186.

24. L. A. Erenberg and S.E. Hirsch, *The War in American Culture: Society and Consciousness during World War II*. Chicago: University of Chicago Press, 1969, p. 2.

25. William H. Chafe, Raymond Gavins, and Robert Korstad, et al., *Remembering Jim Crow*. New York: Center for Documentary Studies for the Behind the Veil Project, 2001.

Bibliography

Adorno, T. W. "Television and Patterns of Mass Culture." *Mass Culture: The Popular Arts in America*. Ed. Bernard Rosenburg and David Manning. New York: Free Press, 1957. 479-91.
Agee, James. *Agee on Film: Reviews and Comments*. Boston: Beacon Press, 1958.
Allen, Robert C. "Audience-Oriented Criticism and Television." *Channels of Discourse Reassembled: Television and Contemporary Critics*. 2nd ed. Ed. Robert C. Allen. Chapel Hill: University of North Carolina Press, 1992. 101-37.
Allen, Robert L. *The Port Chicago Mutiny: The Story of the Largest Mass Mutiny Trial in U.S. Naval History*. New York: Warner Books, 1989.
Althusser, Louis. "Ideology and Ideological State Apparatuses." *Lenin and Philosophy and Other Essays*. Trans. Ben Brewster. New York: Monthly Review Press, 1971.
Ambrose, Stephen E. *Citizen Soldiers: From the Normandy Beaches to the Surrender of Germany*. New York: Simon & Schuster, 2002.
American History Project, "How to Tell a Chinese from a Jap." 27 April 2011 < http://historymatters.gmu.edu/d/6795>.
Anderson, Karen Tucker. "Last Hired, First Fired: Black Women Workers during World War II." *Journal of American History* (1982) 69: 84- 85.
Anderson, Paul Russell. "Universal Military Training and National Security." *Annals of the Academy of Social and Political Science* (1945) 24: 198-214.
Andrews, James. "Reflections of the National Character in American Rhetoric." *Central States Speech Journal* (1971) 42: 316-24.
Aptheker, Herbert. *Afro-American History: The Modern Era*. New York: Citadel Press, 1971.
Asante, Molefi K. *The Afrocentric Idea*. Philadelphia: Temple University Press, 1987.
Astor, Gerald. *The Right to Fight: A History of African Americans in the Military*. Cambridge, MA: Da Capo Press, 1998. A Welcome to Britain, 1943. British Ministry of Information film.
British Imperial War Museum archives. Original film transcription by author.
Baer, H.A. *African-American Religion in the Twentieth Century*. Knoxville: University of Tennessee Press. 1992.
Bhabba, H.K. "The Other Question: Difference, Discrimination, and the Discourse of Colonialism." *Out There: Marginalization and Contemporary Cultures*. Eds. R. Ferguson, M. Gaver, T.T. Hinh-ha, and C. West. Cambridge, MA: MIT Press, 1990. 71-87.
———. "Introduction: Narrating the Nation." *Nation and Narration*. Ed. H.K. Bhabba. New York: Routledge, 1990. 1-7.
Bailey, Beth, and David Farber. "The 'Double V' Campaign in World War II Hawaii: African Americans, Racial Ideology, and Federal Power." *The American Experience in World War II: The American People at War: Minorities and Women in the Second World War*, Vol. 10. Ed. Walter L. Hixson. New York: Routledge, 2003. 163-88.

———. "The Double V Campaign in World War II Hawaii: African Americans, Racial Identity, and Federal Power." *Journal of Social History* (1993) 13: 817–43.
Barker, Lucius J., and Mack H. Jones. *African Americans and the American Political System*. Englewood Cliffs, NJ: Prentice Hall, 1994.
Barry, Jonathan, and Joseph Melling. "The Problem of Culture." *Culture in History: Production, Consumption and Values in Historical Perspective*. Eds. Joseph Melling and Jonathan Barry. Devon, UK: University of Exeter Press, 1992. 3–27.
Barthes, Roland. *Mythologies*. London: Paladin, 1973.
Bassett, John Spenser. *Life of Andrew Jackson*. New York: Macmillan Company, 1925.
Bendix, Reinhard. *Nation-Building and Citizenship*. New York: John Wiley & Sons, 1964.
Benedict, Ruth. *Patterns of Culture*. New York: Houghton Mifflin, 1934.
Benedict, Ruth, with Gene Weltfish. *The Races of Mankind: Public Affairs Pamphlet No. 85*. New York: Public Affairs Committee, Inc., 1943.
Bennett, Lerone. *The Shaping of Black America*. New York: Penguin Books, 1969.
Bercovitch, Sacvan. *The American Jeremiad*. Madison: University of Wisconsin Press, 1978.
Berger, John. *Ways of Seeing*. New York: Penguin, 1972.
Bernard, Daniel. *The Birth of Whiteness: Race and the Emergence of U.S. Cinema*. New Brunswick, NJ: Rutgers University Press, 1996.
Bethel, Elizabeth Rauh. *The Roots of African-American Identity: Memory and History in Antebellum Free Communities*. New York: St. Martin's Press, 1997.
Bielakowski, Alexander. *African American Troops in World War II*. Westminster, MD: Random House, 2007.
Billington, Monroe. "Freedom to Serve: The President's Committee on Equality of Treatment and Opportunity in the Armed Forces, 1949–1950." *Journal of Negro History* (1966) 51: 262–74.
Bird, Elizabeth, and R. Dardenne. "Myth, Chronicle, and Story: Exploring the Narrative Qualities of News." *Media, Myths and Narratives: Television and the Press*. Ed. James Carey. Newbury Park, CA: Sage, 1988. 67–86.
"Black Americans in Defense of Our Nation." Department of Defense, 1985. 6 February 2013 <http://www.shsu.edu/~his_nep/AfrAmer.html>.
Blassingame, John et al. *The Frederick Douglass Papers: Series One–Speeches, Debates and Interviews*, Vol. 1. New Haven: Yale University Press, 1979.
Bloom, Jack M. *Class, Race, and the Civil Rights Movement*. Bloomington: University of Indiana Press, 1987.
Blum, John Morton. *V Was for Victory: Politics and American Culture during World War II*. New York: Harcourt Brace Jovanovich, 1976.
Blumer, Herbert. "Morale." *American Society in Wartime*. Ed. William Fielding Ogburn. Chicago: University of Chicago Press, 1943. 207–32.
Bogart, Leo. "Introduction." *Project Clear: Social Research and the Desegregation of the U.S. Army*. Ed. L. Bogart. Chicago: Markham, 1951. ix–liii.
———. *Project Clear: Social Research and the Desegregation of the U.S. Army*. New Brunswick, NJ: Transaction, 1992.
Bogle, Donald. *Toms, Coons, Mulattoes, Mammies, and Bucks: An Interpretive History of Blacks in American Films*. New York: Viking Press, 1973.
———. *Prime Time Blues: African Americans on Network Television*. New York: Farrar, Straus and Giroux, 2001.

Bond, Horace Mann. "The Negro in the Armed Forces of the United States Prior to World War I." *Journal of Negro Education* (1943) 12: 68–287.
Botsch, Carol, et al. *African-Americans and the Palmetto State*. Columbia, SC: South Carolina State Department of Education, 1994.
Bowser, Pearl. "Pioneers of Black Documentary Film." *Struggles for Representation: African American Documentary Film and Video*. Eds. Phyllis R. Kotman and Janet K. Cutler. Bloomington: Indiana University Press, 1999. 1–33.
———. 1982. "Sexual Imagery and the Black Woman in Cinema." *Black Cinema Aesthetics: Issues in Black Filmmaking*. Ed. Gladstone Yearwood. Columbus: Ohio University's Centre for Afro-American Studies, 1982. 42–52.
Boyd, James. "Letter to the Editor." *Nation* (June 26, 1943) 156: 884–87.
Bradley, Patricia. *Slavery, Propaganda, and the American Revolution*. Jackson: University Press of Mississippi, 1999.
Bray, Mayfield S., and William T. Murphy. *Audiovisual Records in the National Archives of the United States Relating to World War II*. Washington, DC: National Archives and Records Service 1974.
Brink, William, and Louis Harris. *The Negro Revolution in America*. New York: Simon & Schuster, 1964.
Broderick, Francis L., and August Meier. *Negro Protest Thought in the Twentieth Century*. Indianapolis, IN: Bobbs-Merrill, 1965.
Brown, Earl, and George Leighton. *The Negro and the War*. New York: Americas Press, 1942.
Brown, Sterling A. *The Negro in American Fiction*. Manchester, NH: Ayers Co., 1969.
Buchanan, A. Russell. *Black Americans in World War II*. Santa Barbara, CA: Clio, 1977.
Buck, Pearl S. "Too Much Unity is a Danger." *Opportunity* (April 1941):110–11.
Burk, James. "Citizenship Status and Military Service: The Quest for Inclusion by Minorities and Conscientious Objectors." *Armed Forces & Society* (1995) 21: 503–29.
Burke, Kenneth. "The Range of Rhetoric." *A Rhetoric of Motives*. Oakland: University of California Press, 1950.
Cameron, Kenneth M. *America on Film: Hollywood and American History*. New York: Continuum, 1997.
Campbell, Craig W. *Reel America and World War I: A Comprehensive Filmography and History of Motion Pictures in the United States, 1914–1920*. Jefferson, NC: McFarland, 1985.
Campbell, Joseph. *The Hero with a Thousand Faces*. New York: Meridian, 1949.
Capra, Frank. *The Name Above the Title: An Autobiography*. New York:Macmillan, 1971.
Carey, James. *Communication as Culture: Essays on Media and Society*. Boston: Unwin Hyman, 1989.
Carruthers, Susan L. *The Media at War: Communication and Conflict in the Twentieth Century*. New York: St. Martin's Press, 2000.
Cayton, Horace R. "Negro Morale." *Opportunity: Journal of Negro Life* (1941) 19: 371–75.
Chafe, William H., Raymond Gavins, and Robert Korstad, et al. *Remembering Jim Crow*. New York: Center for Documentary Studies for the Behind the Veil Project, 2001.
Chamberlain, Charles D. *Victory at Home: Manpower and Race in the American South during World War II*. Athens: University of Georgia Press, 2003.
Chambers, J. W., and D. Culbert. *World War II: Film and History*. New York: Oxford University Press, 1996.
Cheh, Mary M. "VMI Essays: An Essay on VMI and Military Service: Yes, We Do Have to be Equal Together." *Washington and Lee Law Review* (1993) 50: 49–61.

Chicago Commission on Race Relations. *The Negro in Chicago, A Study of Race Relations and a Race Riot*. Chicago: University of Chicago Press, 1922.

Christensen, Terry, and Peter J. Haas. *Projecting Politics: Political Messages in American Films*. Armonk, NY: M.E. Sharpe, 2005.

Clark, Kenneth B. "Morale of the Negro on the Home Front: World Wars I and II." *Journal of Negro Education* (1943) 12: 417–28.

Colley, David P. "On the Road to Victory: The Red Ball Express." 11 November 2003. <http://www.military.com/Content/MoreContent?file=PRredball>.

Condit, Celeste M., and John L. Lucaites. *Crafting Equality: America's Anglo-African Word*. Chicago: University of Chicago Press, 1993.

Converse, Elliott V., Daniel K. Gibran, John A. Cash, Robert K. Griffith, and Richard H. Kohn. *The Exclusion of Black Soldiers from the Medal of Honor in World War II: The Study Commissioned by the United States Army to Investigate Racial Bias in the Awarding of the Nation's Highest Military Decoration*. Jefferson, NC: McFarland, 1997.

Cook, Timothy E. "The Bear Market in Political Socialization and the Costs of Misunderstood Psychological Theories." *American Political Science Review* (1985) 79: 1079–93.

Corner, John. *A Critical Introduction to Documentary*. Manchester, UK: Manchester University Press, 1996.

Cox, Clinton. "From Columbus to Hitler and Back Again." *Race & Class* (2002) 43: 39–49.

Cripps, Thomas. "Film." *Split Image: African Americans in the Mass Media*. Eds. Jannette L. Dates and William Barlow. Washington, DC: Howard University Press, 1993. 131–85.

———. *Hollywood's High Noon: Moviemaking & Society before Television*. Baltimore: Johns Hopkins University Press, 1997.

———. "Racial Ambiguities in American Propaganda Movies." *Film & Radio Propaganda in World War II*. Ed. K.R.M. Short. Knoxville: University of Tennessee Press, 1983. 125–45.

———. *Slow Fade to Black: The Negro in American Film, 1900–1942*. New York: Oxford University Press, 1977.

———. "The Noble Black Savage: A Problem in the Politics of Television Art." *Journal of Popular Culture* (1975) 8: 687–95.

Cripps, Thomas, and David Culbert. "The Negro Soldier (1944): Film Propaganda in Black and White." *American Quarterly* (1979) 31: 616–40.

Cruse, Harold. *The Crisis of the Negro Intellectual: From Its Origins to the Present*. New York: William Morrow, 1967.

Culbert, David. "Walt Disney's Private Snafu: The Use of Humor in World War II Army Film." *Prospects: An Annual Journal of American Cultural Studies* (1975) 1: 80–96.

Dabbs, James McBride. *Who Speaks for the South?* New York: Funk & Wagnalls, 1964.

Dabney, Virginius. "Nearer and Nearer the Precipice." *Atlantic Monthly* (January 1943): 94–100.

Dalfiume, Richard M. *Desegregation of the Armed Forces: Fighting on Two Fronts*. Columbia: University of Missouri Press, 1969.

———. "Desegregation of the United States Armed Forces, 1939–1953." University of Missouri: Unpublished doctoral dissertation, 1966.

———. "Military Segregation and the 1940 Presidential Election." *Freedom's Odyssey: African American History Essays from Phylon*. Eds. Alexa Benson Henderson and Janice Sumler-Edmond. Atlanta: Clark Atlanta University Press, 1999. 353–70.

———. "The 'Forgotten Years' of the Negro Revolution." *The American Experience in World War II: The American People at War: Minorities and Women in the Second World War*, Vol. 10. Ed. Walter L. Hixson. New York: Routledge, 2003. 146–62.

Dates, Jannette L., and William Barlow. "A War of Images." *Split Image: African Americans in the Mass Media*. Eds. Jannette L. Dates and William Barlow. Washington, DC: Howard University Press, 1993. 1–22.

———. "Split Images and Double Binds." *Split Image: African Americans in the Mass Media*. Eds. Jannette L. Dates and William Barlow. Washington, DC: Howard University Press, 1993. 523–28.

Davis, Arthur P. "Will a Long War Aid the Negro?" *Negro Digest* (November 1943) 2: 43–46.

Davis, Ralph N. "The Negro Newspapers and the War." *Sociology and Social Research* (1943) 27: 373–80.

D-Day 24 Hours That Saved the World. 70th Anniversary Tribute. New York: Time Magazine, 2014.

Debord, Guy. *Society of the Spectacle and Other Films*. London: Rebel Press, 1992.

Dennis, Rutledge. "W.E.B. Du Bois's Concept of Double Consciousness." *Race and Ethnicity: Comparative and Theoretical Approaches*. Eds. John Stone and Rutledge Dennis. London: Blackwell Publishing, 2003. 13–17.

DeSantis, A.D. "Selling the American Dream Myth to Black Southerners: The Chicago *Defender* and the Great Migration of 1915- 1919." *Western Journal of Communication* (1998) 62: 474–511.

Deutsch, Morton, and Mary Evans Collins. "Interracial Housing." *American Social Patterns*. Ed. William Petersen. Garden City, NY: Doubleday Anchor, 1956. 7–61.

Diawara, Manthia. "Black Spectatorship: Problems of Identification and Resistance." *Black American Cinema*. Ed. Manthia Diawara. New York: Routledge, 1993. 211–20.

Dobak, William, and Phillips, Thomas. *The Black Regulars, 1866-1898*. Norman: University of Oklahoma Press, 2001.

Dollard, C., and D. Young. "In the Armed Forces." *Survey Graphic* (1947) 36: 66–68, 111–16.

Dougherty, Thomas. *Projections of War: Hollywood, American Culture and World War II*. New York: Columbia University Press, 1993.

Dower, John W. *War without Mercy: Race & Power in the Pacific War*. New York: Pantheon, 1986.

Du Bois, W.E.B. "Close Ranks." *Crisis* (July 16, 1918): 111.

———. "Niagara Movement," *Horizon* (September 1908) 4: 1–9.

———. "Returning Soldiers." *Crisis* (May 1919) 18: 13–14.

———. *The Souls of Black Folk*. Chicago: A.C. McClurg, 1903. (Edition cited is Greenwich, CT: Fawcett Publications, 1961.)

Durden, Robert F. *The Gray and the Black: The Confederate Debate on Emancipation*. Baton Rouge: Louisiana State University Press, 1972.

Eastland, James O. "Are Negroes Good Soldiers?" *Negro Digest* (December 1945): 29–33.

Eberwein, Robert. *The Hollywood War Film*. West Sussex, UK: Wiley-Blackwell, 2010.

Edwords, F. "The Religious Character of American Patriotism." *Humanist* (1987) 47: 20–25.

Eisenhower, Dwight D. "Farewell Address to the Nation." January 17, 1961. <http://www.ourdocuments.gov/doc.php?flash=true&doc=90>.

Ellis, Mark. "'Closing Ranks' and 'Seeking Honors': W.E.B. Du Bois in World War I." *Journal of American History* (1992) 79: 96–124.

Entman, Robert M., and Andrew Rojecki. *The Black Image in the White Mind*. Chicago: University of Chicago Press, 2000.
"Erasing Color Lines." *Wall Street Journal* (October 19, 1942): 14.
Erenberg, Lewis A., and Susan E. Hirsch. *The War in American Culture: Society and Consciousness during World War II*. Chicago: University of Chicago Press, 1996.
Eriksen, Thomas Hylland. *Ethnicity and Nationalism: Anthropological Perspectives*. Boulder, CO: Pluto Press, 1993.
Ernst, Wolfgang. "DIStory: Cinema and Historical Discourse." *Journal of Contemporary History* (1983) 18: 397–409.
Escobar, E.J. "Zoot-Suiters and Cops: Chicano Youth and the Los Angeles Police Department during World War II." *The War in American Culture: Society and Consciousness during World War II*. Eds. Lewis A. Erenberg and Susan E. Hirsch. Chicago: University of Chicago Press, 1996. 284–309.
Farley, Reynolds. "The Urbanization of Negroes in the United States." *Journal of Social History* (1968) 1: 241–58.
Finkle, Lee. *Forum for Protest: The Black Press during World War II*. Cranbury, NJ: Associated University Presses, 1975.
Finnemore, Martha, and Kathryn Sikkink. "International Norm Dynamics and Political Change." *International Organization* (1998) 52: 912–31.
Fishel, Leslie H., and Benjamin Quarles. *The Negro American: A Documentary History*. Glenview, IL: Scott, Foresman, 1967.
Fisher, Walter R. *Human Communication as Narration*. Columbia: University of South Carolina Press, 1987.
———. "Narration, Reason, and Community." *Memory, Identity, Community: The Idea of Narrative in the Human Sciences*. Eds. Lewis P. Hinchman and Sandra K. Hinchman. Albany: State University of New York Press, 1997. 307–27.
Fiske, John. "British Cultural Studies." *Channels of Discourse: Television and Contemporary Criticism*. Ed. Robert Allen. Chapel Hill: University of North Carolina Press, 1987. 254–89.
———. *Television Culture: Popular Pleasures and Politics*. London: Methuen, 1987.
———. *Understanding Popular Culture*. Winchester, MA: Unwin Hyman, 1989.
Flynn, George Q. "Selective Service and American Blacks during World War II." *Journal of Negro History* (1984) 69: 14–25.
Foley, Barbara. *Spectres of 1919: Class and Nation in the Making of the New Negro*. Urbana, IL: University of Urbana Press, 2003.
Folkerts, Jean, and Stephen Lacy. *The Media in Your Life*. Boston: Pearson, 2004.
Foner, Eric. *Reconstruction: America's Unfinished Revolution, 1863-1877*. New York: Harper & Row, 1988.
"For Manhood in National Defense." *Crisis* (December 1940) 47: 375.
Foreman, Clark. "Race Tension in the South." *New Republic* (September 21, 1942) 107: 340–42.
Foss, Sonja K. "Visual Imagery as Communication." *Text & Performance Quarterly* (1992) 12: 85–96.
Foucault, Michel. *Discipline and Punish: The Birth of the Prison*. New York: Pantheon, 1977.
———. "Film and Popular Memory." *Radical Philosophy* (1975) 11: 24–29.
———. "The Order of Discourse." *Language and Politics*. Ed. Michael J. Shapiro. New York: New York University Press, 1984. 124–45.
Fowler, Arlen. *The Black Infantry in the West, 1861-1868*. Westport, CT: Greenwood and Negro University Press, 1971.

Franklin, John Hope. "History of Racial Segregation in the United States." *The Making of Black America: The Black Community in Modern America*, Vol. 2. Ed. August Meier and Elliott Rudwick. New York: Atheneum, 1969. 3–13.

Franklin, John Hope, and Alfred A. Moss. *From Slavery to Freedom*. New York: McGraw-Hill, 1994. Frazier, E. Franklin. *The Negro Church in America*. New York: Schocken Books, 1964.

———. *The Negro in the United States*. New York: Macmillan, 1957.

Fredrickson, G.M. *The Black Image in the White Mind: The Debate on Afro-American Characters and Destiny, 1817–1914*. New York: Harper and Row, 1971.

Fyne, Robert. *The Hollywood Propaganda of World War II*. Lanham, MD: Scarecrow Press, 1997.

G-2 Memorandum to Assistant Secretary of War McCloy. (June 27, 1942). ASW 291.2, Record Group 335.

Galloway, J.L. "The Last of the Buffalo Soldiers." *U.S. News & World Report* (May 6, 1996) 117: 45–46.

Garfinkel, Herbert. "Negroes in the Defense Emergency." *Blacks in White America Since 1865*. Ed. Robert C. Twombly. Philadelphia, PA: David McKay, 1971.

———. *When Negroes March: The March on Washington Movement in the Organizational Politics for FEPC*. Glencoe, IL: Scott Foresman, 1959.

German, Kathleen M. "Hollywood Goes to War: An Analysis of Frank Capra's 'Why We Fight' Series." *Western Journal of Speech Communication* (1990) 54: 237–48.

Geyer, Michael. "War and the Context of General History in an Age of Total War." *Journal of Military History* (1993) 57: 152–53.

Gluck, Sherna Berger. *Rosie the Riveter Revisited: Women, the War, and Social Change*. New York: Meridian, 1987.

Goldzwig, Stephen R. "Civil Rights and the Cold War: A Rhetorical History of the Truman Administration's Desegregation of the United States Army." *Doing Rhetorical History*. Ed. Kathleen J. Turner. Tuscaloosa: University of Alabama Press, 1998. 143–69.

Gramsci, Antonio. *Selections from the Prison Notebooks*. Trans. Quintin Hoare and Geoffrey Nowell-Smith. New York: International Publishers, 1971.

Granger, Lester B. "Negroes and War Production." *Survey Graphic* (November 1942) 31: 469–71.

Graves, John Temple. "The Southern Negro and the War Crisis." *Virginia Quarterly Review* (1942) 18: 500–17.

Gray, Herman. "Television and the New Black Man: Black Images in Prime-Time Situation Comedy." *Media, Culture and Society* (1986) 8: 223–42.

———. *Watching Race: Television and the Struggle for "Blackness."* Minneapolis: Regents of the University of Minnesota, 1995.

Green, J. Ronald. "'Twoness' in the Style of Oscar Micheaux." *Black American Cinema*. Ed. Manthia Diawara. New York: Routledge, 1993. 26–48.

Griffin, Charles J. "The Rhetoric of Form in Conversion Narratives." *Quarterly Journal of Speech* (1990) 76: 152–63.

Griffin, Michael. "The Great War Photographs: Constructing Myths of History and Photojournalism." *Picturing the Past: Media, History & Photography*. Eds. Bonnie Brennen and Hanno Hardt. Urbana: University of Illinois Press, 1999. 122–57.

Griffith, Richard. "The Use of Films by the U.S. Armed Services." *Documentary Film*. Ed. Paul Rotha. London, UK: Faber and Faber, 2011. 44–358.

Griggs, William E. *The World War II Black Regiment That Built the Alaskan Military Highway: A Photographic History*. Jackson: University Press of Mississippi, 2002.

Gronbeck, Bruce E. "Reconceptualizing the Visual Expedience in Media Studies." *Communication: Views from the Helm for the 21st Century*. Ed. Judith S. Trent. Boston: Allyn and Bacon, 1998. 289–93.

———. "Tradition and Technology in Local Newscasts." *Critical Approaches to Television*. Eds. Leah R. Vande Berg, Lawrence A. Wenner, and Bruce E. Gronbeck. Boston: Houghton Mifflin, 1998. 124–39.

Gurr, Ted. *Why Men Rebel*. New Haven: Princeton University Press, 1970.

Guzman, Jessie P. *Negro Year Book: A Review of Events Affecting Negro Life 1941–1946*. Tuskegee: Tuskegee Institute, 1947.

Hachey, Thomas. "Walter White and the American Negro Soldier in World War II: A Diplomatic Dilemma for Britain." *Freedom's Odyssey: African American History Essays from Phylon*. Eds. Alexa Benson Henderson and Janice Sumler-Edmond. Atlanta: Clark Atlanta University Press, 1999. 455–64

Hall, E.T. "Race Prejudice and Negro-White Relations in the Army." *American Journal of Sociology* (1947) 52: 401–9.

Hall, Stuart. "Encoding/decoding." *Culture, Media, Language*. Eds. Stuart Hall, D. Hobson, A. Lowe, and P. Willis. London: Hutchinson, 1980. 128–38.

Hall, Stuart. "Gramsci's Relevance for the Study of Race and Ethnicity." *Journal of Communication Inquiry* (1986) 10: 5–27.

———. "The Narrative Construction of Reality." *Southern Review* (1984) 17: 1, 3–17.

———. "The Whites of their Eyes: Racist Ideologies and the Media." *Silver Linings: Some Strategies for the Eighties*. Eds. George Bridges and Rosalind Brunt. London, UK: Lawrence & Wishart, 1981. 28–52.

Hamilton, C.V. *The Black Preacher in America*. New York: Morrow, 1972.

Hare, Nathan. "Recent Trends in the Occupational Mobility of Negroes, 1930–1960: An Intracohort Analysis," *Social Forces* (1965) 44: 166–73.

Hardt, Hanno. "The Site of Reality: Constructing Photojournalism in Weimar Germany, 1928–33." *Communication Review* (1996) 1: 373–402.

Hastie, William H. "The Negro in the Armed Forces in World War II." *Crisis* (February 1935) XLII: 41, 52.

———. "The Negro in the Army Today." *Annals of the American Academy of Political Science* (1942) 223: 55–59.

Hattaway, Allison M., And Susan L. Brinson. "Race and Radio: The Alabama Negro Extension Service Broadcasts, 1940–1945." *Journal of Radio Studies* (2001) 8: 372–87.

Herman, Gerald. "Documentary, Newsreel, and Television News as Factual Resources in the History Classroom." *Image as an Artifact: The Historical Analysis of Film and Television*. Ed. John E. O'Connor. Malabar, FL: Robert E. Krieger, 1990. 203–16. "A Hero from the Galley." *Pittsburgh Courier*. (January 3, 1942): 8.

Hershey, Lewis. "They're in the Army." *Negro Digest* (December 1942) 41: 70–72.

High, Stanley. "How the Negro Fights for Freedom." *Reader's Digest* (July 1942) 41: 113–18.

Hilmes, Michelle. *Radio Voices: American Broadcasting, 1922–1952*. Minneapolis: University of Minnesota Press, 1997.

Hintze, Otto. "Military Organization and the Organization of the State." *The Historical Essays of Otto Hintze*. Ed. Felix Gilbert. New York: Oxford University Press, 1975.

Hjort, Mette, and Scott Mackenzie. *Cinema & Nation*. New York: Routledge, 2000.

Hodges, Robert. "Buffalo Soldiers' Assault on the Gothic Line." 11 April 2012 <*Http://www.military.com/Content/General*>.
Honey, Maureen, ed. *Bitter Fruit: African American Women in World War II*. Columbia: University of Missouri Press, 1999.
hooks, bell. *Outlaw Culture: Resisting Representations*. New York: Routledge, 1994.
———. *Yearning: Race, Gender, and Cultural Politics*. Boston: South End Press, 1990.
Howard-Pitney, David. "The Enduring Black Jeremiad: The American Jeremiad and Black Protest Rhetoric, from Frederick Douglass to W.E.B. Du Bois, 1841-1919." *American Quarterly* (1986) 38: 481-92.
"How to Tell Japs from the Chinese." *Life* (December 22, 1941) 11: 81.
"Intelligence Report: White Attitudes Toward Negroes." OWI: Bureau of Intelligence. "The Polls: Race Relations." *Public Opinion Quarterly* (August 5, 1942) XXVI: 137-48.
Iser, Wolfgang. *The Act of Reading: A Theory of Aesthetic Response*. Baltimore: Johns Hopkins University Press, 1978.
Jacobs, Ronald N. *Race, Media, and the Crisis of Civil Society*. Cambridge, UK: University of Cambridge Press, 2000.
James. C.L. R., George Breitman, Edgar Keemer, et al. *Fighting Racism in World War II*. New York: Monad, 1990.
Jaynes, Gerald. "The Expansion of Economic Rights since World War II." *African American Citizenship, 1865-Present*. Eds. Henry Louis Gates Jr., et al. New York: Oxford University Press, 2012. 323-54.
Jenkins, McKay. *The South in Black and White: Race, Sex, and Literature in the 1940s*. Chapel Hill: University of North Press, 1999.
Janowitz, Morris. "Military Institutions and Citizenship in Western Societies." *Armed Forces and Society* (1976) 2: 185-204.
———. *Political Conflict*. Chicago: Quadrangle Books, 1970.
———. "The All-Volunteer Military as a 'Sociopolitical' Problem." *Social Problems* (1975) 22: 435.
———. *The Reconstruction of Patriotism*. Chicago: University of Chicago Press, 1983.
Jerome, V.J. *The Negro in Hollywood Films*. New York: Masses & Mainstream, 1950.
"Jim Crow in the Camps." *Nation* (March 20, 1943) 156: 429.
Johnson, Charles S. "The Negro and Organized Labor." *The Black American: A Documentary History*. Eds. Leslie H. Fishel and Benjamin Quarles. Glenview, IL: Scott, Foresman, 1923. 417-19.
———. *To Stem This Tide: A Survey of Racial Tension Areas in the United States*. Boston: Pilgrim Press, 1943.
Jones, Dorothy B. "The Hollywood Film: 1942-1945." *Hollywood Quarterly* (1945): 1-19.
Jones, G. William. *Black Cinema Treasures: Lost and Found*. Denton: University of North Texas Press, 1991.
Jones, Lester M. "The Editorial Policy of Negro Newspapers of 1917-1918 as Compared with That of 1941-1942." *Journal of Negro History* (January 1944) XXIX: 24-31.
Jordan, William G. "The Damnable Dilemma: African American Accommodation and Protest during World War I." *Journal of American History* (1995) 81: 1562-83.
Jordan, Winthrop E. *The White Man's Burden: Historical Origins of Racism in the United States*. New York: Oxford University Press, 1974.
Karst, Kenneth L. "The Supreme Court 1976 Term-Foreword: Equal Citizenship Under the Fourteenth Amendment." *Harvard Law Review* (1977) 91.

Karsten, Peter. *Soldiers and Society: The Effects of Military Service and War on American Life*. Westport, CT: Greenwood, 1978.

Katz, William Loren. *Breaking the Chains: African-American Slave Resistance*. New York: Ethrac Publications, 1990.

———. *The Black West*. Garden City, NY: Anchor Press, 1973.

Kerber, Linda K. *No Constitutional Right to Be Ladies*. New York: Hill and Wang, 1998.

Kelly, J.W. "Storytelling in High-Tech Organizations: A Medium for Sharing Culture." Paper presented at the Annual Meeting of the Western Speech Communication Association, Fresno, CA, February 16-19, 1985.

Kelso, William M. "The Archaeology of Slavery at Thomas Jefferson's Monticello: 'A Wolf by the Ears.'" *Journal of New World Archaeology* (1986) 6: 5–20.

Killens, John Oliver. "Hollywood in Black and White." *The State of the Nation*. Ed. David Boroff. Englewood Cliffs, NJ: Prentice-Hall, 1965. 100–7.

Klinkner, Philip, and Rogers Smith. *The Unsteady March: The Rise and Decline of Racial Equality in America*. Chicago: University of Chicago Press, 1999.

Klotman, Phyllis R. "Military Rites and Wrongs: African Americans in the U.S. Armed Forces." *Struggles for Representation: African American Documentary Film and Video*. Eds. Phyllis R. Kotman and Janet K. Cutler. Bloomington: Indiana University Press, 1999. 34–70.

Knoppes, C., and G. Black. "What to Show the World: The Office of War Information and Hollywood, 1942–45." *Journal of American History* (1977) LXIV: 87–105.

Kolker, Robert. *Film, Form, and Culture*. 2nd ed. Boston: McGraw Hill, 2002.

Kornweibel, Theodore. "The Most Dangerous of All Negro Journals." *American Journalism* (1994) 11: 154–68.

Kraay, Hendrik. "Slavery, Citizenship and Military Service in Brazil's Mobilization for the Paraguayan War." *Slavery & Abolition: A Journal of Slave and Post-Slave Studies* (1997) 18: 228–56.

Kracauer, Siegfried. *History: The Last Things Before the Last*. New York: Oxford University Press, 1963.

———. "National Types as Hollywood Presents Them." *Public Opinion Quarterly* (1949) 13: 53–72.

———. *Theory of Film: The Redemption of Physical Reality*. New York: Oxford University Press, 1960.

Krebs, Ronald R. "A School for the Nation? How Military Service Does Not Build Nations, and How it Might." *International Security* (2004) 29: 85–124.

———. *Fighting for Rights: Military Service and the Politics of Citizenship*. Ithaca, NY: Cornell University Press, 2006.

Kryder, Daniel. *Divided Arsenal: Race and the American State during World War II*. Cambridge: Cambridge University Press, 2000.

Krysan, Maria. "From Color Cast to Color Blind, Part II: Racial Attitudes during the Civil Rights and Black Power Eras, 1946–1975." *African American Citizenship, 1865–Present*. Eds. Henry Louis Gates Jr. et al. New York: Oxford University Press, 2012. 178–94.

Kuhn, Annette. *Family Secrets: Acts of Memory and Imagination*. London, UK: Verso, 1995.

Lardner, Joyce. "Introduction to Tomorrow's Tomorrow: The Black Woman." *Feminism and Methodology*. Ed. S. Harding. Bloomington: Indiana University Press, 1972.

Leab, Daniel J. "A Pale Black Imitation: All Colored Film 1930–1950." *Journal of Popular Film* (1975) 4: 345–56.

———. *From Sambo to Superspade: The Black Experience in Motion Pictures*. Boston: Houghton Mifflin, 1975.
Leadership and the Negro Soldier. Army Service Forces Manual M5. Washington, DC: United States Government Printing Office, 1944.
Leckie, William, and Shirley Leckie. *The Buffalo Soldiers: A Narrative of the Black Cavalry in the West*. Norman: University of Oklahoma Press, 2003.
Lee, Alfred M., and Norman D. Humphrey. *Race Riot*. New York: Dryden Press, 1943.
Lee, Felicia R. "From Noah's Ancient Curse to Slavery's Rationale." *New York Times* (November 11, 2003): A13, 15.
Lee, Robert E. *The Wartime Papers of R.E. Lee*. Ed. Clifford Dowdey. New York: Bramhall House, 1961.
Lee, Ulysses. "The Draft and the Negro." *Current History* (July 1968): 28–33, 47–48.
———. *The Employment of Negro Troops*. Washington, DC: Office of the Chief of Military History, United States Army, 1966.
Lee, Wallace. "Are Negroes Good Soldiers? Negro Digest Poll." *Negro Digest* (December 1945): 28.
Lewis, David Levering. *W.E.B. Du Bois: Biography of a Race 1868–1919*. New York: Henry Holt, 1993.
Lewis, Roscoe E. "The Role of Pressure Groups in Maintaining Morale among Negroes." *Journal of Negro Education* (1943) 12: 464–73.
Lincoln, C. Eric, and Lawrence H. Mamiya. *The Black Church in the African-American Experience*. Durham: Duke University Press, 1990.
Lindholm, Charles, and John A. Hall. "Frank Capra Meets John Doe: Anti-politics in American National Identity." *Cinema & Nation*. Eds. Mette Hjort and Scott Mackenzie. New York: Routledge, 2000. 32–44.
Lipsitz, George. *Time Passages: Collective Memory and American Popular Culture*. Minneapolis: University of Minnesota Press, 1990.
Lochard, Metz T.P. "Negroes and Defense." *Nation* (June 4, 1941) 152: 14–16.
Logan, Rayford W. *What the Negro Wants*. Chapel Hill: University of North Carolina Press, 1944.
Lommel, Cookie. *African Americans in Film and Television*. New York: Chelsea House, 2003.
Long, H.H. "The Negro Soldier in the Army of the United States." *Journal of Negro Education* (1943) 12: 314.
Longmate, Norman. *The GIs: The Americans in Britain 1942–1945*. London, UK: Charles Scribner, 1975.
Lovejoy, Arthur O. *The Great Chain of Being: A Study of the History of an Idea*. New Brunswick, NJ: Transition, 1936. 2009 reprint.
MacCann, Richard Dyer. *The People's Films: A Political History of U.S. Government Motion Pictures*. New York: Hastings House, 1973.
MacGregor, Morris J. *Defense Studies: Integration of the Armed Forces, 1940–1965*. Washington, DC: Center of Military History, 1981.
MacGregor, Morris J., and Bernard C. Nalty. *Blacks in the United States Armed Forces: Basic Documents*. Wilmington, DE: Scholarly Resources, 1977.
Magee, General James C. "Memo to Assistant Secretary of War John J. McCloy." (Sept. 3, 1941). ASW 291.2, Record Group 335. Washington, DC: National Archives.
Mahon, John K. *History of the Militia and the National Guard*. New York: MacMillan, 1983.

Malcomson, Scott L. *One Drop of Blood: The American Misadventure of Race*. New York: Farrar Straus Giroux, 2000.
Manvell, Roger. *Films and the Second World War*. South Brunswick, NJ: A.S. Barnes, 1974.
Marc, David. *Democratic Vistas: Television in American Culture*. Philadelphia: University of Pennsylvania Press, 1984.
Marshall, General George C. "Memo to all Commanding Generals." (July 13, 1943). NARG 18, 291.1-C, AAF.
Marshall, T.H. "Citizenship and Social Class." *Class, Citizenship, and Social Development*. Ed. T.H. Marshall. Chicago: University of Chicago Press, 1975. 71–134.
———, ed. *Citizenship and Social Class*. Cambridge, UK: University of Cambridge Press, 1950.
Martin, Charles H. "Negro Leaders, the Republican Party and the Election of 1932." *Freedom's Odyssey: African American History Essays from Phylon*. Eds. Alexa Benson Henderson and Janice Sumler-Edmond. Atlanta, GA: Clark Atlanta University Press, 1999. 443–54.
Martin, Harold. "How Do Our Negro Troops Measure Up?" *Saturday Evening Post* (June 16, 1951): 13.
Martinez, J. Michael. *A Long Dark Night: Race in America from Jim Crow to World War II*. New York: Rowman & Littlefield, 2016.
May, L. "Making the American Consensus: The Narrative of Conversion and Subversion in World War II Films." *The War in American Culture*. Eds. Lewis A. Erenberg and Susan E. Hirsch. Chicago: University of Chicago Press, 1996. 71–102.
Mazon, Mauricio. *The Zoot-Suit Riots: The Psychology of Symbolic Annihilation*. Austin: University of Texas Press, 1984.
McGee, Michael C. "The Ideograph: A Link between Rhetoric and Ideology." *Quarterly Journal of Speech* (1980) 66: 1–16.
McGuire, Philip. *Taps for a Jim Crow Army: Letters from Black Soldiers in World War II*. Lexington, KY: University of Kentucky Press, 1993.
McPherson, James M. *For Cause & Comrades: Why Men Fought in the Civil War*. New York: Oxford University Press, 1997.
———. *The Negro's Civil War: How American Negroes Felt and Acted during the War for the Union*. Urbana: University of Illinois Press, 1982.
McWilliams, Carey. "Race Tensions: Second Phase." *Common Ground* (1943) IV: 7–12.
———. "What We Did about Racial Minorities." *While You Were Gone: A Report on Wartime Life in the United States*. Ed. J. Goodman. New York: Simon & Schuster, 1946. 89–111.
Meckiffe, D., and M. Murray. "Radio and the Black Soldier during World War II." *Critical Studies in Mass Communication* (1998) 15: 337–56.
Mennell, Stephen. "Momentum and History." *Culture in History: Production, Consumption and Values in Historical Perspective*. Eds. Joseph Melling and Jonathan Barry. Devon, UK: University of Exeter Press, 1992. 228–46.
Merrill, Francis E. *Social Problems on the Homefront*. New York: Harper and Bros., 1948.
Mershon, S., and S. Schlossman. *Foxholes & Color Lines: Desegregating the U.S. Armed Forces*. Baltimore: Johns Hopkins University Press, 1998.
Miller, James A. "The Case of Early Black Cinema." *Critical Studies in Mass Communication* (1993) 10: 181–83.
Millett, Allan R., and Peter Maslowski. *For the Common Defense: A Military History of the United States of America*. New York: Free Press, 1984.
Milner, Lucille B. "Jim Crow in the Army." *New Republic* (March 13, 1944) 110: 429.

Minutes of the Meeting of the Board of Directors, NAACP, 8 December 1941; Box #38, Arthur B. Spingarn Papers, Library of Congress.

Modell, John, Marc Goulden, and Sigurdur Magnusson. "World War II in the Lives of Black Americans: Some Findings and an Interpretation." *The American Experience in World War II: The American People at War: Minorities and Women in the Second World War*, Vol. 10. Ed. Walter L. Hixson. New York: Routledge, 2003. 120–30.

Moon, Bucklin. *The High Cost of Prejudice*. New York: J. Messner, 1947.

Morehouse, Maggi M. *Fighting in the Jim Crow Army: Black Men and Women Remember World War II*. Lanham, MD: Rowman & Littlefield, 2000.

Moskos, Charles C. "Racial Integration in the Armed Forces." *The Making of Black America: The Black Community in Modern America*, Vol. 2. Eds. August Meier and Elliott Rudwick. New York: Atheneum, 1969. 425–47.

Moskos, Charles C., and John S. Butler. *All That We Can Be: Black Leadership and Racial Integration the Army Way*. New York: HarperCollins, 1996.

Moss, Carlton. "Interview." *Time* (March 27, 1944): 94–96.

Motley, Mary Patrick. *The Invisible Soldier: The Experience of the Black Soldier, World War II*. Detroit: Wayne State University Press, 1975.

Moyers, Bill. "The Propaganda Battle." *A Walk Through the 20th Century* television broadcast. 11 March 2009. <www.mtv.com/movies/movie/171843/moviemain.jhtml>.

Mullane, Deirdre. *Crossing the Danger Water*. New York: Doubleday, 1993.

Mullen, Robert W. *Blacks in America's Wars*. New York: Monad Press, 1973.

Mumby, Dennis K. *Communication and Power in Organizations: Discourse, Ideology, and Domination*. Norwood, NJ: Ablex, 1988.

———. "The Political Function of Narrative in Organizations." *Communication Monographs* (1987) 54: 113–27.

Murray, James. *To Find an Image: Black Films from Uncle Tom to Super Fly*. Indianapolis: Bobbs-Merrill, 1973.

Myrdal, Gunnar. *An American Dilemma: The Negro Problem and Modern Democracy*. New York: Harper & Bros., 1944.

NAACP Press Release. (April 27, 1944). NAACP 1940–55, General office file, films; *The Negro Soldier*, 1944–45, NAACP Microfilm.

Nakagawa, Gordon. "Deformed Subjects, Docile Bodies: Disciplinary Practices and Subject-Construction in Stories of Japanese-American Internment." *Narrative and Social Control: Critical Perspectives*. Ed. Dennis K. Mumby. Thousand Oaks, CA: Sage, 1993.

Nalty, Bernard C. *Strength for the Fight: A History of Black Americans in the Military*. New York: Macmillan, 1986.

———. *The Right to Fight: African-American Marines in World War II*. Washington, DC: Marine Corps Historical Center, 1995.

"Nazi Plan for Negroes Copies Southern U.S.A." *Crisis* (March 1941) 48: 71.

"Negro Morale," 1942. Survey S-1. Field 4-15-42 to 5-11-42, RG 208, Entry 3d, Box 6, Folder "Negro Morale," 1942.

"Negroes in the Armed Forces." *New Republic* (October 18, 1943) 109: 542–43.

Nelson, Keith L. "The 'Black Horror on the Rhine': Race as a Factor in Post-World War I Diplomacy." *Journal of Negro History* (December 1970) 41: 607–11.

Newby, Idus A. *Jim Crow's Defense: Anti-Negro Thought in America, 1900–1930*. Baton Rouge: University of Louisiana Press, 1965.

Nichols, Lee. *Breakthrough on the Color Front.* New York: Three Continents Press, 1954.
"No Closed Ranks Now, Says *Crisis.*" *Pittsburgh Courier* (January 17, 1942): 2.
Noble, Peter. *The Negro in Films.* London: Knapp, Drewett & Sons, 1948. "Now Is the Time Not to be Silent." *Crisis* (January 1942): 7.
Norrell, Robert J. *The House I Live In: Race in the American Century.* New York: Oxford University Press, 2005.
O'Connor, John E. *Image as an Artifact: The Historical Analysis of Film and Television.* Malabar, FL: Robert E. Krieger, 1990.
Odum, Howard W. *Race and Rumors of Race: Challenge to Crisis.* Chapel Hill: University of North Carolina Press, 1943.
———. "Social Change in the South." *Journal of Politics* (1948) 10: 247–48.
Office of War Information. "The Negro Looks at War." May 1942. Schomburg Collection, Appendixes III, IX (Typescript).
Olsen, Peter. "The Negro Maritime Worker and the Sea." *Negro History Bulletin* (1971) 34: 38–41.
Omi, Michael, and Harold Winant. "Racial Formations." *Race, Class, and Gender in the United States.* Ed. Paula S. Rothenberg. New York: St. Martin's Press, 1995. 13–22.
"Oral History Interview with Judge William H. Hastie." January 5, 1972. Truman Presidential Museum & Library Online. 12 October 2011. <http://ww.trumanlibrary.org/oralhist/hastie.htm>.
O'Reilly, Kenneth. "The Roosevelt Administration and Black America: Federal Surveillance Policy and Civil Rights during the New Deal and World War II Years." *Freedom's Odyssey: African American History Essays from Phylon.* Ed. Alexa Benson Henderson and Janice Sumler-Edmond. Atlanta, GA: Clark Atlanta University Press, 1999. 465–83.
Osborn, Michael. "Rhetorical Depiction." *Form, Genre, and the Study of Political Discourse.* Eds. Herbert W. Simons and A.A. Aghazarian. Columbia: University of South Carolina Press, 1986. 79–107.
Osur, Alan M. *Blacks in the Army Air Forces during World War II: The Problem of Race Relations.* Washington, DC: Department of Defense, Department of the Air Force, Office of Air Force History. US Government Printing Office, 1977.
———. *Separate & Unequal: Race Relations in the AAF during World War II.* Honolulu: University Press of the Pacific, 2004.
Park, Robert E. "Racial Ideologies." *American Society in Wartime.* Ed. William Fielding Ogburn. Chicago: University of Chicago Press, 1943. 165–84.
Parker, Christopher. "War and African American Citizenship, 1865–1965: The Role of Military Service." *African American Citizenship, 1865– Present.* Eds. Henry Louis Gates Jr. et al. New York: Oxford University Press, 2012. 425–63.
Patton, George S., Jr. *War as I Knew It.* Boston: Houghton Mifflin, 1947.
Patton, Gerald W. *War and Race: The Black Officer in the American Military, 1915–1941.* Westport, CT: Greenwood Press, 1981.
Pauley, G.E. "Rhetoric and Timeliness: An Analysis of Lyndon B. Johnson's Voting Rights Address." *Western Journal of Communication* (1998) 62: 26–53.
Phillips, Kimberly L. "Did the Battlefield Kill Jim Crow?" The Cold War Military, Civil Rights, and Black Freedom Struggles." *Fog of War: The Second World War and the Civil Rights Movement.* Eds. Kevin M. Kruse and Stephen Tuck. New York: Oxford University Press, 2012. 208–29.

Pines, Jim. *Blacks in Films: A Survey of Racial Themes and Images in American Film*. London: Cassell & Collier Macmillan, 1975.

"Plessy v. Ferguson-163 US 537 (1896): Justia US Supreme Court Center." 22 December 2012. <http://www.Supreme.justia.com>.

Pollenberg, Richard. *America at War: The Home Front, 1941–1945*. Englewood Cliffs, NJ: Prentice-Hall, 1968.

Prattis, Percival L. "The Morale of the Negro in the Armed Services of the United States." Percival L. Prattis Papers. University of Pittsburgh Archives. Box 2, Folder 72–73: 355–63.

———. "The Role of the Negro Press in Race Relations." *Phylon* (1946) 7: 273–83.

Price, Clement Alexander. "*Men of Bronze* (U.S., 1980) and *Liberators* (U.S., 1992): Black American Soldiers in Two World Wars." *World War II: Film and History*. Eds. J.W. Chambers and D. Culbert. Oxford, UK: Oxford University Press, 1996. 123–36.

Putney, Martha S. *When the Nation Was in Need: Blacks in the Women's Army Corps during World War II*. Metuchen, NJ: Scarecrow Press, 1992.

Quarles, Benjamin. *The Negro in the American Revolution*. New York: W.W. Norton, 1961.

———. *The Negro in the Civil War*. New York: Da Capo Press, 1953.

———. *The Negro in the Making of America*. New York: Touchstone, 1964.

Raack, R.C. "Historiography as Cinematography: A Prolegomenon to Film Work for Historians." *Journal of Contemporary History* (1983) 18: 411–38.

"Race Support of War Effort Is Lukewarm, Say Conferees." *Pittsburgh Courier* (January 17, 1942): 1.

Randolph, A. Philip. "Keynote Speech." *Official Proceedings of the Second National Negro Congress*. Philadelphia: October 15–17, 1937.

Rankin, John. "The Question of Transfusing Blood." *Atlantic Monthly* (January 1943): 95.

Ransom, William L. "Military Training: Compulsory or Volunteer?" *Proceedings of the Academy of Science in the City of New York* 6, no. 4. 1916.

Reddick, Lawrence D. "The Negro in the United States Navy during World War II." *Journal of Negro History* (1947) XXXII.

Reich, Elizabeth. *Militant Vision: Black Soldiers, Internationalism and the Transformation of American Cinema*. New Brunswick, NJ: Rutgers University Press, 2016.

Reid, Ira De. A. "Special Problems of Negro Migration during the War." *Milbank Memorial Fund Quarterly* (1947) 23: 284–92.

Reid, Mark A. *Redefining Black Film*. Berkeley: University of California Press, 1993.

Renshon, Stanley A. "Assumptive Frameworks in Political Socialization Theory." *Handbook of Political Socialization: Theory and Research*. Ed. Stanley A. Renshon. New York: Free Press, 1977. 3–44.

Rhines, Jesse Algeron. *Black Film/White Money*. New Brunswick, NJ: Rutgers University Press, 1996.

Rhodes, Jane. "The Visibility of Race and Media History." *Critical Studies in Mass Communication* (1993) 10: 184–90.

Robinson, Cedric J. *Forgeries of Memory & Meaning: Blacks & the Regimes of Race in American Theater & Film before World War II*. Chapel Hill: University of North Carolina Press, 2007.

Rocchio, Vincent F. *Reel Racism: Confronting Hollywood's Construction of Afro-American Culture*. Boulder, CO: Westview Press, 2000.

Roosevelt, Franklin D. Statement on Peace Time Universal Selective Service on September 16, 1940. 6 June 2013. <Http://www.presidency.ucsb.edu/site/docs>.

Rosenbaum, Jonathan. "Multinational Pest Control: Does American Cinema Still Exist?" *Film and Nationalism*. Ed. Alan Williams. New Brunswick, NJ: Rutgers, 2002. 217-29.

Rosenblum, Karen E., and Toni-Michelle C. Travis. *The Meaning of Difference: American Constructions of Race, Sex and Gender, Social Class, and Sexual Orientation*. New York: McGraw-Hill, 1996.

Rosenstone, Robert A. "History in Images/History in Words: Reflections on the Possibility of Really Putting History onto Film." *American Historical Review* (1988) 43: 1178-95.

Ross, Karen. *Black and White Media: Black Images in Popular Film and Television*. Cambridge: Blackwell, 1996.

Said, Edward W. *Orientalism*. New York: Random House, 1978.

Salyer, Lucy E. "Baptism by Fire: Race, Military Service, and U.S. Citizenship Policy, 1918-1935." *Journal of American History* (2004) 91: 847-76.

Samuel, L.R. *Pledging Allegiance: American Identity and the Bond Drive of World War II*. Washington, DC: Smithsonian Institution Press, 1997.

Sancton, Thomas. "A Southern View of the Race Question." *Negro Quarterly: A Review of Negro Life and Culture* (1942) 1: 197-200.

———. "The Negro Press." *New Republic* (April 26, 1943) 108: 557-60.

Sandler, Stanley. "Homefront Battlefront: Military Racial Disturbances in the Zone of the Interior, 1941-1945." *The American Experience in World War II: The American People at War: Minorities and Women in the Second World War*, Vol. 10. Ed. Walter L. Hixson. New York: Routledge, 2003. 131-45.

———. *Segregated Skies: All-Black Combat Squadrons of WW II*. Washington, DC: Smithsonian Institution Press, 1992.

Santosuosso, Antonio. *Soldiers, Citizens, and the Symbols of War: From Classical Greece to Republican Rome, 500-167 b.c.* Boulder, CO: Westview, 1997.

Scarborough, Robert "Foreigners Find Military Fast Track to Citizenship." *Washington (DC) Times* (August 22, 2002): 11.

Schacter, Daniel. *Searching for Memory*. New York: Basic Books, 1996.

Sherman, Lt. Colonel John H. "Are Negroes Good Soldiers?" *Negro Digest* (December 1945): 32-33.

Schindler, C. *Hollywood Goes to War: Films and American Society, 1939-52*. London, UK: Rutledge & Kegan Paul, 1979.

Schlesinger, Arthur M., Jr. "Political and Social Change: 1941-1968." *Interpreting American History: Conversations with Historians*. Ed. John A. Garraty. New York: Macmillan, 1970. 265-88.

Schlesinger, Philip. "The Sociological Scope of 'National Cinema.'" *Cinema & Nation*. Eds. Mette Hjort and Scott Mackenzie. New York: Routledge, 2000. 19-31.

Schubert, Frank. *Black Valor: Buffalo Soldiers and the Medal of Honor, 1870-1898*. Wilmington, DE: SR Books, 1997.

Schudson, M. "The Present in the Past Versus the Past in the Present." *Communication* (1989) 11: 105-13.

Schyler, George. "The Double V (Pt. II)." *Courier* (January 10, 1942): n.p.

Scott, Samuel F. "The French Revolution and the Professionalization of the French Officer Corps, 1789-1793." *On Military Ideology*. Eds. Morris Janowitz and Jacques Van Dorrn. Rotterdam: University of Rotterdam Press, 1971. 5-56.

Sears, Stephen W. *Gettysburg*. Boston: Houghton Mifflin, 2003.

Seelye, Katharine Q. "When Hollywood's Big Guns Come Right from the Source." *New York Times* (June 10, 2002): A1, A19.
Segal, David R. *Recruiting for Uncle Sam: Citizenship and Military Manpower Policy.* Lawrence: University of Kansas Press, 1989.
Shapiro, Herbert. *White Violence and Black Response: From Reconstruction to Montgomery.* Amherst: University of Massachusetts Press, 1988.
Sherry, Michael S. *In the Shadow of War.* New Haven: Yale University Press, 1995.
Shklar, Judith. *American Citizenship.* Cambridge, MA: Harvard University Press, 1991.
Shockley, Megan Taylor. *"We, Too, Are Americans": African American Women in Detroit and Richmond, 1940–54.* Urbana: University of Illinois Press, 2003.
Short, K. "Hollywood: An Essential War Industry." *Historical Journal of Film, Radio and Television* (1985) 5: 90–99.
Short, K.R.M. *Feature Films as History.* Knoxville: University of Tennessee Press, 1981.
Shuler, Jack. *Calling Out Liberty: The Stono Slave Rebellion and the Universal Struggle for Human Rights.* Jackson: University Press of Mississippi, 2009.
Silberman, Charles E. *Crisis in Black and White.* New York: Vintage, 1964.
Silk, Catherine, and John Silk. *Racism and Anti-racism in American Popular Culture.* Manchester, UK: Manchester University Press, 1990.
Silvera, J.D. *The American Negro, His History and Literature: The Negro in World War II.* New York: Arno Press, 1969.
Simmons, Charles A. *The African American Press: With Special Reference to Four Newspapers, 1827–1965.* Jefferson, NC: McFarland, 1998.
Simon, Rita James. *Public Opinion in America: 1936–1970.* Chicago: Rand McNally, 1974.
Sitkoff, Harvard. *A New Deal for Blacks: The Emergence of Civil Rights as a National Issue—The Depression Decade.* New York: Oxford University Press, 2008.
———. "African American Militancy in the World War II South: Another Perspective." *Remaking Dixie: The Impact of World War II on the American South.* Eds. Neil McMillen and Morton Sosna. Jackson: University of Mississippi Press, 1997. 70–92.
———. "Racial Militancy and Interracial Violence in the Second World War." *Journal of American History* (1971) 58: 661–81.
———. "The Detroit Race Riot of 1943." *Blacks in White America Since 1865.* Ed. Robert C. Twombly. Philadelphia: David McKay, 1971.
———. *The Struggle for Black Equality 1954–1980.* Toronto: Collins, 1981.
Sklar, Robert. *Movie-Made America: A Cultural History of American Movies.* New York: Random House, 1975.
Sklar, Robert, and Vito Zagarrio. *Frank Capra: Authorship and the Studio System.* Philadelphia: Temple University Press, 1998.
Slonaker, John. *The U.S. Army and the Negro.* Carlisle Barracks, PA: US Army Military History Research Collection, 1971.
Smith, Archie, Jr., and Gill G. Barnes. *Navigating the Deep River: Spirituality in African American Families.* Cleveland, OH: United Church Press, 1997.
Smith, Graham. *When Jim Crow Met John Bull: Black American Soldiers in World War II Britain.* New York: St. Martin's Press, 1987.
Snead, J.A. "Images of Blacks in Black Independent Films." *Critical Perspectives on Black Independent Cinema.* Eds. M.S. Cham and C. Andrade-Watkins. Cambridge, MA: MIT Press, 1988. 16–25.

Snyder, R. Claire. *Citizen-Soldiers and Manly Warriors: Military Service and Gender in the Civic Republican Tradition*. Lanham, MD: Rowman & Littlefield Publishers, 1999.

———. "The Citizen-Soldier Tradition and Gender Integration of the U.S. Military." *Armed Forces & Society* (2003) 29: 185–204.

Social Science Institute, Fiske University. *Monthly Summary of Events and Trends in Race Relations*, Vol. 1, 1944.

Solomon, Mark. *The Cry was Unity: Communists and African Americans, 1917–1936*. Jackson: University Press of Mississippi, 1998.

Sontag, Susan. *On Photography*. New York: Farrar, Strauss & Giroux, 1977.

Sosna, Morton. "More Important than the Civil War? The Impact of World War II on the South." *Perspectives on the American South: An Annual Review of American Society, Politics, and Culture*. Eds. James Cobb and Charles Wilson. New York: Gordon and Breach Science Publishers, 1987.

Steele, R., and Charles Redding. "The American Value System." *Western Speech* (1962) 26: 83–91.

Stone, I.F. "Capital Notes." *Nation* (January 23, 1043) 156: 115.

Stott, William. *Documentary Expression and Thirties America*. New York: Oxford University Press, 1973.

Stouffer, Samuel A., et al. *The American Soldier, Adjustment during Army Life*, Vol. 1. Princeton, NJ: Princeton University Press, 1949.

Stouffer, Samuel, et al. *Studies in Social Psychology in World War II: Vol. III, Experiments on Mass Communication*. Princeton, NJ: Princeton University Press, 1949.

Strother, T. Ella. "The Black Image in the Chicago *Defender*, 1905–1975." *Journalism History* (1977–78) 4: 137–41, 156.

Sturken, Marita. "Absent Images of Memory: Remembering and Reenacting the Japanese Internment." *Perilous Memories: The Asia-Pacific War(s)*. Eds. G.T. Fujitani, M. White, and L. Yoneyama. Durham, NC: Duke University Press, 2001. 33–49.

Sturken, Marita, and Lisa Cartwright. *Practices of Looking: An Introduction to Visual Culture*. New York: Oxford University Press, 2001.

Susman, Warren. *Culture as History: The Transformation of American Society in the Twentieth Century*. New York: Pantheon, 1984.

Takaki, Ronald. *A Different Mirror: A History of Multicultural America*. Boston: Little, Brown, 1993.

———. *Double Victory: A Multicultural History of America in World War II*. New York: Little, Brown, 2000.

Taylor, Clyde. "Paths of Enlightenment: Heroes, Rebels, and Thinkers." *Struggles for Representation: African American Documentary Film and Video*. Eds. Phyllis R. Klotman and Janet K. Cutler. Bloomington: Indiana University Press, 1999. 122–50.

Terrett, Dulany. *The Signal Corps: The Emergency (To December 1941)*. Washington, DC: Office of the Chief of Military History, US Army, GPO, 1956; rpt. 1941.

"The Colors of War: Anchors Aweigh." History Channel television broadcast. February 18, 2002.

"The Courier's Double 'V' for a Double Victory Campaign gets Country-Wide Support." *Pittsburgh Courier* (February 14, 1942): 1.

The Negro Sailor, 1945. US Department of War. National Archives. Original film transcript by author.

The Negro Soldier. 1944. Signal Corps Film: National Archives NA 1110F-51. Original film transcript by author.

"The Negro's War." *Fortune* (June 1942) 25: 78.
"The Polls: Race Relations." *Public Opinion Quarterly* (Spring 1962) XXVI: 137–48.
The Rhetoric of Aristotle. Trans. Lane Cooper. New York: Appleton Century-Crofts, 1932/1960.
The Use of Negro Manpower in War. Carlisle Barracks, PA: US Army War College, 1925.
Thelen, D. "Memory and American History." *Journal of American History* (1989) 75: 1117–29.
"These Truly Are the Brave." *Ebony* (August 1968) 123: 164–77.
This Is Our War: Selected Stories of Six War Correspondents–Six Who Were Sent Overseas by the Afro-American Newspapers. Baltimore: Afro-American Company, 1945.
Thompson, Chas H. "The American Negro and the National Defense." *Journal of Negro Education* (1940) 9: 547–52.
———. "The American Negro in World War I and World War II." *Journal of Negro Education* (1943) 12: 263–67.
Thompson, George Raynor, and Dixie R. Harris. *The Signal Corps: The Outcome (Mid-1943 through 1945)*. Washington, DC: Department of the Army, 1966.
Thompson, George Raynor, et al. *The Signal Corps: The Test (December 1941 to July 1943)*. Washington, DC: Department of the Army, 1957.
Thompson, James G. "Should I Sacrifice to Live 'Half-American?'" *Pittsburgh Courier* (January 31, 1942): 3.
Thompson, Mark. "Army Strong: The Ban on Women in Combat Ends. Now What?" *Time* (February 11, 2013) 181: 15.
Thompson, Victor. "The Strange Career of Racial Science, Racial Categories, and African American Identity." *African American Citizenship, 1865-Present*. Eds. Henry Louis Gates Jr. et al. New York: Oxford University Press, 2012. 151–77.
Thorne, Christopher. "Britain and the Black GIs: Racial Issues and Anglo-American Relations in 1942." *New Community* (Summer 1974): n. p.
Tilly, Charles. "A Primer on Citizenship." *Theory and Society* (1997) 26: 599–602.
———. "Citizenship, Identity and Social History." *International Review of Social History* (1995) 40: 1–17.
Toll, Robert C. *Blacking Up: The Minstrel Show in Nineteenth Century America*. New York: Oxford University Press, 1974.
Toplin, Robert Brent. "The Filmmaker as Historian." *American Historical Review* (1988) 43: 1210–27.
Tuck, Stephen. "African American Struggles for a New Place in Popular Culture." *Fog of War: The Second World War and the Civil Rights Movement*. Eds. Kevin M. Kruse and Stephen Tuck. New York: Oxford University Press, 2012. 103–25.
Tucker, Linda G. *Lockstep and Dance: Images of Black Men in Popular Culture*. Jackson: University Press of Mississippi, 2007.
Turner, Graeme. *Film as Social Practice*. New York: Routledge, 1993.
Turner, Patricia A. *Ceramic Uncles & Celluloid Mammies*. New York Anchor, 1994.
US Bureau of the Census. *16th Census of the United States, 1940: Population. The Labor Force*. Washington, DC: Government Printing Office, 1943. Table 1.
US Selective Service System. *Selective Service, 4th Report of Director, 1944–45 and 1946–47: Selective Service and Victory*. Washington, DC: US Government Printing Office, 1948.
"Used Men as Seagoing Chambermaids, Bell Hops, Dishwashers." *Pittsburgh Courier* (October 5, 1940): 1.
Valbrun, Marjorie. "Military Track to Citizenship: Acceptance through Service." *Wall Street Journal* (April 2, 2003): 9.

Vande Berg, Leah R., Wenner, Lawrence A., and Gronbeck, Bruce E. *Critical Approaches to Television*. Boston: Houghton Mifflin Company, 1998.

Van Deburg, W.L. *Slavery & Race in American Popular Culture*. Madison: University of Wisconsin Press, 1984.

van Dijk, Teun A. "Stories and Racism." *Narrative and Social Control*. Ed. Dennis K. Mumby. Newbury Park, CA: Sage, 1993. 121–42.

Vann, R.L. "Letter to the Editor." *Pittsburg Courier* (January 19, 1939): 51.

Vickery, William Edward. *The Economics of the Negro Migration, 1900– 1960*. New York: Ayer, 1977.

"Voices of Defeat." *Life* (April 13, 1942): 77–89.

Walton, Hanes. "Black Voting Behavior in the Segregation Era: 1944–1964." *Black Politics and Black Political Behavior: A Linkage Analysis*. Ed. Hanes Walton. Westport, CT: Praeger, 1994. 115–36.

Ward, Brian. *Media, Culture, and the Modern African American Freedom Struggle*. Gainesville: University Press of Florida, 2001.

Washburn, Patrick S. *A Question of Sedition: The Federal Government's Investigation of the Black Press during World War II*. New York: Oxford University Press, 1986.

———. "J. Edgar Hoover and the Black Press in World War II." *Journalism History* (1986) 13: 26–33.

Waskow, Arthur I. *From Race Riot to Sit-In: 1919 and the 1960s*. New York: Doubleday, 1966.

Weaver, Robert C. "Racial Employment Trends in National Defense." *Phylon* (1941) II: 337–58.

Weber, Max. "The Meaning of Discipline." *From Max Weber: Essays in Sociology*. Eds. H.H. Gerth and C. Wright Mills. New York: Oxford University Press, 1946. 253–61.

Wedin, Carolyn. *Inheritors of the Spirit: Mary White Ovington and the Founding of the NAACP*. New York: John Wiley, 1998.

Weigley, Russell F. "Armed Forces." 23 August 2004. <http://college.hmco.com/history/readerscomp/rcah/html.>.

———. *History of the United States Army*. Bloomington: Indiana University Press, 1984.

Wesley, Charles H. "World War II: Reaching Toward Desegregation." *National Guard* (1989) 43: 30–33.

White, Hayden. "The Value of Narrativity in the Representation of Reality." *Critical Inquiry* (1980) 7: 5–27.

White, Walter. *A Rising Wind*. New York, 1945.

———. "It's Our Country, Too: The Negro Demands the Right to be Allowed to Fight for It." *Saturday Evening Post* (December 14, 1940) 213: 27, 61–68.

———. "What the Negro Thinks of the Army." *Annals of the American Academy of Political and Social Science* (1942) 223: 67.

White, Walter, et al. "A Declaration by Negro Voters." *Crisis* (January 1944) LI: 16–17.

White, William. "Speech to Hollywood Writer's Mobilization Congress." Writer's Congress, Los Angeles, October 1, 1943. Series II, Box A, 277.

Wilkins, Roy. "Letter to the Editor." *Crisis* (March 9, 1939) 46: 93.

Williams, Alan. "Introduction." *Film and Nationalism*. New Brunswick, NJ: Rutgers, 2002.

Williams, Lee, and Lee Williams II. *Anatomy of Four Race Riots: Racial Conflict in Knoxville, Elaine (Arkansas), Tulsa, and Chicago, 1919–1921*. Jackson: University Press of Mississippi, 2008.

Williams, Patricia J. *The Alchemy of Race and Rights*. Cambridge, MA: Harvard University Press, 1991.

Williamson, Chilton. *American Suffrage: From Property to Democracy.* Princeton, NJ: Princeton University Press, 1960.

Wills, Garry. *Lincoln at Gettysburg: The Words That Remade America.* New York: Simon & Schuster, 2006.

Wilmore, Gayraud S. *Black Religion and Black Radicalism: An Interpretation of the Religious History of Afro-American People.* Maryknoll, NY: Orbis Books, 1994.

Wilson, Sondra K. *The Crisis Reader: Stories, Poetry, and Essays from the NAACP's Crisis Magazine.* New York: Random House, 1999.

Wilson, W. "Old Jim Crow in Uniform." *Crisis* (February 1939) 46: 42–44; (1939, March) 46: 71–73, 82, 93.

Wilson, William Julius. *The Truly Disadvantaged: The Inner City, the Underclass, and Public Policy.* Chicago: University of Chicago Press, 1987.

Winik, Jay. *April 1865: The Month That Saved America.* New York HarperCollins, 2001.

Winter, Thomas. "*The Training of Colored Troops*: A Cinematic Effort to Promote National Cohesion." *Hollywood's World War I: Motion Picture Images.* Eds. Peter C. Rollins and John E. O'Connor. Bowling Green, OH: Bowling Green State University Popular Press, 1997. 3–25.

Wood, David. "Pentagon Does Not Track Thousands of Foreigners in U.S. Military." 22 May 2004. <http://www.newhouse.com/archive/story1a061102.html>.

Woods, Wilma. Personal interview, August 12, 2007.

Woodson, Carter G. *The History of the Negro Church.* Washington, DC: Associated Publishers, 1921.

Woodward, C. Vann. "The Negro in American Life: 1865–1918." *Interpreting American History: Conversations with Historians.* Ed John A. Garraty. New York: Macmillan, 1970. 43–68.

Wynn, Neil A. *The Afro-American and the Second World War.* New York: Holmes and Meier, 1975.

Wyschogrod, Edith. An Ethics of Remembering: History, Heterology and the Nameless Others. Chicago: University of Chicago Press, 1998.

Yearwood, Gladstone L. *Black Film as a Signifying Practice: Cinema, Narration and the African-American Aesthetic Tradition.* Trenton, NJ African World Press, 2000.

Yinger, J. Milton. *A Minority Group in American Society.* New York: Unesco Press, 1965.

Young, Betty. Personal interview, June 25, 1989.

Zangrando, Robert L. "About Lynching." *The Reader's Companion to American History.* Eds. Eric Foner and John A. Garraty. New York: Houghton Mifflin, 1991. 27–29.

Index

AAF Intelligencer, The, 130
acts of valor, 4
Adjutant General's Office, 131, 203
Advisory Committee on Negro Troop Policies, 119, 138
African American: actors and actresses, 80; film productions, 7, 54; leadership, 68, 73, 79–80, 112, 127–33; military history, 12, 15–16, 41, 74, 83, 96, 114, 143, 206; movie theaters, 61, 71, 138; newspapers, 68–71, 114, 159–65, 171–87; organizations, 51–52, 57, 115, 136, 141, 153, 168–69; religion, 50, 74, 79, 165; as savages, 11, 63; women, 3, 29, 31, 36, 61, 63, 70, 78, 88, 140–41, 160, 165, 167, 175, 187
African Blood Brotherhood, 141, 153
Almond, Edward M., 129
American Dilemma, 90
American Federation of Labor, 141, 153
Americanization, 34
Amos 'n' Andy, 50, 55
anti-slavery agitation, 25
Aristotle, 8
Army General Classification Test, 116
Army Information and Education Division, 69, 71
Army Plan for Mobilization, 113
Army Service Forces Manual M5, 124
Army War College, 111
Army Air Corps, 112, 114, 122, 133
Arnold, Henry H., 122, 129, 132
Aryan philosophy, 17, 74, 93, 163, 195
Asian immigrants, 11–12, 14, 16–17, 30, 39
At Their Side, 61
Attucks, Crispus, 75, 80

Bacon's Rebellion, 15
Baltimore Afro-American, 174, 177, 183
Bamber Bridge, England, 143–44

Barnes, George, 68
Battle of the Bulge, 65, 67, 108, 113
Benedict, Ruth, 18
Benny, Jack, 50
Biddle, Francis, 128, 183–85
Birth of a Nation, 41
blackface, 49–50
black film production, 53, 62
blood quantum, 12
Boise Valley Herald, 185
British Information Services, 135
Brotherhood of Sleeping Car Porters, 113
Brown, Henry B., 13
Brown, William Wells, 29
Brown v. Board of Education, 4, 13
Bureau of Public Relations, 184
Bush, George W., 40
bushido code, 21

Cabin in the Sky, 50
Capra, Frank: and the American Dream, 43; as a director, 43, 45–47, 73; films of, 42, 45; *Why We Fight* series, 69
Carver, George Washington, 75, 85
Chase, William Calvin, 171
Chicago Defender, 172, 174, 177, 183
Chicago Tribune, 183
cinematic mode of address, 93–102
citizenship: conditions of, 19, 22, 28–32; immigration and, 22–23, 26; relationship to race, 15, 26
citizen-soldier: evolution of concept, 21–24; popular conception of, 21
Civil Rights Bill of 1964, 4
civil rights movement, 5, 20, 65–66, 84, 89–90, 121, 146–51, 155, 188, 196, 202, 207
Civil War, 3, 12, 28–33, 50, 56, 73, 75, 82, 85, 107–9, 157, 163, 173

Civil War, The, 4
Clark, Kenneth B., 154–155
Close Harmony, 91, 96–98
Coast Guard, 37, 67, 148, 176, 187
colonial wars, 3, 28, 212n73
Colored Troops Disembarking, The, 56
comic books, 43, 68–69
Command of Negro Troops, 120
Committee on Public Information (CPI), 42, 57
communism, 17, 14, 37, 130, 133, 147
communist *Daily Worker*: appeal to African Americans, 172; class struggle, 172
community celebrations, 33, 192
Congress of Racial Equality (CORE), 136, 153
Connelly, Marc, 73
conscription, 6, 109
conversion narrative, 7, 9, 77–79, 81, 84, 89, 191, 194, 196
Cooke, Elliot D., 120
Coolidge, Calvin, 140
Crisis, The, 141, 153, 164, 172, 174–81, 185
Croix de Guerre, 110, 175

Dabney, Virginius, 17
Davis, Arthur, 156
Davis, Benjamin O., 123, 144, 169
Davis, Elmer, 70
Davis, H. L., 32
Debt, The, 48
Department of Agriculture, 96–97, 169
Dick Act, 43, 109. *See also* Militia Act of 1903
Don't Be a Sucker, 91, 96
Doris "Doris" Miller, 4, 75, 92, 165, 175–76
double consciousness, 37
"Double V" Campaign, 6, 130, 147, 150, 177–78, 187–88
Dred Scott decision, 6, 28, 108
DuBois, W. E. B., 32, 37, 51, 87, 152, 154, 156, 174

Eastland, James O., 212
Edison, Thomas, 53
Eisenhower, Dwight D., 24, 61, 124
Emancipation Proclamation, 4, 28, 35
eugenics theories, 13
Everett, Edward, 33
Executive Order 2594, 57

Executive Order 8890, 70, 113
Executive Order 8891, 204

Fahy, Charles, 205
fifth columnist activity, 183
Fish, Hamilton, 165
Flynn, Edward J., 120
Flynn, John C., 43, 60
Four Freedoms, 139, 142, 161, 163, 165, 181
Fourteenth Amendment, 13
Frederick Douglass, 3, 28–29, 37, 166
Freedmen, 3, 25, 28
Freedom's Journal, 172
French and Indian Wars, 26
French Revolution, 27, 107
Frissell, Hollis B., 35, 152

Garvey, Marcus, 51
G. I. Bill of Rights, 204
Gillem Commission, 203
Glory, 4
Goldberg, Jack, 62, 70–71
Gone with the Wind, 41
Granger, Lester, 147, 155, 166
Great Chain of Being, 11
Great Depression, 78, 103, 150–51, 153, 155, 166, 181
Great Migration, 51, 158–59
Greece, 21, 23
Green Pastures, 50
Griffith, D. W., 55

Hallelujah, 54
Ham and Eggs at the Front, 49
Harlan, John Marshall, 13–14
Harlem Renaissance, 51
Hastie, William, 114, 123, 131, 138–39, 146, 169, 186
Hawaiian racial categories, 18
Hecht, Ben, 73
Hegel, Georg Wilhelm Friedrich, 23
Heisler, Stuart, 73
Henry Browne, Farmer, 90–91, 96–98
historical memory, 150, 204–5
Hitler, Adolf, 74, 79, 93, 167–68, 185
Holcomb, Thomas, 115, 129

Index

Hollywood: budgets, 41, 43; cooperation with government, 46–47, 59–60, 73, 133, 167, 198; distribution, 43; popularity of films, 20, 45; wartime activities, 33–44, 103, 202
homosexuals, 16, 36
Hoover, J. Edgar, 147, 183
House I Live In, The, 84, 91, 100
Houston, Charles H., 113
Hunger, Frank, 127

identity: National, 5, 8, 20–21, 31, 34, 44, 77–79, 84, 159, 193–95, 199, 207; racial, 11–20, 62, 85, 148, 170, 188, 190–99
immigration: and national identity, 11, 30, 32–33; pressures, 33–34, 108, 158; restrictions, 26, 114
Immigration Exclusion Acts, 158
Indian Citizenship Act, 73, 220n73
Indian Reorganization Act of 1934, 13
Indian wars, 26, 107–8
Industrial Workers of the World, 141, 153
inferiority: African American, 13, 20, 51, 55, 61–62, 100, 162, 177, 201; belief, 22, 32, 54, 122, 126, 133; social, 29, 39, 108, 130–31, 189, 198
In Slavery Days, 48

Jane Doe v. The State of Louisiana, 14
Japanese racial propaganda, 111, 133, 156
Jazz Singer, The, 50
Jim Crow, 50, 54, 59, 65, 73, 75, 82, 95, 99, 102, 110, 112, 114–15, 122, 125, 131, 134, 137, 142, 144–45, 148, 155, 172, 175, 177, 179, 188, 202, 207
Johnson, Campbell, 124
Johnson, Charles S., 160
Johnson, Henry, 110, 175
Jolson, Al, 50

King, Martin Luther, Jr., 90
Knox, Frank, 120, 129, 137, 148, 179
Korean War, 36, 64, 113, 124, 202, 206
Kracauer, Sigfried, 93–94
Kubie, Lawrence, 145

Launching of the Booker T. Washington, The, 91, 96

leadership: African American, 165–67; military, 126–33; religious, 39, 74, 79, 165
Leadership and the Negro Soldier, 68, 130
Liberty Ship, 91, 96
Lifeboat, 60–61, 104
Lincoln, Abraham, 33, 73, 75
Lost Boundaries, 62–63, 104
Louis, Joe, 74, 85, 180
Lovett, Robert A., 122
lynching, 134, 141–43, 152–53, 155, 162, 164, 168, 173–74, 178, 180

MacArthur, Douglas, 128, 213
MacDill riot, 143–44
Machiavelli, Niccolò, 23
Magee, James C., 167
Marine Corps, 115, 129, 148, 176
Marshall, George, 68, 120, 131
masculinity and military service, 33
mass media: influence of, 41–44, 56; popularity of, 42, 51
McCarran-Walter Act, 26
McCloy Committee, 119, 184, 186
Mechanical Aptitude Test, 117
Meredith, Burgess, 60, 99
Military Affairs Committee, 17
military industrial complex, 24
military service: and citizenship, 21–26; and discrimination, 37, 65, 68, 98, 107, 109, 112, 126, 137–38, 145, 164, 171, 176, 182, 198
militia: colonial, 22–23, 26, 90; compulsory, 26, 28; history of, 3, 25–30; part-time, 22, 107; state, 29
Militia Act of 1792, 27, 107, 109
Militia Act of 1903, 34, 109. *See also* Dick Act
minstrel: images, 9, 48–49, 55, 77; tradition, 7, 19, 50, 61, 198
mob violence, 28, 141–43, 161
Moss, Carlton, 70, 73–75, 87
Moton, Robert, 110, 154
Muson, Lyman, 68
Myrdal, Gunnar, 90, 163, 181

Nate Turner Rebellion, 12
National Association for the Advancement of Colored People (NAACP), 136, 139, 174

National Brotherhood Workers of America, 141, 153
National Defense Act of 1920, 109
National Liberty Congress of Colored Americans, 141
National Negro Congress, 71, 168
National Negro Publishing Association, 176
National Urban League, 51, 147, 155, 160, 166, 168, 174, 180
Native Americans, 3, 11–13, 22, 28, 30–31, 39, 212n73
Navy: African American attitudes toward, 121, 138–39, 145, 164–65, 179; history of discrimination, 32, 84, 91–92, 109–10, 115, 121, 129, 175; recruitment, 93, 148
Navy Cross, 4, 176
Navy Steward, The, 46, 59, 100–102, 192
Nazi: Aryan racial superiority, 16, 44, 79, 168; racial philosophies, 21; racial propaganda, 16, 163
Negro Colleges in Wartime, 90–91, 98
Negro Digest, 156, 174, 212
Negro in American Fiction, The, 53
Negro Sailor, The, 84, 90–95, 100–103, 170, 179, 190, 192, 195, 197, 200, 202, 206
Negro Soldier, The, 7–9, 17, 19, 40, 45–47, 57, 59, 65–91, 93–95, 100, 102–3, 106, 127, 130, 136, 148, 179, 198, 190, 194–95, 197, 200, 202, 205, 207
New Army Act, 107
New Deal, 158
newspapers: advertising, 6; African American, 68, 70–71, 114, 136, 141, 159, 162, 164–65, 170–79, 181–88; black journalists, 9, 70, 91, 173, 175, 177, 179–80, 188; circulation figures, 153; mainstream, 60, 110; private letters, 127, 179
New York Messenger, 141, 153
New York Militant, 185
Nimitz, Chester W., 4
Ninth Negro Cavalry Watering Horses, The, 53, 56
Norfolk *Journal and Guide*, 174, 177, 183
North American Aviation, 166
Northern Pump Company, 167

Office of the Civilian Aide to the Secretary of War, 114

Office of War Information (formerly Office of Facts and Figures), 130, 136, 165, 180, 185–87, 199
Operation Iraqi Freedom, 40
Opportunity, 160, 174, 180
one drop rule, 13
Oriental exclusion laws, 17
other, the, 16
Ottley, Roi, 140, 175
Our Colored Fighters, 57
Ovington, Mary White, 153
Owens, Jesse, 180
Ozawa, Takao, 26

patriotism, 9, 19, 33, 44, 47, 72, 75, 77–78, 82, 91, 95, 111, 142, 155, 199–200
Palmer, A. Mitchell, 173
Pan African Congress, 51
Park, Robert E., 155
Patterson, Robert P., 211
Patton, George S., 129, 139
Pearl Harbor, 4, 16, 42, 75, 92, 114, 137–38, 155, 162, 177
Pearl Harbor (film), 4, 167
persuasion, 8, 77, 94, 200
Picture History of World War II, 45
Plessy v. Ferguson, 13–14
Pittsburgh *Courier*, 51, 174, 176–82, 184, 186
Poitier, Sidney, 63, 104
Port Chicago Mutiny, 87, 91, 119–21, 138, 140, 144–45
President's Committee on Equality of Treatment and Opportunity in the Armed Services, 205
Price, Charles F. B., 134–35
production quality, 62, 97
professional army, 30–32
Project Clear, 201
propaganda: documentary film as, 42, 77, 201; enemy, 17–18, 46, 70, 134, 142, 148, 181; World War I, 57; World War II, 42–45, 67–68, 186–87
Provisional Army Act of 1798, 107
public opinion: concerning race, 126, 164, 170, 181, 188, 202; during World War I, 157; during World War II, 38, 42, 44, 57, 71, 95, 155; polls, 126, 136

Quartermaster Corps, 110, 111, 114, 121
Queen, Colonel Howard Donovan, 136

race: attitudes toward, 4, 6, 14, 16, 20, 22, 31, 36, 44, 48–50, 55, 59, 66, 69, 76, 90, 103, 108, 124, 128–29, 136, 154, 179, 181, 198; definitions of, 12–13, 119; depictions of, 73, 80, 87, 205; hierarchy, 3, 11, 14, 37, 100, 140, 161, 192, 202; laws regarding, 27, 107–9, 113, 167; and Japanese aggression, 5, 16–17, 46, 79; and military segregation, 115–16, 130–31, 205; patriarchy, 72, 99; riots, 17, 111, 139, 142–46, 161–62, 164
Racial Integrity Act, 13
radio, 12, 42, 50, 52, 55–56, 70, 104–5, 122, 170, 175
Randolph, S. Philip, 90, 113, 166
Rankin, John, 14
Reconstruction, 29, 75, 82
Red Ball Express, 104, 114, 130
Red Summer of 1919, 161
representations: historical, 73, 175, 181, 196; racial, 52, 58, 120, 188, 192–94, 198; stereotyped, 23, 44, 49, 171
Revolutionary War, 26–27
rhetorical mode of address, 8, 101
Rice, Thomas Dartmouth, 49
Roberts, Cecil, 135
Roberts, Needham, 110
Robinson, General Ray A., 148
Rochester, 80
Rome, 21, 23
Roosevelt, Franklin Delano, 38, 43, 67, 79, 113, 115, 120–24, 139, 142, 146–48, 151, 163, 165, 168–69, 179, 181, 184–85
Roosevelt, Theodore, 34–35
Rowe, James, 120

Schmeling, Max, 74, 85, 180
Scott, Emmett J., 152
Second Amendment, 27–28, 184
Second Continental Congress, 26
segregation, 28–29, 35–36, 38–39, 62, 64–65, 68, 70, 72–75, 82–91, 94–98, 99–104, 109, 111–28, 130, 133, 137–40, 145–49, 152, 155, 157–64, 167, 171, 177, 180, 188–89, 191–94, 202–5

selective service system: and Franklin Roosevelt address, 38; prior to World War II, 38; Public Law 783 (also known as the 1940 Selective Service Bill), 113, 121–24, 169; and race, 119
Sherman, John H., 212
Shoeshine Boy, 91, 96
Signal Corps, 19, 41, 43–47, 57, 61–62, 65, 73, 148, 169
slave codes, 25, 28
slave revolts, 25
slavery, 3, 6, 11–12, 22, 29–31, 40, 48–51, 60, 62, 70, 73, 75, 82
Soldier's National Cemetery at Gettysburg, 33
Southern colonies, 3
Southern plantation myth, 48–49, 77, 100, 195
Southern Theater Federation, 54
Spanish-American War, 3, 28, 75, 81, 108–9
Standard Steel Corporation, 166
stereotypes: and media, 9, 41, 47, 49–59, 73, 80, 87, 91, 98, 142, 148, 193; of African Americans, 15–16, 18, 62–63, 77, 83, 89, 130, 135, 137, 174–75, 182, 188; of Japanese, 14, 16–18, 21, 111
Stimson, Henry L., 112, 120, 128, 132, 165
Stoddard, Lothrop, 161
Stouffer, Samuel, 71
suffrage, 15, 27
Swerling, Jo, 73

Tarzan of the Apes, 20, 62–63
Teamwork, 70, 84, 90–91, 96, 98
Temple, Shirley, 49
Thompson, James G., 177
Tobias, Channing H., 120
To Secure These Rights, 204
Training of Colored Troops, The, 57
Trooper of Company K, 52, 56
Truman, Harry S., 35, 64, 70, 113, 203–6
Tuskegee Airmen, The, 4
Tuskegee pilots, 115, 123

Uncle Tom's Cabin, 6, 50
universal military service, 26
Universal Negro Improvement Association, 51

Unknown Soldier Speaks, The, 62
USS *Philadelphia*, 179

"Vale of Tears," 160
Vietnam War, 4, 36, 47
Virginia Military Institute, 36
voting, 22, 28, 31–32, 212n73

Walker, Jimmie, 214n39
Walker, Frank, 185
War Department Personnel Division, 112
War of 1812, 28, 75, 107
War Production Board, 185
Washington Bee, 171
Washington, Booker T., 75, 80, 152, 154, 170
Washington, George, 75, 107
Way of the Subject, The, 46
Welcome to Britain, A, 60, 98–99
We've Come a Long, Long Way, 70–71

Whiskey Rebellion, 107
White, Walter, 52, 120, 139
Wilkins, Roy, 164, 174
Willcox, William G., 35, 152
Wilson, Woodrow, 35, 57, 110, 140–154
Wings, 46
Wings for This Man, 133
women in military service, 27, 36, 39, 47, 160, 167, 208n3
World War I, 3, 34–35, 42, 56–59, 75, 108–10, 141–42, 150–54, 157, 160, 164, 175
World War II: attitudes, 16–17, 151–56, 161–63, 165–66, 170–74, 185, 190–91, 195–96, 201–2; discrimination, 4–5, 19, 35–35, 39, 104, 106, 112–13, 121–22, 124–25, 137, 143, 203–5, 207; as a race war, 13–14, 139, 142, 150–51; role of mass media, 43–45, 59–64, 78, 86
Wright, Cleo, 186

www.ingramcontent.com/pod-product-compliance
Lightning Source LLC
Chambersburg PA
CBHW030338240426
43661CB00052B/1676